A Tenant's Town
Québec in the 18th century

Yvon Desloges

Translated from the original French

Studies in Archaeology,
Architecture and History

National Historic Sites
Parks Service
Environment Canada

Available in Canada through associated book stores and other book sellers or by mail from Canada Communication Group/Publishing, Supply and Services Canada, Ottawa, Ontario, Canada K1A 0S9.

Published under the authority of the Minister of the Environment, Ottawa, 1991

Editing: Sheila Ascroft
Design: Louis D. Richard
Desktop Production: Suzanne Rochette
Cover: Rod Won
Cover photo: Jacques Beardsell
Translation: Department of the Secretary of State

Parks publishes the results of its research in archaeology, architecture and history. A list of publications is available from Research Publications, Parks Service, Environment Canada, 1600 Liverpool Court, Ottawa, Ontario, Canada K1A 0H3.

Canadian Cataloguing Publication Data

Desloges, Yvon

A Tenant's Town: Québec in the 18th Century
(Studies in Archaeology, Architecture and History, ISSN 0821-1027)
Also published in French under the title: Une ville de locataires: Québec au XVIIIe siècle
Includes bibliographical references
ISBN: 0-660-14204-X
Cat. No.: R61-2/9-54E

1. Quebec (Quebec) — 18th century — Social conditions. 2. Quebec (Quebec) — 18th century — Economic conditions. 3. Quebec (Quebec) — History. 4. Quebec (Quebec) — Population. I. Canadian Parks Service, National Historic Sites. II. Title. III. Title: Québec in the 18th century. IV. Series.

FC2946.4D4413 1991   971.4'47102   C91-098708-4
F1054.5QD4413 1991

TABLE OF CONTENTS

Submitted for publication in 1987 by Yvon Desloges, Environment Canada, Parks Services, Québec Region.

ACKNOWLEDGEMENTS

This study would not have been possible without the collaboration of many individuals and institutions. I would like to thank the staff the Archives du séminaire de Québec and the Archives nationales du Québec in Québec for their help in locating the required sources.

Apart from various institutions and their staff, many people have been closely associated with various phases of this project. Louise Déry, Adrienne Labbé, Johanne Lacasse, Rénald Lessard and Gérald Sirois carried out documentary research under difficult conditions.

Involved in a study of the leisure activities of the population of Québec in the 18th century, based on the same sources, our colleague Gilles Proulx shared the required documentary research. His understanding of the period and experience working at Louisbourg, have made him an indispensible resource person.

The debt to computer "guru," Pierre Vézina, is enormous. Without his patience and marvellous didactic sense, this study would have had to content itself with much more restricted horizons.

One more person, Marc Lafrance, has been part of this research project from start to finish. This study benefited greatly from his knowledge of the city of Québec and his innumerable references on the subject. I am immeasurably indebted to him. And I would like to acknowledge the valuable collaboration of Jacques Mathieu of the Department of History of Université Laval. His critique of this manuscript made it possible for me to solve a thousand and one ambiguities. I will always be grateful to him.

INTRODUCTION

As the night quietly slips away lifting the dark veil on the Laurentian colony, the first faint glimmerings of dawn appear along the majestic St. Lawrence River. During the cool night, the residents of the capital were able to recover a little from the overwhelming humidity that has weighed upon the town for the last few days. Here and there, wisps of fog conceal the river, as calm and flat as a mirror. As day breaks, the rooster belonging to Madame Corbin on Notre-Dame Street, makes haste to announce it.

Shortly after, the merchant, Yves Arguin, jumps out of bed. The day ahead will be a busy one: he has a meeting with the notary to sign a lease; then, he has to visit the Colonial Administrator to settle a few small business problems, and stop in Upper Town to see a client. What a day! To say nothing of the possible arrival of stock, since the ship is already at anchor in Bellechasse cove, waiting for favourable winds before approaching Québec. Inevitably, the arrival of the ship means that he will have to deal with a mountain of paper and regulations; but, never mind! This evening, the Governor will receive the town's upper crust at the Château Saint-Louis. Our man will finally have a chance to have some fun with congenial company.

Jean-Baptiste, a slave from Martinique, is already up. He is setting out the toiletries for his master, laying out his clothes and preparing his breakfast. Once the ritual has been completed, our merchant moves closer to the window for a breath of fresh air. Surprise! The delicate stench of manure that lay heavy upon the town the night before seems to have disappeared. Things are already stirring in the street below; the first cart is moving in the direction of Sault-au-Matelot. The coastal sailing ships in port aimlessly rise and fall with the tide: the wind refuses to blow. Oblivious of the suffocating heat of the advancing day, Gilbert the smith, hammers away on his anvil; while carpenter Joseph Delorme works on the roof of the neighbouring house. There is a clear message in all this jangle of noise: the capital is stirring again after a short night of rest.

However, during the night's low tide some new arrivals built temporary camps on the river shore. This morning they are suddenly and brutally awakened by the constabulary: their presence represents an infraction against two "municipal" regulations, one prohibiting fires on a public place and the other preventing anyone from "camping" on the beach. In the opinion of our merchant, who would otherwise rush to their aid in the hope they might some day become faithful clients, these Nouvelle-Beauce migrants could plead ignorance of the law.

But, as he leans out of his window, our hero is suddenly brought back to reality. The clerk has arrived, and they have to go over the good and bad debts. And he's very worried about the latter; some of the people named in the cash book disappeared from circulation a long time ago. These people, temporary residents of Québec, have vanished without a trace. Fortunately, our friend was farsighted enough to ensure that their credit was limited. Still he will have to take a sharp loss. Once the books have been revised, he will have to look at the order invoice; if the vessel arrives before he comes back, the merchant has delegated his faithful clerk to go to the Admiralty's Receiver and the Crown Office.

With his usual flustered gesture, Arguin consults his pocket watch. How time flies! He has already been working with his clerk for two hours. And he still has to go to the notary where his tenant is waiting to renew a lease. The malodorous manure produced by the cow belonging to Laporte, the innkeeper, assaults his sensitive nose as he rushes away. His attention is soon drawn by a grunting pig wallowing in one of the many mud holes that dot the street. Another one that got away he mumbles to himself. Ah, here at last is the notary's house.

The tenant, Widow Renaud, who has been kept out of town, is represented by her niece. It's really only a formality since the rental conditions remain the same as they were in the previous lease. However, what with looking for witnesses, reading the act and finally signing the document, the whole thing takes up a lot of precious time. Lunch time nears. Our man decides that it would be better to return to the store than to go to the Administrator's office; civil servants are known to take such long lunches.

As far as the servant Jean-Baptiste is concerned, he was asked to go shopping; today is market day, and on this beautiful Tuesday in August, meats, vegetables and fruits are plentiful. Back at the house, the meal is prepared. The menu consists of onion soup and veal brisket with green peas, accompanied by thinly sliced root vegetables, everything liberally flavoured by red wine. For dessert, berries of the season. The meal is eaten in the kitchen, in the same room where Widow Levasseur did the cooking. The clock strikes two. On this signal, our merchant leaves to hail a carriage to take him to the Administrator's office; the drive will cost very little, barely equivalent of one-quarter of a loaf of bread.

On the way back, the driver will let the merchant off on the square in Upper Town, where he has a meeting with Brassard, the beadle. Arguin, who already sells to the Recollects, is trying to win the contract to supply the Cathedral Church. Once this business is completed, the merchant goes to Gatien the roofer, who lives nearby, to ask him to come and repair the roof of his store. On the way he meets Father Jacrau, the parish priest, who is coming back from visiting with the Tourangeaus, the parents of a large family who have just lost their newborn daughter. And the priest launches into a long-winded philosophical view of life and death that is nevertheless timely, because this is the fourth infant who has died in the last ten days.

As he makes his way back in the increasing heat, Arguin stops at the inn kept by Couturier to slack his thirst, gossip a little and inquire about the barrel stock. Before crossing the threshold, he scrutinizes the horizon on the side of Île d'Orléans to see if the vessel carrying his cargo of cloth, beverages and household sundries is already in sight. If so his stop at the inn will have to be a short one. Alas, the lack of good wind has forced the captain to stay a day longer in Bellechasse cove. Maybe tomorrow....

With a quick look at his watch, our merchant realizes that it is already 5:15 p.m., and that the afternoon has flown by. As he leaves the inn, he steps aside to let in a group of men doing fatigue-duty on the site of the fortifications. They are exhausted but happy to be celebrating their last day of work. Tomorrow they will be replaced by the team from Beauport parish. The merchant thinks he may be able to substitute his servant Jean-Baptiste if he is called up to serve. Alas, there is nothing he can do about the taxes imposed to construct the fortifications and maintain the barracks.

But enough of this idle speculation. He must rush home to wash, tidy himself and dress suitably for this evening's Governor's ball. It's an event that will attract the best society in the colony. Arguin can already see himself succumbing to the charms of beautiful ladies, moved by the conversation of Madame de Beauharnois, and flitting from group to group, enjoying all the chitchat, and each one of these encounters....

*****

Many daily gestures that today seem to form part of our normal, not to say commonplace, ritual are hidden behind this scenario.[1] Today we look at our watches almost instinctively; however, the same was not true in the age of Louis XV when only a few well-heeled people could take advantage of the benefits of clocks and watches. And yet, time became one of the major preoccupations of the 18th century. Most Québec citizens had to content themselves with consulting public or institutional clocks and sun dials. In the 20th century measuring time is no longer a problem. Also, although in the late 20th century infant mortality in Québec seems to be a marginal phenomenon, in the 18th century it was an inevitable preoccupation. How times have changed! The Rent Control Board has replaced the notary as the arbitrator between owners and tenants, and leases are arranged by agreement between the parties.

But beyond this brief consideration of a few daily practices, the scenario described must serve to remind us that there are three principal topics that we can study to better understand daily life in Québec in the 18th century. These three topics — demography, housing and wealth, gravitate around the central idea of tenancy. Derived from the premise that everyone has to live somewhere, the primary purpose of this study is to isolate the pace of growth of the capital, not only in time but also in space; that is, neighbourhood by neighbourhood. This initial stage will lead to an observation of the rates of growth and the demographic movement of the residents of the capital as a function of marriage, birth and inevitable mortality. When these data are put together with those drawn from the analysis of housing conditions, it's possible to assess

Québec's society in terms of the legal status of its members as owners or tenants. Initially this demographic analysis will reveal a certain mobility in the population. Rental records for houses or apartments tend to confirm this movement, so that the logical conclusion is that geographic mobility was one of the fundamental characteristics of Québec society in the 18th century. However, it is important to emphasize that housing is not only concerned with buildings, in the most common use of the term, it also refers to the urban landscape, the management of real estate and urban amenities. Once these components are understood, it then becomes possible to place property in its proper perspective.

Although Québec became a tenant's town during the course of the 18th century, it is important to travel the length of the various streets and lanes of the capital in order to scout the domestic environment, from the stable or shed to the contents of the living quarters, without forgetting the accoutrements of the garden and the larder. The elements of decoration and the modes of transportation are also manifestations that are characteristic of urban life. In this case, they also indicate a growing poverty caused by heavy competition.

The competition that is rampant within the territorial boundaries of cities revealed itself in various ways: from the competition provided by new workers recently arrived from adjacent parishes to that of French or foreign-finished products. Some sectors of activity have to deal with both of these problems; while others were affected only by the first. Nevertheless, the results were the same: competition leads to mobility, as it pares down one's share of the market and consequently one's income. Thus the three key words that support the conclusions of this study and that characterize urban life in the 18th century are: mobility, competition and impoverishment.

It is important to emphasize this concept of urban life, because in terms of competition it is significantly different from life in a rural environment. And cities grow partly on the basis of an influx of rural immigrants. For some, the economic dynamism of the city can offer important job opportunities. For others, it represents a market for their products. So behind these three terms, we can glimpse partially the phenomenon of the city, which can manifest itself in very different ways depending upon whether we look at it with the eyes of an American or European geographer or historian.[2]

According to the French historian Jean-Claude Perrot, economic policy analysts in the 18th century had already emphasized the relationship that existed between commerce, industry and population, mortality and wealth, and housing and the size of families, in the core of the cities. There, a market capitalism had been deliberately assumed and consequently it was necessary to show how the entire city resonated to the tune called by trade.[3] In summary, the city bids an open welcome, but represents nothing but a turnstile for both goods and people. In this context, many are called, few are selected and even fewer can buy a home where they can settle down.

NOTE TO READERS

All references to money in this text are given in French currency: *livres*, *sols* and *deniers*.

PART I

THE POPULATION

All urban bases grow at their own pace; particular conditions impose upon them movement or inertia, growth, population loss, or even stagnation. Québec, the capital of New France and the continental port of entry to and exit from the Laurentian colony, was cut off from France for six months every year. Québec is a garrison town and a fortress that also harboured, among other things, the mother houses of the most important religious communities. These various roles played by the city attracted many craftsmen and traders as well as various kinds of administrators and officials. Québec was a complex demographic and social network that operated deliberately upon a background of market capitalism.

CHAPTER 1

DEMOGRAPHIC CHARACTERISTICS, 1688-1755

To describe an urban settlement and draw a picture of its evolution is impossible without first attempting to say a few words about the population. After the first few years of settling down, and male over-representation,[1] the population of Québec started to balance out. An observation of this balancing process will evidently lead to an examination of the characteristics of the population such as age and sex. This involves a study of the components of the urban group. Thus, one must consider the size of the households, and at the same time extract the dominant socio-demographic characteristic: mobility, which is linked to the economic climate.

Sources

In order to study demography, it is necessary to carry out a few statistical calculations. As far as the period covered by this study is concerned, the researcher is usually confronted not with a lack of data but with an abundance of such.

It is important to emphasize that the colonial administrators[2] ordered the execution of 23 statistical censuses between 1690 and 1739, without counting the two nominal rolls that were carried out in 1716 and 1744 respectively by Thibault and Jacrau, priests in charge of the Parish of Notre-Dame in Québec. The Government of Canada has published nine of these statistical censuses,[3] and the nominal rolls have been the sub-

ject of two publications each,[4] without including the publication of the
registers of births, marriages and deaths. How can we explain the fact
that no monograph has yet been published on this subject?

Another mystery will emerge from the comparison of the two 1716
censuses. According to the civil administration, there were a total of
2408 people in Québec. On the other hand, the most recent version of
the census carried out by the parish priest, which was published by
demographers of the Université de Montréal, shows that the number of
residents in the capital was 2281. Moreover, according to the Notre-
Dame parish priest, there were more households than the number listed
in the civil census, which would mean that Québec families may have
had many fewer children. Who is telling the truth?

According to the civil census figures, it appears that the parish priest
underestimated the population by 5.5% and overestimated the number of
households by 11.2%. There are many explanations for this phenomenon. Even though the criteria used by demographers today to calculate
the number of households appear to be less accurate than those used by
the census-takers of the time, we have to accept the number of families
shown in the civil census, especially when we consider that the difference between the two population totals is entirely due to factors outside
the realm of demography. The parish priest may have failed to include
Protestants or even foreign merchants in his figures. It is also possible
that the area covered by the ecclesiastic administration was different
from that covered by the civil administration. All these explanations are
possible but which is the right one?

Since it is impossible to say, it may be more prudent to retain the figures produced by the statistical civil censuses and to compare them with
the nominal rolls produced by the religious censuses. As arbitrary as
these choices may appear, they cannot be accepted without a final examination of the statistical censuses. Since the 1712 census contains only
incomplete figures, it seems useless to use it in the various tables. Furthermore, we must also reject the 1698 census, which reveals a certain
amount of unreliability in terms of the figures shown. Thus we are left
only with the 21 statistical censuses.

Apart from the population totals, the data contained in these documents indicates the number of children, boys and girls, under and over
15 years of age (majority was legally attained only at the age of 25, at

least in the case of men). The documents also show the number of married women and widows, followed by the number of married men under and over 50 years of age. Starting in 1707, there were more or less regular entries indicating the number of families.[5] We also find the number of men absent from their homes after 1720. On the other hand, only the nominal rolls make it possible to establish with a certain amount of accuracy the socio-professional categories and trades of the population.

These data can lead to an analysis of population growth not only in absolute terms, but more importantly as a function of the distribution between its male and female components, and its rate of renewal. They may even make it possible to identify the contributions made by immigration to natural growth, which in turn implies an evaluation of mortality, both infant and other.

The Population, 1660-90

Starting out from the postulate that a colonial population, where immigration dominates, shows clear signs of a serious lack of balance in its male-female ratio, R. Chénier has demonstrated the significant disparity between the two sexes, after placing the population of Québec in its colonial context. Before drawing a table of the period between 1690 and 1755, it is important then to obtain a balance for the preceding years and, if need be, to compare it with known data for Montréal.

Before the royal administration took charge of the colony in 1663, New France came under the responsibility of fur trading companies. The population was growing slowly. From 28 winter colonists in 1608, it rose to 2000 people in 1653. Once the King had assumed direct charge of the fate of the colony, the number of inhabitants grew at an increasingly fast pace: to 3215 in 1666 and 10 303 in 1688, which represents an annual rate of growth of 4.7% for these years.[6]

However, the capital grew more slowly than the colony during these 22 years: from 547 people in 1666 to 1407 in 1688, for an average annual rate of growth of 3.99%.[7] Evidently, these figures do not take into account the population of the suburbs nor the floating population consisting of sailors, soldiers, foreign merchants and immigrants in transit.

The population of Québec accounted for 17% of the total population of the colony in 1666 and for 13.7% in 1688.[8]

Characteristically, the major portion of the population of the colony was made up of men: 63.3% in 1666 and 52.8% in 1688.[9] The proportion was 61.1% and 55.1% respectively for the same years in Montréal.[10] As far as Québec is concerned, it had even more men than the colony as a whole; in 1666, the proportion was 65.8% and in 1688, it was 54.8%. This male over representation was slowly decreasing both in Québec and in the rest of the colony. It seems that this phenomenon can be explained by an increase in the birth rate[11] as the result of the arrival of girls of marriageable age.[12]

In terms of marriage itself, from the previous picture we may infer that men were not only more numerous, but that they were also more likely to be unmarried than the women. On the other hand, the percentage of married women in Québec was consistently higher than that of married men,[13] a situation caused by male overrepresentation, which nevertheless tended to balance out toward the end of this period.

These observations lead to a consideration of the age pyramid. In comparison with 1666, the average age of the population was much lower 15 years later;[14] and this was true both for the colony as a whole and for the cities of Québec and Montréal.

In sum, the period between 1660 and 1690 corresponds to a settlement stage. Does this mean that the next generation would find itself in a stable situation and that the next one after that will ensure renewal? An analysis of the censuses carried out between 1692 and 1755 will serve to confirm or refute this.

Demographic Structures, 1692-1755

Taking into account the difficulties involved in assessing and evaluating the censuses,[15] it seemed more just to single out some of these rather than attempting to justify the "anomalies." Thus, we will use the first of the statistical censuses of this period, carried out in 1692, then the civil census of 1716, which will make it possible to compare with the census compiled the same year by the parish priest; then the 1739 census, and finally the census carried out by Father Jacrau in 1744.

TABLE 1

POPULATION AND GROWTH RATE (%)
1628-1755

Year	Canada	Rate	Québec	Rate	Montréal	Rate
1628	76		76			
1653	2000	7.4	600	6.2		
1666	3215		547	4.0		
1688	10303	3.9	1407			
1692 (a)	11114		1659			
1697 (a)					1150	
1707 (b)			1779		1327	
1716	20896	2.4	2574	1.9		
1731					2980	3.2
1739	43264	3.0	4609	2.7	3450	1.8
1744 (c)			5004	1.6		
1755			7215	3.3		

(a) War of the Augsburg League (1689-1697)
(b) War of the Spanish Succession (1701-1713)
(c) War of the Austrian Succession (1740-1748)

These five key sources will make it possible to determine the pace of urban growth, and to compare it with that of the colony of Montréal and even some American cities.

Pace of Growth

The population of Canada grew from 11 114 people in 1692 to 20 896 in 1716 and to 43 264 in 1739.[16] The annual rate of growth was 2.5% for the first period and 3% between 1716 and 1739. Montréal grew at approximately the same pace as the colony as a whole: by 3.2% between 1707 and 1731.[17] As far as Québec is concerned, the pace of growth seemed to be slightly lower than that of the colony as a whole for the 17th century, but quite similar to the latter in the 18th century.

By isolating blocks of data at intervals of approximately 25 years (1692-1716, 1716-39 and 1739-55) [Table 1],[18] we can produce a rather

TABLE 2
GROWTH RATES (%) OF SEVERAL AMERICAN CITIES
1660-1755

Year	Philadelphia	Rate	Boston	Rate	New York	Rate	Charleston	Rate	Portsmouth	Rate	Newport	Rate	Providence	Rate
1660			3000		2400									
1685	2500						700		900					
1690	4000	9.2	7000	2.7	3900	1.6	1100	4.4						
1708											2204		1443	
1730											4645	3.2	3910	4.2
1743	13000	2.0	16382	1.5	11000	1.8	6800	2.7	3300	1.9				
1748											5529	0.9	3464	-0.6
1755											6769	3.4	3162	-1.5

homogeneous curve that shows that war, in particular, was responsible for a significant slow-down in population growth not only in Québec, but in the entire colony. At the same time, when we compare it to the rates prevailing during the previous one hundred years, we can see that the pace of growth decreased in the 18th century. The situation could not have been otherwise, taking into account the small numbers of people, and the even lower proportion of individuals of reproductive age in the 17th century.

Furthermore, this slow-down in population growth is a phenomenon that was not exclusively limited to New France. It was also evident in the largest cities of the English colonies (Table 2).[19] Even though these towns were generally more heavily populated, only one of them grew at a faster pace than the capital: the city of Charleston in Carolina. All these cities, with the exception of New York, suffered a significant slow-down in growth during the 18th century.

Seen from our point of view so many years after, another phenomenon may nevertheless be in danger of being ignored: growth was by no means regular and even; it proceeded by jumps and starts characterized by interruptions and quick advances. Already, the rates of growth shown on Table 1 for the periods of 1739-44 and 1745-55 in Québec, and 1731-39 in Montréal, show significant fluctuations in relation to the average rate.

Moreover, a simple observation of the number of families in the statistical censuses is very revealing in terms of the situation prevailing in the capital during the 18th century. From 290 in 1707, the number of families increased regularly to reach 449 in 1716;[20] between 1717 and

TABLE 3
POPULATION GROWTH
IN QUÉBEC
1692-1755

Year	Population	Inter-censal Rate (%)	Periodic Rate (%)
1692 (a)	1658		
1707 (b)	1779	0.47	1.25
1716	2574	4.10	
1726	2550	-0.13	
1737	4508	5.04	
1744 (c)	5004	1.49	3.29
1755	7215	3.29	

(a) War of the Augsburg League (1689-1697)
(b) War of the Spanish Succession (1701-1713)
(c) War of the Austrian Succession (1740-1748)

1723, this figure underwent many variations, so that we can say that during these six years high inflation and the re-evaluation of the currency negatively affected population growth in Québec.[21] From 1724 on, the population stabilized and, between 1727 and 1730, the capital showed a spectacular increase in the number of families; in the order of 33%. This phenomenon was the result of Québec's maritime activities. At that time the city was experiencing significant growth in its foreign trade, which attracted large numbers of skilled and unskilled workers.[22] Subsequently, the numbers increased more moderately, and even dropped between 1737 and 1739, probably due to the 1737-38 crisis caused by a poor harvest that led to a one-third drop-off in trade.[23]

Thus, the population of the capital was nervous: it reacted rapidly to the slightest economic permutations. In order to understand these movements, we must attempt to bring these situations into the open. The political and economic context divides the period between 1692 and 1755 into two stages: 1692-1726 and 1727-55, during the course of which the annual rate of population growth was 1.25% and 3.29% respectively, reflecting the generally accepted premise that the period between 1692

TABLE 4

COMPOSITION OF THE POPULATION OF QUÉBEC, 1692-1739

Year	Men						Women					Total		Population of Québec (%)
	+50yrs	25-49	15-24	-15 yrs	Total	%	+24 yrs	15-24	-15 yrs	Total	%	Québec	Canada	
1692	63	238	235	356	892	53.8	314	161	292	767	46.2	1659	11114	14.9
1695	84	207	285	329	905	54.5	320	178	257	755	45.5	1660	12786	13.0
1698	137	243	257	483	1120	52.0	366	192	477	1035	48.0	2155		
1706	62	230	180	277	749	45.4	299	183	420	902	54.6	1651	16788	9.8
1707	54	240	185	310	789	44.3	290	180	520	990	55.6	1779	17615	10.1
1713	61	272	181	300	814	43.0	373	248	462	1083	57.0	1897	18467	10.2
1714	119	330	296	674	1419	55.5	470	295	371	1136	44.5	2555	18741	13.6
1716	137	284	335	545	1301	50.5	460	327	486	1273	49.5	2574	20996	12.3
1718	452		754		1206	48.9	459	803		1262	51.1	2468	23125	10.7
1719	160	270	260	510	1200	46.5	450	310	620	1380	53.5	2580	22530	11.4
1720	180	325	206	478	50 +1189	55.3	349	182	469	1000	44.7	2239	24544	9.1
1721	182	217	217	480	53 +1096	53.1	351	191	472	1014	46.9	2163	24949	8.7
1722	130	220	210	490	54 +1050	51.5	360	199	480	1039	48.5	2143	25106	8.5
1723	180	267	215	494	50 +1156	51.3	463	191	489	1143	48.6	2349	25972	9.0
1724	189	269	219	493	36 +1170	51.0	463	194	499	1156	48.9	2362		
1726	200	293	252	500	50 +1245	50.8	525	210	520	1255	49.2	2550	29836	8.5
1727	210	312	250	593	22 +1365	52.1	528	199	549	1276	47.9	2663	31169	8.5
1730	145	636	336	720	44 +1837	46.0	719	730	754	2203	53.9	4084	34188	11.9
1732	150	640	345	732	40 +1867	50.4	724	378	771	1873	49.5	3780	35525	10.6
1736	189	600	330	904	40 +2023	48.0	889	442	909	2240	52.0	4303	39220	11.0
1737	216	738	427	953	2334	51.8	837	494	843	2174	48.2	4508	40143	11.2
1739	247	617	322	993	50 +2179	48.4	884	519	971	2374	51.6	4609	43264	10.6

and 1726 was less favourable to an economic boom than that of 1727 to 1755 when there was a resurgence of intercolonial trade. However, the population curve went through several ups and downs. Table 3 underscores this phenomenon rather eloquently. When the War of the League of Augsburg (1689-97) and the beginning of the War of the Spanish Succession (1701-13) dampened population growth, the resulting increase in military expenditures and upsurge in intercolonial trade attracted a number of artisans and labourers to Québec. The city underwent a spectacular increase in its annual rate of growth (4.1%) between 1707 and 1716.[24]

After the Treaty of Utrecht (1713) and the death of Louis XIV (1715), France was confronted with the depressing reality of a public purse reeling under a staggering national debt. It was necessary to implement a recovery plan and this did not spare Canada: the Canadian *livre* underwent a devaluation in the order of 62.5%. Even though there was a delay in the announcement of this policy, already rumours were rampant in the streets of the capital. Popular dissatisfaction was gaining strength and the prices of goods and services were reaching previously unheard-of levels. In this context it was not surprising to find evidence of a massive exodus. Those newly arrived during the period of prosperity went back, some to the surrounding countryside and others to the territories of their respective governments.

It was only in 1725-26 that the prices stabilized. The basic elements of the infrastructure of the great intercolonial trade had been organized for a few years. Thus, 1727 corresponds to a significant leap forward in trade so that Québec experienced a phenomenal rate of growth in its population of 5% per year. After this period of population growth, there were a series of poor harvests that rendered the new citizens particularly vulnerable; the capital suffered a significant slow-down in the growth of its population. However, massive public investment (1745-54) in military and maritime public works, and even convents (the cathedral in Québec), again enticed those living in the outskirts of the town as well as foreigners to settle in the city.[25] Although the strong rates of growth seemed to be a phenomenon exclusive to the 17th century, one has to think again and examine more closely the situation prevailing during the 18th century. In sum, the people of Québec and even those in the surrounding countryside, were aware of the economic situation and reacted

GRAPH 1
MALE POPULATION OF QUÉBEC
1692-1739

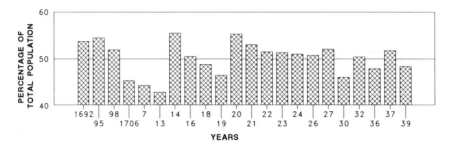

in an excitable and fretful way: wildly ebbing and flowing. Québec throbs to the beat of its economy. This is the mark of an established and balanced society, of an urban community.

The Balance of Forces

The lack of balance in male-female ratio evened out during the course of the 17th century, corresponding to the period of settlement.[26] In Montréal, male dominance eclipsed quickly between 1666 and 1681, and the ratio reached equilibrium toward 1695 when the proportion of men was 51.6%. This situation persisted until about 1710 when the percentage of women became slightly higher, a situation that is considered to be normal.[27] In Québec in 1688 men represented 54.8% of the population.[28] Four years later, they accounted for 53.8%; for 50.5% in 1716 and for 48.4% in 1734 (see Table 4 and Graph 1). Notwithstanding a few statistical stops and starts,[29] men were slightly more numerous than women in Québec during the course of the entire period, which is entirely comparable to the situation prevailing in the colony as a whole.[30]

The nominal rolls obtained by the parish priest in 1716 confirm this situation: females made up 51.7% of the population. Thus, there was a difference of 2.2% between the two (civil and religious) censuses, which demonstrates the parity of the sexes. According to Father Jacrau, in 1744 the proportion of women was 50.6%. Thus, the male-female ratio

TABLE 5

**ENDOGAMY IN MARRIAGES PERFORMED
IN QUÉBEC, 1692-1755**

Years	Total marriages	Both from Qué.	%	Husband from Qué.	%	Wife from Qué.	%
1692-1706	323	92	28.5	36	11.1	170	52.6
1707-1713	202	48	23.8	18	8.9	101	50.0
1714-1726	504	154	30.5	29	5.7	240	47.6
1727-1736	468	187	39.9	33	7.1	175	37.4
1737-1744	354	137	38.7	12	3.4	170	48.0
1745-1755	667	465	69.7	43	6.4	138	20.7
Total	2518	1083	43.0	171	6.8	994	39.5

stabilized during the course of the 18th century, at least from the point of view of the population as a whole.

The Composition of the Population

This evidence of periods of strong growth alternating with slower population increases leads to a more profound consideration of the composition of the population. At this point, we must support the hypothesis formulating a significant increase in male immigration. In the marriages celebrated in Notre-Dame Church in Québec between 1690 and 1755,[31] the two spouses came from the capital in 43% of the cases (Table 5).[32] Even though there was a marked increase in this endogamy rate after 1727, in 48% of the marriages recorded for the period the future wife resided in the capital, but her husband came from outside the parochial boundaries. This newcomer originated from two different sources: one of every three came from the colony (especially the government of Québec), and two out of every three came from France (Graph 2).[33] Overseas immigration was much higher than expected, a phenomenon that may be partly explained by the administrative functions of the capital.

We may certainly form the hypothesis that the marriage was being celebrated in the bride's parish. The objection is well taken; however, here

GRAPH 2
ORIGIN OF SPOUSES
QUÉBEC, 1690-1749

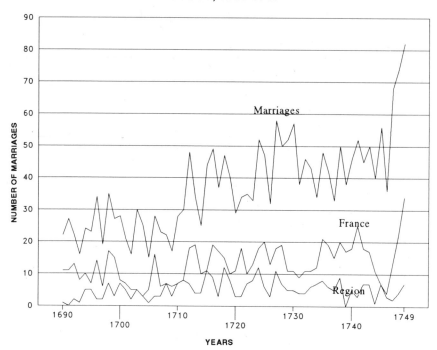

again, endogamy must be measured against the economical background. Thus, between 1737 and 1744, which were difficult years, three out of every five Québec women married foreigners (55% of the cases); while in the subsequent years, during the period when the great public works were being carried out, three out of every four women married other Quebeckers (77%). This situation is similar to that of 1727-36 when Quebeckers accounted for 52% of the husbands.

During the course of the 18th century, these couples tended to reproduce more and we see an increase in the proportion of children (Table 6).[34] On the other hand, the working population experienced a high mortality rate as indicated by the significant decrease in those aged 15 to 49. This could have been due to more difficult working conditions. As far as the elderly were concerned, their place in the age pyramid seemed

TABLE 6

COMPOSITION OF AGE GROUPS IN THE QUÉBEC POPULATION, 1692-1739

Year	Population	Percentage by age group		
		0-14	15-49	50 and +
1692	1659	39.0	53.3	7.6
1716	2574	40.0	49.3	10.6
1739	4609	42.6	46.5	10.7

to be stable. In sum, in comparison with European residents, the population of Québec was very young; in this, it compared favourably with Montréal.[35] Nevertheless, the working population was more often threatened by death.

The increase in the group of those aged 15 years or less, together with the decrease in those aged 15 to 49 (the group more likely to marry and have children), also means that there would be an increase in the number of people per household. An analysis of the censuses indicates that in 1681 there were 4.55 people per household and that this average had increased to 4.94 by 1716.[36] According to the 1739 census the number was 6.3 people per household.[37]

Thus, during the course of the 18th century the population of Québec grew at a moderate pace interspersed with sudden leaps and bounds. Aware of the economic situation, the population owed a significant proportion of its growth to an influx of male immigrants. Even though they were having more children, Québec couples in the 18th century were nevertheless faced with a high mortality rate so that the balance between the sexes that had been reached since the end of the 17th century was often compromised.

The Precariousness of the Balance, 1690-1749

In the opinion of a number of historians, the statistical censuses of the period often reveal "some curious anomalies" or at least significant though temporary imbalances. However, these are the two fundamental

GRAPH 3
DISTRIBUTION OF MARRIED AND WIDOWED PEOPLE, BY SEX
1692-1739

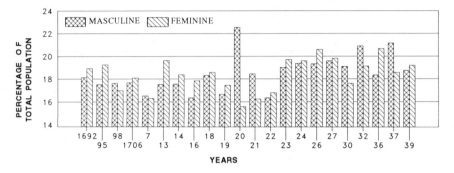

characteristics of the population of the *ancien régime* (before 1789).[38] Without otherwise having to answer for these "errors" in the census, it would be appropriate to study more closely the population of Québec in the 18th century, especially from the point of view of its behaviour in terms of marriage and reproduction.

Marriage

The registers of births, marriages and deaths represent a treasure trove of pieces of information one as revealing as the next. From the beginning, there is a very surprising revelation: between 1690 and 1749, while the Notre-Dame priests baptized over 11 000 children, they only conducted about 7000 funeral services, which left a surplus of a little over 4000 people. Between 1692 and 1744 then the population of the capital increased only by about 3300 people. The city did not absorb all these births. At the same time, the massive arrival of male immigrants translated into a very high degree of mobility in the population. However, this mobility was not exclusive to the colony; it was one more of the characteristics of populations during the *ancien régime*.

These new arrivals married Québec women. In principle (and to a very large extent in practice also since the parish priests made sure of it!), all procreation took place within the framework of the marriage union.

TABLE 7

MARITAL STATUS AT TIME OF MARRIAGE, 1690-1749

	Single (W)	%	Widowers	%	Total	%
Single (M)	1606	72.7	290	13.1	1896	85.8
Widows	201	9.1	113	5.1	314	14.2
Total	1807	81.8	403	18.2	2210	

Thus, it is important to obtain an evaluation of the marriage patterns. Even though the registers consulted do not indicate the ages of the spouses, we may assume that they were quite close to those of the colonial average; that is, 26.8 years for men and 21.9 years for women.[39] The age of women at the time of marriage therefore may have affected the fertility rates; on the other hand, men were hesitant to settle down, possibly as a result of the economic situation, but more probably as a function of their having to learn a trade.

Furthermore, the ratio between married and widowed people of both sexes illustrates that there was almost always (68% of the cases) a larger number of widows, which is the result of the higher male mortality; a situation that is easily comparable with the situation in France (Graph 3). Women should have enjoyed a better life expectancy, but the reality seems to have been somewhat different since an analysis of the deceased in the parish indicates that, in the group aged 15 to 49, female mortality was higher in the order of 54.7% (Table 12). We must conclude that there was higher male mobility; at least, this is the explanation suggested by Graph 2 and Table 5, while in periods of prosperity, larger numbers of foreigners settled in Québec.[40]

The death of one of the spouses marked the end of a union that would have lasted 14.5 years on the average;[41] even though it is important to point out that three out of every five marriages did not last as long. Almost one out of every five lasted less than five years. While a widow in France would find it somewhat difficult to marry again due to the opposition of the children produced during her first marriage, this situation did not seem to occur in Québec since remarriages account for 27.3% of all unions contracted in Québec during the course of the 18th century[42] (Table 7). However, contrary to the Canadian average for the 18th cen-

TABLE 8

SEASONAL FLUCTUATION OF MARRIAGES
1690-1749

Month	1	2	3	4	5	6	7	8	9	10	11	12	Total
Absolute number	245	229	45	191	172	125	148	184	224	275	375	43	2256
Daily number	7.90	8.10	1.40	6.40	5.50	4.20	4.80	5.90	7.50	8.90	12.50	1.40	74.60
Monthly rate	1.27	1.30	0.22	1.03	0.88	0.67	0.77	0.95	1.21	1.43	2.01	0.22	12.00

GRAPH 4

MONTHS OF MARRIAGES
QUÉBEC, 1690-1749

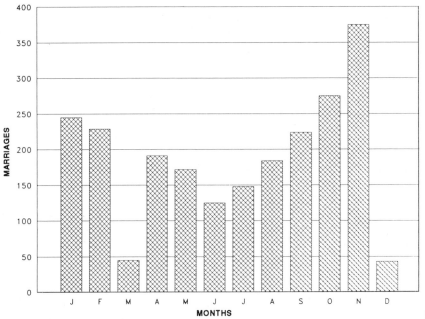

tury, more widows than widowers married a second time, while unions between widows and widowers were the least frequent. These figures confirm the brief span of a good number of marriages[43] and suggest that the economic situation was forcing widows to remarry. However, as a corollary, we should add that living conditions seemed to be more difficult in an urban than in a rural environment, especially for the possibilities of employment.

Regardless of their origins, the future spouses religiously respected the edicts of the Church, which prohibited marriages during Lent and Advent (Table 8).[44] Even though most people displayed a marked preference for the fall, particularly for November, they increasingly got married during the winter, especially in January and February (Graph 4). In this way, they approached the averages for Canada as a whole and for the city of Montréal.[45] From the beginning of October to the end of February (five months), the parish priest performed over half of all the marriages for the year.

This profile of the marriage behaviour of Quebeckers during the course of the 18th century could be summarized as follows: an increasing rate of endogamy and a trend for women to marry foreigners one out of every two times, except in periods of prosperity. The union took place primarily in the fall or winter and in many cases was of brief duration.

Generation Renewal

But what happened once the union was consummated? Already the short duration of the marriage leads us to believe that the proverbial fertility of Québec women did not in fact correspond to the reality of the 18th century. Since there are certain physiological considerations, we should rather speak of the constraints that must be respected. As Pierre Goubert wrote, there are four factors that allow us to evaluate legal fertility. These elements are the age at which girls marry, the age at which women cease to be "fertile," the intervals between siblings (between births) and finally the duration of the union.[46]

An evaluation of these factors is not possible except as a function of reconstructing the structure of the families, which is far beyond the

TABLE 9

NUMBER OF BIRTHS PER MARRIAGE
1690-1749

Decade	Births	Marriages	Quotient
1690-1699	1145	249	4.6
1700-1709	1192	225	5.3
1710-1719	1308	382	3.4
1720-1729	1848	422	4.4
1730-1739	2611	429	6.1
1740-1749	2880	549	5.2
Total	10 984	2256	4.9

TABLE 10

SEASONAL FLUCTUATION OF MARRIAGES AND CONCEPTIONS
1690-1749

Month of conception	4	5	6	7	8	9	10	11	12	1	2	3	
Month of birth	1	2	3	4	5	6	7	8	9	10	11	12	
													Total
Absolute number	831	796	979	952	955	869	977	1024	1025	1042	959	762	11 171
Daily number	26.81	28.18	31.58	31.73	30.81	28.97	31.52	33.03	34.17	33.61	31.97	24.58	366.96
Monthly Rate	0.88	0.93	1.03	1.04	1.01	0.95	1.03	1.08	1.12	1.10	1.04	0.80	12

scope of this study. Even though it is possible that the marriage age of the wife was about 21, and that physiological fertility is a phenomenon that stops at age 50,[47] which provides an indication of the duration of the period of fertility, we still do not have interval data respecting the lying-in periods, the duration of the period of widowhood (with all that these data imply) or the duration of the period of breast-feeding, temporary sterility, etc.

However, there is a more unrefined method that can be used to analyze the number of children per family: it consists of dividing the number of births in a parish by the number of marriages celebrated during the same period. For the 18th century,[48] this calculation method produces a figure of 5.6 children per family in Canada and 5 in Montréal. Between 1690 and 1749 the priests of Notre-Dame in Québec recorded 4.9 births per family (Table 9).[49] Since the capital represents only a

TABLE 11
DISTRIBUTION OF BIRTHS, BY SEX
1690-1749

Period	Total	Boys		Girls	
		Number	%	Number	%
1690-1699	1145	579	50.6	566	49.4
1700-1709	1192	609	51.1	583	48.9
1710-1719	1308	688	52.6	620	47.4
1720-1729	1848	923	49.9	925	50.0
1730-1739	2611	1348	51.6	1263	48.4
1740-1749	2880	1467	50.9	1413	49.1
Total	10 984	5614	51.1	5370	48.9

fraction of the colonial population, we must primarily see this as an example of an urban behaviour that is different from what would be more characteristic of a rural setting: living conditions in town are more difficult and this leads to a lower birth rate.

Québec also deviates from the standards for Canada and Montréal in terms of the seasonal movement of births (Table 10).[50] While in Montréal, the end of the spring is the peak season for conception, particularly the months of May and June, and June is the peak month for conceptions in the colony, the situation is entirely different in Québec.[51] Many more children were born in Québec during the months of July to November; in accordance with an arbitrary back reckoning of nine months to determine the months of conception, we find then that these would have been November, December and January. A sign of the balance between the sexes was that during the course of these 60 years (Table 11)[52] births were rather evenly distributed between boys and girls.

Furthermore, these physiological considerations respecting conception correspond to the end of the sailing season on the St. Lawrence River. Thus, nature also played a role in determining the pace of life in Québec; however, this was the flip side of the way things were done in Montréal! It was not spring that ensured renewal in Québec, but rather the season when the weather is grey and rainy, or the snowy, cold long

TABLE 12
MORTALITY IN QUEBEC
1690-1749

Period	Children				Adults				Total		
	0 - 1 yr		1 - 14 yrs		15 - 49 yrs		50 yrs and +				
	B	G	B	G	M	F	M	F	M	F	M+F
1690-1699	137	70	32	28	42	26	36	22	247	146	393
1700-1709	122	100	84	86	98	119	55	37	359	342	701
1710-1719	122	105	113	107	78	93	59	34	372	339	711
1720-1729	172	141	115	114	70	87	78	46	435	388	823
1730-1739	312	298	212	252	95	113	95	67	714	730	1444
1740-1749	401	344	227	247	144	191	131	121	903	903	1806
	1266	1058	783	834	527	629	454	327	3030	2848	5878
%	54.5	45.5	48.4	51.6	45.6	54.4	58.1	41.9	51.5	48.5	
Total	2324		1617		1156		781		5878		
%	39.5		27.5		19.7		13.3		100		

Infant mortality: B: 2049 (52 %) G: 1892 (48 %) Total : 3941
Adult mortality: M : 981 (51%)   F : 956 (49 %) Total : 1937

GRAPH 5
NUMBER OF CHILDREN PER FAMILY
QUÉBEC, 1690-1749

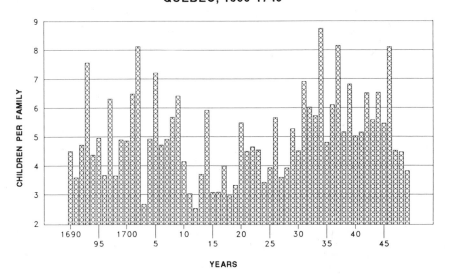

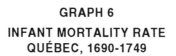

GRAPH 6
INFANT MORTALITY RATE
QUÉBEC, 1690-1749

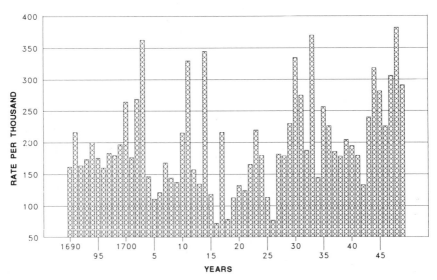

nights of the fall and winter. This may have been a way to keep warm while the stove fires slowly died down.

Affected by the seasons and particularly the times when navigation was possible, the residents of Québec did not seem particularly interested in reproducing themselves. In part this is why widows found it easier to remarry. Again, we must explain this lack of enthusiasm on the part of Quebeckers for a large family either on the basis of living conditions, which as most demographers admit are more difficult in an urban environment; on the basis of deliberate choices made by a sector of the population; on the basis of the premature end of marital unions, or even high infant mortality.

Struggle for Survival

Obviously, we should beware of the ratio of births per marriage, since at no time does this take into account the deaths that balance the growth of populations.[53] In France, infant mortality (0-1 year) fluctuated around and could even rise above one-fourth of all live births and the same was most likely true of Canada.[54] And since the cities in the past were considered to be "devourers of men"[55] these rates must have been even higher in Québec. The deaths recorded by the priests of Notre-Dame in Québec show that two out of every five newborns died soon after birth (Table 12).[56] But, even though during the period between 1710 and 1730, the number of births per family plunged (Graph 5) as the result of the difficult times (see below) and deaths followed the same trend; after 1730, infant mortality increased as the century drew to a close (Graph 6). Children (1-14 years) accounted for 27% of all deaths. In sum, during the course of the 18th century two out of every three children never reached the age of 15.[57]

On the whole, slightly more boys (52%) than girls died over the course of these 60 years. This proportion is also true in the case of newborn and elderly people; on the other hand, girls 1 to 14 and women between 15 and 49, died in greater numbers; the first probably as the result of domestic work[58] and the second childbirth. A baby boy that successfully reached his first year of existence had a better chance to grow old than his sister or the girl next door.

Nevertheless, it is important to remember that these are minimum estimates of deaths and that, during the mortality crises that assailed Québec during the course of the 18th century, especially during the first twenty years, many deaths may not have been recorded. As Graph 7 shows there were six mortality peaks in Québec between 1702 and 1748, of which four took place between 1702 and 1718. The epidemics of smallpox of 1702-03 and 1733 were the most cruel blows and were subsequently followed by the crises of 1714-15, 1717 and 1748.

Pierre-Georges Roy estimated that about 350 people died in Québec as the result of the smallpox epidemic of 1702-03.[59] This figure represents about 20% of the population of the capital and, if we believe the words of Governor Callières and Colonial Administrator Beauharnois, this was equivalent to about 30% of all deaths that occurred in the colony at that time.[60] The epidemic of smallpox led to a veritable "mortality crisis." We could even say that it was a "major crisis" with a magnitude of four according to Dupâquier's scale.[61] During these initial years of the 18th century, death rode through the streets of Québec causing greater

GRAPH 7
BAPTISMS, MARRIAGES AND BURIALS
QUÉBEC, 1690-1749

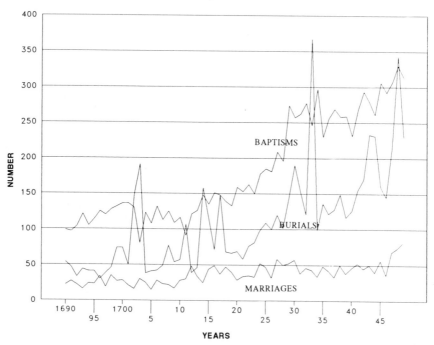

ravages than in Montréal, where 8% of the European population perished.[62]

But Quebeckers were not at the end of their pain. They would have to confront death three more times during the course of the second decade of the 18th century. The worst of these crises, the calamity of 1714-15 was as bad as that of 1702-03. In terms of its index, it also represents a "major crisis" despite the fact that it killed only 6.6% of the population.

According to Dupâquier's evaluation, the crisis of 1717 represented only a "minor crisis." In accordance with the same method, no crisis was caused by the 1711 epidemic of "Siam fever" despite the peaks in the figure.[63] Subsequently, two new crises stunned the Canadian population during the course of 1730 and 1740.[64] As was the case during the crisis of 1702-03, smallpox achieved its worst ravages in the capital. Again in

1733, death cut down more victims in Québec than in Montréal when
a crisis, measuring four in the scale, killed 9.7% of the population. In
1748 there was a similar situation when 6.5% of the population perished.

The people of Québec were familiar with the face of death. From their
first breath, first the newborns then the children and then the future moth-
ers, who were at the time the main three categories of victims, had to
engage in an incessant struggle for life. As far as men over 50 are concerned, they seemed to have died of old age after a full life. The path
through life was strewn with snares.

During the course of these years, the capital had to face a constant
battle with famine and poor harvests. As J. Hamelin pointed out, "there
is a remarkable correspondence, if we consider that, on the figure (representing fluctuations in the price of wheat in Québec), a poor harvest
results in a peak the following year."[65] Thus, in 1700-01 the price of
wheat was high, and the years 1713-19 were also characterized by high
prices and high inflation; during this time, the inhabitants of Québec
had to face one poor harvest after another. When grain was scarce they
had to depend upon the products of their own hunting and fishing. The
population also had to grapple with vitamin deficiencies during the
winter, which created a more fertile ground for epidemics like those of
1702-03 and 1732.[66] Although sombre, this picture is probably less
dreary than the situation prevailing on the other side of the Atlantic.

*****

The population of Québec grew at a relatively modest pace of 2% per
year between 1690 and 1755, a rate that was lower than that of the colony as a whole. But behind this seeming stability are often hidden spectacular leaps and bounds orchestrated around the economic climate. The
town attracted a number of foreigners seeking new job opportunities;
and it was they who ensured that society carried on since Quebeckers
were dying in large numbers. Furthermore the capital was not absorbing
its excess births. A frightful thing occurred: people, even entire
families, had to move away. Québec became something like a revolving
door through which passed not only goods, but also people. The population was not only mobile but we would even say volatile. This mobility

is at the origin of the sudden changes in the statistical censuses. It is important to point out that, during the difficult years from 1713 to 1726, the Colonial Administrator ordered 11 censuses in 14 years. The administrators were worried about all this coming and going, and the unsettlement caused by the bad economic conditions.

When things took a turn for the worse, rural people did not hesitate to return to their villages from which their roots had never been completely torn.[67] From our perspective, this human flux is characteristic of urban settlement: despite its surrounding walls Québec was a town open to all comers. However, its evolution is in singular contrast with that of the village, which easily welcomes increasing numbers of foreigners;[68] over the course of the years, the population of the capital tended to turn back upon itself and even to withdraw behind its walls.

This parallel between the town and the countryside also emphasizes the behavioural difference between city and country dwellers. Québec couples had fewer children than those in rural areas, even though the difference diminished during the course of the 18th century, so that over 40% of the population was under 15 years of age. On the other hand, there were fewer children per family in Québec than in the colony. This may have been due to the fact that children were dying at a young age; a total of two out of every three children never reached the age of 15. This sad reality partly explains why widows were able to marry again in such high numbers. Nevertheless, this explanation can be only partial, because we should also take into account working conditions and consequently, economic conditions, as well as the behaviour of the population in terms of their propensity toward marriage and the timing of births: in Québec, a port open to navigation for six months every year, the pulse of the city beats to the cadence of the tides. Maritime and therefore, economic activities, modulated the demographic behaviour. Statistical "anomalies" can be explained and thus no longer exist. Statistical censuses reflect the economic situation.

CHAPTER 2

OF MEN, NEIGHBOURHOODS AND TRADES

To reduce the capital's population to a general statistic does not really capture its vital cadence. Just like today, each neighbourhood had its own characteristics; each sought to distinguish itself. If Place Royale claimed to be the heart of Lower Town since it was the harbour district and thereby the centre of trade, what was the situation in Upper Town, the Palace Quarter or the suburbs, (that is, the area bordering the Saint-Charles River, Côte Saint-Jean and the Canardière)? Do the nominal rolls of the priests make it possible to understand social change or only the pace of urban development? In short, we must be able to glean information about the growth of the city, each of its districts and, as far as possible, of its various streets.

Evolution of the Urban Base

Whether influenced by geographic or economic criteria, by cultural or social factors, Québec's residents, new or old, demonstrated their preferences by choosing the neighbourhood where they wanted to live. There is no doubt that this development was based on economic, social or cultural considerations.[1] Already the general demographic traits have produced evidence of great mobility and consequently of rapid evolution. Therefore, the change must be measured not only from the point of view of numbers, but also in terms of social change.[2]

TABLE 13
NATURAL POPULATION GROWTH
QUÉBEC, 1690-1749

Decade	Births	Deaths	Increase	Annual Average
1690-1699	1148	448	700	70.0
1700-1709	1195	764	431	43.1
1710-1719	1312	875	437	43.7
1720-1729	1859	958	901	90.1
1730-1739	2643	1583	1060	106.0
1740-1749	2910	2010	900	90.0
Total	11 067	6638	4429	442.9
Ten-year average	1844.5	1106.3	738	73.8

Growth

A survey of its four districts leads the observer of 18th-century Québec to note that by the end of the 17th century Lower Town was, according to the Jesuit Antoine Silvy, "crowded with houses"; it had hardly any lots available for building. Consequently Upper Town had to absorb this surplus population and experienced marked growth between 1700 and 1713.[3]

For his part, and as a function of his urban expansion projects, the engineer Gaspard Chaussegros de Léry observed that around 1745[4] the population was growing by 130 people annually. Apart from natural growth, this figure undoubtedly includes the increase due to immigration. If he had only taken into account natural growth, he would have realized that the capital's population increased by 74 people annually between 1690 and 1749. The high points of this increase would have been between 1730 and 1739, with an average of 106 people per year (Table 13). The engineer's way of forecasting the growth in the population base, although simplistic, nevertheless helped him estimate the urban area that Québec's population could occupy.

The plans for urban expansion show, however, that the engineer was concerned with the city's commercial needs, at least as far as Lower

TABLE 14
GROWTH RATE BY DISTRICT, QUÉBEC
1716 AND 1744

District	Population		Rate
	1716	1744	(%)
Upper Town	707	2242	3.72
Lower Town	1379	1831	1.01
Palace Quarter	146	411	3.40
St-Roch Suburb		248	
Suburbs	44	272	5.15
Total	2276	5004	2.68

Town and the harbour were concerned. He anticipated an increase in shipping activity and predicted that some of the jobs thus created would attract new residents and merchants. Consequently, he planned to house part of the population in the harbour district. As for Upper Town, he planned to develop his main hubs for urban expansion there.

Chaussegros de Léry attempted to create a more homogeneous urban environment. Having gone to see Father Jacrau in 1745 to find out about the demographic growth of the capital, he was forced to recognize that, since 1716, the territorial expansion had been carried out in a haphazard manner. He more than likely looked not only at the registers of births, marriages and deaths, but also at the censuses carried out by the priests, one of which was conducted in 1716 and the other, which was still "current" in 1744.

Based on this data, the engineer noted that between 1716 and 1744 Québec's population grew at a rate of 2.7% annually, and that only one neighbourhood had below-normal expansion: Lower Town (Table 14),[5] where geography prevented the demographic growth of the sector.[6] To overcome the natural obstacles (quite apart from defensive considerations), the military engineers and especially Chaussegros de Léry strove to propose urban expansion projects in this district.

As for Upper Town, which showed a significant rate of growth, expansion was hampered by the Chevalier de Beaucour's ramparts. Since the population in this district increased greatly at the beginning of the 18th

Fig. 1 Chaussegros de Léry's draft for the fortifications, which was accepted by the Court in 1718, created a new zone for construction inside the walls. The map shows the limits of Upper Town as defined by the Chevalier de Beaucour's enclosure (1693). The ramparts further west belong to the new layout proposed by Chaussegros in 1740. *Chaussegros de Léry, 1716 and 1740, Baudouin copy. National Archives of Canada, C 15735.*

century, if its new inhabitants wanted to benefit from the protection of the ramparts, they had to occupy the lots surrendered by the religious communities. According to the maps of the time, most of those who arrived in Upper Town settled inside the walls; for example, in the Cap-aux-Diamants sector, around the Hotel-Dieu Hospital, near the Seminary and in the Jesuit enclosure. Only Saint-Louis Street actually went beyond Beaucour's fortifications (Figure 1).

The Palace Quarter grew just as rapidly as Upper Town. The establishment of a ship-building yard on the riverbank encouraged tradesmen and day labourers to settle near their place of work. As for the rate of growth of the suburbs, it cannot be explained by the establishment of the shipyard alone; if Father Thibault had included the whole suburb in his 1716 census, the rate of growth (5.15%) would have been much more moderate.

Households

These rates of growth can be explained by characteristics that are not only quantitative, but also qualitative or rather, social. According to the nominal rolls of the priests, their flock increased from 2276 to 5004 between 1716 and 1744. These figures do not take into account garrisoned servicemen[7] or members of religious communities. The 2276 souls counted in 1716 were distributed over the whole area and formed 460 households;[8] namely, an average of 4.9 people per household. Twenty-eight years later, Father Jacrau enumerated 5004 people within the limits of his parish, distributed among 1054 households,[9] for an average of 4.7 people per household.[10] In short, considering the long period of time involved, the size of the households had tended to decrease. However, we must remember that this phenomenon sometimes hides the true picture.[11]

According to the information supplied by the priests, the age of the adult population increased over the course of the 18th century; the presence of younger children in 1744 may be explained not by the use of effective contraceptives,[12] but by the fact that people were marrying later in life, or that widows did not remarry for a long time after the death of their spouses. In the typical 1716 household, the man was aged about 42 and his wife or widow, 36.5; they were guardians of 2.6 children and housed 0.2 other people or apprentices. To carry out their domestic tasks, they were helped by 0.3 domestics.[13] According to Father Jacrau, in 1744 the man was one year older and his companion about three years older. The couple had fewer children (2.4), put up fewer relatives or other people, but had the same number of domestics.

Two phenomena arise out of these general figures: on one hand, the true number of children could hardly have been higher in 1744 since the average age of the woman was 39.5, which marked the true end (as opposed to the theoretical end) of her period of fertility.[14] On the other hand, since the number of children decreased and the proportion of domestics remained the same, we should not interpret this as a need for help during the time when the families were getting established,[15] but by a desire to "look good" or for a "taste for ostentation."[16] In such a context, perhaps it is better to introduce a new variable that could affect demographic behaviour: social and professional class.

Trades

In the 18th century, the priests in Québec listed about 60 trades practised by the heads of households. But since the priests were a bit "careless" regarding the professional status of their flocks,[17] this led to some lack of precision in the naming of trades. However, the concept of "sectors of activity" taken from L. Dechêne,[18] makes it possible to group together the various trades and thus to analyze the urban economic structure. These four sectors include most of the trades: service, business, artisans and unskilled workers.

The service sector includes Councillors, officers, public servants, surgeons and sergeants. The business sector includes, apart from shopkeepers and merchants, carriers (sailors, carters, masters of small craft and others) as well as trades related to food (butchers, bakers, hotel- and inn-keepers). The artisan sector includes the construction (masons, carpenters, framers), iron (blacksmiths, edge-tool makers, locksmiths), clothing (especially tailors and wig-makers), leather (tanners, shoemakers and saddle-makers) and the woodworking trades (cask-makers, ship carpenters). The last sector is mainly limited to day labourers.

TABLE 15

DISTRIBUTION OF HEADS OF HOUSEHOLDS, BY SECTOR OF ACTIVITY AND DISTRICT, QUÉBEC, 1716 AND 1744

District	Services		Business		Artisan		Unskilled Labour		Total	
	1716	1744	1716	1744	1716	1744	1716	1744	1716	1744
Upper Town	36	66	17	97	45	144	19	60	117	367
%	30.8	18	14.5	26.4	38.5	39.2	16.2	16.3	37.7	45.1
Lower Town	33	39	77	153	61	114	11	26	182	332
%	18.1	11.9	42.3	46.1	33.5	34.3	6.0	7.8	58.0	40.8
Palace Q. & Saint-Roch	4	17	2	23	7	60	2	15	15	115
%	26.7	14.8	13.3	20.0	46.7	52.2	13.3	13.3	4.7	14.1
Total	73	122	96	273	113	318	32	101	314	814
%	23.2	15.0	30.6	33.5	36.0	39.1	10.2	12.4		

Looked at from the point of view of socio-professional classifications, the capital shows signs of a tangible social change, not based on the general distribution of spheres of activity, but rather on their distribution among the various neighbourhoods (Table 15). In a general distribution, only the service sector shows a pronounced loss in terms of its relative size (from 23% to 15%), a situation that was considered normal in the 18th century since the administrative infrastructure related to the role of the city as capital was already in place.[19] Nevertheless, the void created when the service sector reached its upper limit was distributed equally among the three other sectors; an impression of stability emerges from all this. With regard to the districts this stability appears to be only relative. People moved; work or clients attracted them to one neighbourhood or another. Whereas in 1716 Upper Town was home to artisans first and then to people from the service sector, the situation changed considerably throughout the century. In 1744, the business sector supplanted the service sector, which then fell to third place. In Lower Town and in the Palace Quarter, the withdrawal of officers and public servants allowed the merchants to consolidate their position, although in this district artisans were still the largest group. This situation was to have concrete repercussions on the urban landscape.

TABLE 16
DISTRIBUTION OF HOUSEHOLDS, BY TRADE, QUÉBEC, 1716 AND 1744

Sectors	House-holds		Individuals		No. per household		Age of men		Age of Women		Children		Child. per household		Childless household		Servants		Serv. per household	
	1716	1744	1716	1744	1716	1744	1716	1744	1716	1744	1716	1744	1716	1744	1716	1744	1716	1744	1716	1744
Services																				
Councillor	10	9	77	68	7.7	7.6	53.5	46.0	37.0	36.2	36	32	3.6	3.6	1	3	18	20	1.8	2.2
Public Servant	11	20	51	107	4.6	5.3	43.4	45.8	39.7	41.5	21	48	1.9	2.4	4	7	10	20	0.9	1.0
Officer	11	19	56	97	5.1	5.1	48.9	50.6	39.4	39.4	32	39	2.9	2.0	4	6	5	21	0.4	1.1
Surgeon	7	6	30	40	4.3	6.7	38.1	45.5	34.0	33.1	16	22	2.3	3.7	2	1	1	3	0.1	0.5
Sergeant	7	10	58	61	8.3	6.1	50.0	45.1	37.9	39.2	44	41	6.3	4.1	0	0	0	0	0.0	0.0
	46	64	272	373	5.9	5.8	46.8	46.6	37.6	37.9	149	182	3.2	2.8	11	17	34	64	0.7	1.0
Business																				
Merchant	35	62	184	324	5.3	5.2	43.2	41.4	35.3	35.5	77	135	2.2	2.2	10	21	33	64	0.9	1.0
Tavern-keeper	7	3	49	16	7.0	5.3	39.8	50.7	33.7	41.3	26	9	3.7	3.0	1	0	6	0	0.9	0.0
Butcher	4	17	22	94	5.5	5.5	41.5	42.1	41.2	37.9	10	46	2.5	2.7	1	6	2	6	0.5	0.3
Baker	5	16	36	84	7.2	5.2	42.0	38.4	39.6	31.7	25	48	5.0	3.0	0	4	2	7	0.4	0.4
Carter	9	43	52	251	5.8	5.8	41.4	41.4	32.3	37.7	32	157	3.5	3.6	1	6	1	5	0.1	0.1
Publican	11	39	46	186	4.2	4.8	39.0	43.8	42.2	41.8	27	103	2.4	2.6	2	12	0	2	0.0	0.1
Sailor	18	75	78	315	4.3	4.2	39.8	38.9	32.5	43.5	45	137	2.5	1.8	4	21	0	15	0.0	0.2
	89	255	467	1270	5.2	5.0	41.0	42.4	36.7	37.1	242	635	2.7	2.5	19	70	44	99	0.5	0.4
Artisan																				
Mason	10	27	47	135	4.7	5.0	42.8	40.7	37.9	33.6	25	78	2.5	2.9	2	4	1	2	0.1	0.1
Cabinet-maker	14	39	98	235	7.0	6.0	41.6	43.8	33.1	39.6	68	153	4.9	3.9	0	3	0	2	0.0	0.1
Carpenter	12	85	56	382	4.7	4.5	39.1	39.3	35.7	34.6	31	199	2.6	2.3	3	19	1	2	0.0	0.2
Blacksmith	9	29	50	170	5.5	5.9	38.3	39.4	34.4	35.4	31	86	3.4	3.0	1	4	1	23	0.1	0.8
Cooper	7	25	43	127	6.1	5.1	42.9	37.8	30.2	36.5	23	57	3.3	2.2	0	10	2	11	0.3	0.4
Shoemaker	18	26	88	113	4.9	4.3	35.7	42.4	32.2	35.9	49	56	2.7	2.1	4	8	4	4	0.2	0.1
Tailor	7	16	33	75	4.7	4.7	50.7	37.0	40.8	36.2	17	40	2.4	2.5	1	4	2	2	0.3	0.1
	77	247	415	1237	5.4	5.0	41.9	39.6	34.4	36.2	244	669	3.2	2.7	11	52	10	46	0.1	0.2
Unskilled																				
Labourer	24	96	118	430	4.9	4.5	43.7	40.6	38.2	35.6	68	232	2.8	2.4	3	19	0	3	0	0.3
Total	236	662	1272	3310	5.35	5.1	43.3	42.3	36.7	36.7	703	1718	3.0	2.6	44	158	88	212	0.3	0.4

Households and Trades

If the various heads of household in Québec were grouped together under socio-professional categories we find, for the four professional sectors, a decrease in the size of households[20] between 1716 and 1744 (Table 16). Although the age of the couples remained more or less the same, this situation was due to a general decrease in the average number of children, and a considerable increase in the number of childless couples in the business, artisan and unskilled labour sectors. Paradoxically, while the average number of children decreased in the service sector, the number of domestics increased, a situation that tends to confirm the previous statement on the hiring of domestics.[21]

Neighbourhoods and Streets

Whether they describe the size of the households or the "position" of the heads of households, general statistics dealing with an urban base, whose elements together form the network of its districts, cannot bring to life the various neighbourhoods, with their children's cries or shop noises. Each neighbourhood has its own characteristics.

Upper Town

While Father Jacrau pointed out that Upper Town in 1744 had three times more households and thus a population three times larger than in 1716, it should be emphasized that the number of clergymen decreased almost in the same proportions. Upper Town, which had been the preferred place for the establishment of religious communities since the beginnings of the colony, contained the Seminary, the houses of the Jesuits, Recollects, Hospitalières and Ursulines, not to mention the Bishopric. Whereas in 1716 Upper Town had one person from a religious community for every four laymen; in 1744 the ratio was one to eleven.

In 1744, Father Jacrau found that nearly 45% of the members of his parish lived in Upper Town, a substantial increase in relation to the previous enumeration (Table 17). The average size of the households had

TABLE 17

EVOLUTION OF THE COMPOSITION OF THE POPULATION BY DISTRICT, QUÉBEC, 1716 AND 1744

District	Households		Population		Children and adolescents				Age/Men		Age/Women	
					Total		- 15 yrs					
	1716	1744	1716	1744	1716	1744	1716	1744	1716	1744	1716	1744
Upper Town	136	458	707	2242	405	1175	289	891	44.1	43.3	38.6	39.6
%	29.6	43.4	31.1	44.8	32.8	46.5	32.4	46.8				
Lower Town	295	409	1379	1831	715	869	525	630	40.4	43.1	35.7	39.3
%	64.1	38.8	60.6	36.6	58.0	34.4	58.9	33.1				
Palace Q.	23	91	146	411	91	199	62	164	41.7	37.4	34.9	36.9
%	5	8.6	6.4	8.2	7.4	7.9	6.9	8.6				
Inner Sub.	0	50	0	248	0	123	0	98		42.8		38.2
%		4.7		4.9		4.9		5.1				
Outer Sub.	6	46	44	272	22	160	15	119	31.5	43.2	29.6	40.3
%	1.3	4.4	1.9	5.4	1.8	6.3	1.7	6.2				
Total	460	1054	2276	5004	1233	2526	891	1902	41.8	42.8	36.5	39.4

decreased; a phenomenon due to the lower number of children per household, although the ratio in the neighbourhood remained above the urban average. Thus Upper Town housed 465 of all the children in the parish, an increase that was parallel to the growth in the number of parishioners.

Furthermore, even though artisans were the most numerous representatives in Upper Town society, the beginnings of spatial segregation were starting to be noticeable. In 1716 as well as in 1744, three households of artisans and day labourers out of every five lived north of the area bordered by Buade, de la Fabrique and Saint-Jean streets. Although the proportion of merchants and domestics had increased considerably in Upper Town, the number of domestics in the artisan's enclave remained the same throughout the period: it housed one-third of the district's domestics, although many of them lived on rue des Pauvres (today, Côte du Palais), where many government employees and merchants lived.

In 1716, the Upper Town of Father Thibault had ten streets; in 1744, that of Father Jacrau had twice as many. Without describing the characteristics of the households one by one, we will mention the most important streets either in terms of their population, the size of their households, or their number of children or domestics.

In 1716, with its 244 residents, Saint-Louis Street was the most populous street in Upper Town with about one-third of the population of the district or about 10% of the capital's population living there. The second most populous street in the district was Couillard Street with 108 inhabitants, followed by Saint-Anne and de la Fabrique, which had 74 and 70 residents respectively. The other streets (des Jardins, de la Sainte-Famille, Buade, du Trésor, Saint-Jean, des Carrières) had 50 people or less.

Twenty-eight years later Upper Town had changed considerably. Saint-Louis Street was still the most populous: it had 419 residents, which represented 19% of the residents of the district or 8% of the population of the city. The second most populous street was no longer Couillard, but Saint-Jean, with 16% of the citizens of the district. Thus, over one-third of Upper Town's population was concentrated on these two streets (Figure 2). Next, in descending order were Couillard, Buade, de la Sainte-Famille, Saint-Joseph and des Pauvres; in short, the most populous streets were the oldest ones.

Even though the oldest heads of households lived more or less on the same streets in 1744 (notably de la Sainte-Famille and Couillard); the youngest ones lived on Saint-Flavien Street, de Lavallée and du Séminaire, all three of which were located in the newly developed "fief of Sault-au-Matelot." Most of the streets showed a significant increase in the number of residents, which had doubled or almost doubled except for des Jardins, Sainte-Anne, de la Fabrique and Couillard streets.

As far as the social landscape is concerned, whereas Saint-Louis Street had mostly artisans and day labourers in 1716, by 1744 the picture had changed and it was now inhabited above all by officers and merchants. Consequently, it had a high proportion of domestics, as was the case on Buade and des Jardins streets where there was also a high concentration of officers and merchants. All this leads us to suspect a link between this social concentration and the proximity of the Château Saint-Louis, since Upper Town was above all inhabited by artisans.

In summary, Upper Town, which had a number of unoccupied lots and was easier and easier to reach, became an outlet for those who could not find lodgings in Lower Town or the Palace Quarter. It was the place where religious communities became established; in the middle of the century, they became less visible, even though they still controlled the property base. Certain institutions that faced financial difficulties had to sell lots, and this helped attract young couples, particularly artisans. In this context, the subsequent statement by the engineer Chaussegros de

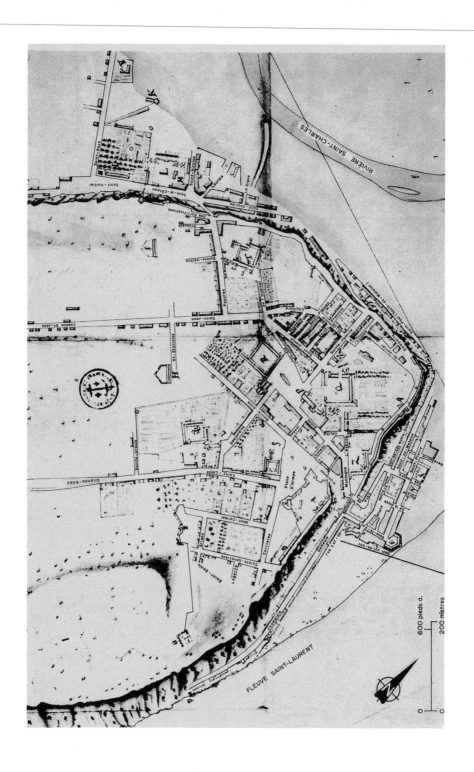

Fig. 2 Streets and laneways in Québec around 1740. At that time, most of the streets had settled on their final names. But there are always exceptions, for example, more often than not Saint Paul Street was called Sault-au-Matelot. The lanes were less firm: "de l'Hôpital" was also called "des Morts." Saint Vallier Street in Upper Town was soon renamed Laval Street in order to avoid any confusion with the one in the Palace Quarter. *Map: F. Pellerin, (86-19G-D3) from a map by Chaussegros de Léry, 1742 (National Archives of Canada, H3/340/Québec/1742/section).*

Léry that it was necessary to "rid" Upper Town of its artisans takes on its full meaning,[22] especially since he lived in Saint-Famille Street himself!

Lower Town

Throughout the period, Lower Town remained the preferred location for merchants. The proximity of the harbour and warehouses provides the reason behind this situation. But it was not only the merchants who settled in Lower Town; ship captains and sailors were also found there. The construction of the Cul-de-Sac shipyard in 1744 undoubtedly helped maintain, if not increase, this preponderance of trading activities in Lower Town.

At the beginning of the 18th century, Lower Town housed 60.6% of the capital's population; consequently, three-fifths (58%) of its children were found there. In 1744, it had only 36.6% of the people in the parish; the district having only gained 114 households and 452 people. Its population, older than that in 1716, assumed fewer responsibilities concerning children, since there were fewer children per family there than the urban average. However, this was still the location of the greatest number of domestics.[23]

While in 1716 the merchants were mainly established on Notre-Dame and Sous-le-Fort streets and on Place Royale, by 1744 they had invaded Saint-Pierre Street. It was also on these streets that the greatest number of domestics were found. One street stood out in 1744; and it deserves to be called a shopping thoroughfare since nine out of ten heads of households living there were artisans; this was rue de l'Escalier. It should be pointed out that on this street children were rare, a situation that can perhaps be explained by the fact that quarters were cramped and that the residents were mostly young couples.

In 1716, the population of Lower Town was concentrated on Sault-au-Matelot Street (28% of the neighbourhood). The de Meulle-Champlain section was second, but had more households; 52% of the households in Lower Town lived on these streets, followed in order by: Sous-le-Fort, Côte de la Montagne, Cul-de-Sac and Notre-Dame. Twenty-eight years later, the situation was similar: Sault-au-Matelot and de Meulle-Champlain, streets were still the most populous thoroughfares, not only of the neighbourhood, but of the capital; in fact, over half of Lower Town's population lived there (54%).

Whereas the youngest couples lived on Sous-le-Fort Street in 1716 as well as in 1744, this was also where the smallest households were found, apart from rue de l'Escalier. On the basis of these demographic indications alone, it seems that Lower Town was frozen in time. We see only a few signs of change, such as the age of the parishioners or the "class" of the residents of Saint-Pierre Street. And yet activity in the harbour imparted a highly dynamic pace to life.

Palace Quarter

The establishment of the shipyard on the banks of the Saint-Charles River explains the fast rate of growth in this district during the 18th century. Whereas in 1716 this neighbourhood accounted for 6.4% of the population, 28 years later it housed 8.2% of it. The presence of the Colonial Administrator's Palace was only a minor attraction for the residents of the neighbourhood as shown by the distribution of the professions of the heads of households. Throughout the 18th century artisans and day labourers predominated in this district. Thus, we should not be surprised to find more male domestics, who were mostly hired as apprentices.

The few public servants attracted by the proximity of the Colonial Administrator's Palace lived not far away on Saint-Nicolas Street. But whereas this street housed 5% of the urban population in 1716, it subsequently reached a plateau and even stagnated. It was supplanted by Saint-Charles Street, where 6% of the capital's population lived in 1744.

In that same year, the head of household was younger than his counterpart in 1716; on the other hand his wife or widow was older, a fact that could not, however, explain why there were much fewer children in the households. Furthermore, these children were younger than the urban average, whereas in 1716 they had been older. At the beginning of the 18th century, families lived and worked there; in the middle of the century, the voices of children had given way to the creaking of cart wheels and the noise made by the pulleys in the shipyard. Over the course of these 28 years, the residents of the district progressively gave more importance to work than to their families, which partially explains the extreme drop in the birthrate there.

The Suburbs

The suburbs were markedly different from the urban area. Despite their rate of growth they remained marginal: in 1716, 2% of the parishioners lived there, and in 1744, 5%. Nevertheless a downward trend was observed in terms of the size of the households. We should add though that there were more children per household there than in the urban neighbourhoods. The suburbs were by definition a rural environment so the demographic behaviour of the people there was necessarily different, based on a conscious ... or imposed policy supporting a rising birthrate. The presence of adolescents in the families compensated for the lack of domestic help.

This rapid overview of the evolution of these districts makes it possible to see behind the screen formed by the apparent lack of change in the urban socio-professional structure. An observer of the scene in Québec in the 18th century can perceive a significant change in the spatial distribution of the population: people no longer sought to settle in Lower Town at any cost; Upper Town was just as attractive, perhaps because of the lots there or the type of housing available for rent. But for harbour workers and sailors, Upper Town had a major inconvenience: its distance from their place of work. A fact arises from the observation of these neighbourhoods: each one developed at a different pace due to the different poles of attraction that were specific to it. However, each neighbourhood had certain nuclei of social structure: in Upper Town, the Château and its immediate surroundings represented a microcosm; in the Palace Quarter the same phenomenon was repeated in Saint-Nicolas Street around the Indendant's Palace.

Furthermore, three observations should be made concerning the movements of the population between 1716 and 1744. First, the streets that were the most populous in 1716 were still the most populous in the middle of the century. In 1744, 41.7% of the capital's population was concentrated on five streets. The second observation, to nobody's great surprise, is that the city grew not only toward the west but also into the heart of Upper Town, when the fief of Sault-au-Matelot was developed: Nouvelle, Saint-Flavien, Saint-Joseph, Saint-François and Lavallé streets were witness to this fact. They housed 18% of Upper Town's population and 8% of the population of the city. Finally, the oldest households preferred to settle in Upper Town. However, it must be added that in this case, a further assumption would prove false: it was not necessarily true that the older the household the larger the family. The residents of Sainte-Anne, de la Fabrique and Notre-Dame streets invalidate this trend. Other variables such as socio-professional class and the economic situation came into play.

Domestic Servants

The occupational structure does not allow for observing the trends followed by domestic staff as such, even though they accounted for a significant proportion of the capital's population. Domestic servants, who made up between 5 and 6% of the "working" population, testify to certain social distinctions, and make it possible to study certain demographic characteristics, especially some socio-economic indicators regarding their employer's households.

First, we should remember that these were live-in domestics, living and working in an urban environment, who could therefore be easily targeted; on the other hand, it is important to determine whether there was a progression or regression in the number of domestics. The fact that domestic servants resided with their employers denotes that the latter were quite well-off. It presupposes that the residence was specially laid out

TABLE 18
SERVANTS, 1716 AND 1744

District	Men				Women				Unspecified		Total	
	+ 15 yrs		- 15 yrs		+ 15 yrs		− 15 yrs					
	1716	1744	1716	1744	1716	1744	1716	1744	1716	1744	1716	1744
Upper Town	6	28	1	17	13	65	4	10		3	24	123
Lower Town	20	42	8	10	45	61	12	7	4	3	89	123
Palace Q. & Inner Sub.		16		2	2	13	1	3	2	1	5	35
Inner Sub.		6		3		1		1	2	0	2	11
Total	26	92	9	32	60	140	17	21	8	7	120	292

and materially organized to accommodate the hired person; the servants' living conditions ensued directly from those of their employers.

In 1716, domestic staff represented 5% of the population. This proportion hardly changed in 28 years; it was 5.9% in 1744. These figures are consistent with those observed in certain French provinces.[24] However, this labour force was employed, in 1716 as well as in 1744, by less than 30% of the households. On the other hand, it should be noted that there was a slight increase in the average number of domestics per household in 1744; but this average was less than two, except in the case of Councillors. This means that between 1716 and 1744, domestic servants were not very common and that often there was only one servant per household. In 1716 and in 1744, the domestic servant, who was most probably a maid since women were in the majority, was over 15 years of age (Table 18). While in 1716 they were first present in Lower Town, by 1744 there were as many of them in Upper Town.

But we must still trace a picture of the employers. According to Table 19, the employers of domestic servants showed an apparent inertia during the 18th century. The main employers of domestic servants were concentrated in the business and service sectors, especially Councillors, public servants, officers and merchants. This situation predominates when only employers are compared amongst themselves. There would seem to have been only a slight shift toward the artisan sector. However, the situation changes considerably when we take into consideration the socio-professional distribution of the urban population. While artisans more or less maintained the same trends (12.4% versus 12.9%) in terms of hiring "apprentice/domestics," the roles were reversed in the service

TABLE 19

SOCIO-PROFESSIONAL DISTRIBUTION
OF EMPLOYERS OF SERVANTS, QUEBEC, 1716 AND 1744

Sector	Employers 1716				Employers 1744			
	Number		%		Number		%	
	Potential	Actual Servants	Actual Servants	By sector	Potential	Actual Servants	Actual Servants	By sector
Services	73	21	26.6	28.8	122	42	22.9	34.4
Business	96	27	34.2	28.1	273	59	32.2	21.6
Artisan	113	14	17.7	12.4	318	41	22.4	12.9
Unskilled	32	0			101	5	2.7	4.9
Unknown		10	12.6			25	13.7	
Widows		7	8.9			11	6.0	
Total	314	79			814	183		

(28.8% versus 34.5%) and business (28.1% versus 21.6%) sectors. Taking into account their proportions in the city as a whole, public servants and other government employees appear to have been the main employers of domestic help in 1744; on the other hand, merchants showed an unequivocal slowing down in their hiring of domestics. If we retain the premise that material affluence is symbolized by the presence of domestic servants, a considerable change in the distribution of wealth among Québec population must have taken place during the 18th century.

A last element will allow us to complete this portrait of the domestic's employer: the servant's tasks. Obviously, we could consult the hiring contracts of servants in order to find this information;[25] however, the enumerations will give us certain indications. Depending upon whether the employer had children or not, or whether he was an artisan, the hired person had to carry out family duties, look after household needs, or carry out professional tasks. The proportion of employers with children, as well as the number of apprentices, fell during the 18th century and a greater place was taken up by employers without children, whether couples, single people or widowers. Clearly domestic staff also met other needs....

In summary, a study of domestic staff gives life to the statistics; it brings out two important considerations from the anonymous figures. Beyond the ostentation of some employers inspired by a certain desire for social emulation, the female domestic servant (since women were in the majority) met material needs and satisfied considerations of a more human nature. Moreover, the desire to emulate by certain merchants became victim, as did the merchants themselves, to a reversal of fortunes during the 18th century, as shown by the drop in the number of employers in the business sector.

*****

Between 1716 and 1744 the face of the capital's neighbourhoods underwent great changes, not only on the socio-professional level, but also on the demographic plane. One after the other, the districts echoed with the cries of children or hummed with artisan's activities. The Palace Quarter became a worksite while Upper Town experienced the beginnings of spatial segregation when artisans and day labourers were driven north of the Saint-Jean/Buade axis.

Households became less crowded especially in the case of artisans and day labourers. Also in spite of a more limited number of children, the Councillors, officers and public servants hired more domestic servants. But while merchants became more numerous, they hired fewer servants, leaving the way open for the hypothesis of a difficult financial situation.

Although death lurked in the streets of Québec and struck blindly in all districts, it was not the only element responsible for these important demographic changes. Despite a serious handicap imposed on the renewal of generations by a high rate of infant and child mortality, this factor only imposed a certain pace on urban life. This cadence was not due strictly to demographic crises, but also to the contributions of the metropolitan and regional populations, in such a way that the pace was transformed into mobility, a mobility that depended upon the economic attractions of the capital. Thus, there was a constant coming and going between France, and other areas in the region or even the colony at large.

This movement was not limited to this direction alone; it also took place from one neighbourhood to another. When the shopkeeper hung out his sign in Upper Town, when the innkeeper attracted military or civilian clients there, or when the carter found a warehouse for his equipment or a shelter for his animals there, all this activity was likely to bring about night and day movement. These events announced a substantial change in the urban landscape. But did the shifting of two Lower Towns toward Upper Town occur strictly because of the congestion of the area circumscribed by the cliff and the river?

PART II

HOUSING CONDITIONS

The mobility of the population is a factor that is likely to affect the urban landscape in terms of architectural development. But the notion of housing conditions is not restricted to architecture alone. It also refers to general considerations such as the use of space and urban legislation, not to mention the use of the property infrastructure for accommodation or speculation purposes.

CHAPTER 3

THE URBAN LANDSCAPE

Québec is divided into Upper Town and Lower Town; the merchants live in Lower Town for easy access to the harbour, where they have built very handsome three-storey houses out of a stone that is as hard as marble. Upper Town is just as splendid and well populated. [...] There is quite a broad road between the two, which is a bit steep, with houses on the left and right. [...] The Intendant lives apart, on the banks of a small river, which joins up to the St. Lawrence River, enclosing the village at a sharp angle [translation].[1]

The illustrious traveller Lahontan, undoubtedly amazed by the urban character of Québec in such an "uncivilized" context at the end of the 17th century, was already aware that the city was divided among three districts at that time: Lower Town, Upper Town and the Palace Quarter. There was no mention of the inner or outer suburbs, which would be in place 65 years later when the Swedish botanist Pehr Kalm visited Québec, and which were created partly as the result of a marked increase in the capital's population in the 18th century.

But to bring out the urban character of Québec and describe its districts or the increase in its population, it would be pretentious to compare it to other French cities of the Enlightenment such as Lyon, Rouen, Nîmes or even Paris. Québec presents the observer with a different situation and a dissimilar pattern of change at both the territorial and human levels; however, all the elements are there, only the scale is changed. Whereas Rouen had some 60 000 inhabitants in 1760 and

Nîmes had about 36 000 around 1765,[2] the total population of Canada barely amounted to some 15 000 more than Rouen, and the capital's population was a little over 7200 in 1755.

But were conditions in Québec crowded? Was it free of problems affecting its water supply and public health as a result of its small size? Colonial administrators issued orders, ordinances and regulations to control urban growth, while the military engineers planned the enlargement of the area. These decisions affected the citizens in their daily lives. Not only did they have to be careful about what they did with their refuse, but they also had to obey the various regulations on fire prevention, which translated onto the urban landscape by the building of channels in the middle of the roads and of fire-proof walls. However, this legislation did not appear spontaneously. It adapted to circumstances and evolved as the population grew.

Québec at the Time of Pehr Kalm

The Swedish botanist described the situation in Québec in detail. In the diary of his travels to Canada he recorded not only the various plants that his hosts pointed out to him or that he discovered himself, but also the most trifling customs of the inhabitants of Québec that struck him as out of the ordinary. His scientific interest was aroused by the houses and their furnishings and by the inhabitants and their habits. The topography had changed little since Lahontan's visit so Kalm could only repeat the physical description already sketched out. But already one of his remarks is astounding: Lower Town was being built "on a promontory formed by rubbish and other things that have been discarded there."[3] This area housed most of the merchants, whose three- or four-storey stone houses were "built tightly against each other." The streets were narrow and uneven.[4]

As for Upper Town, although it was "less crowded," it still covered five or six times more space. Distinguished people lived there and that was where Québec's most important buildings were located including the Château Saint-Louis, the cathedral, the residences of the Jesuits and the Recollects, the Ursulines' convent and the Hôtel-Dieu not to mention the Seminary. Streets were wide and the houses, also made of stone, were on a level with them. Vegetable gardens were common behind the houses. The few remaining wooden houses were slowly giving way to those made of stone.[5]

The Colonial Administrator's or Intendant's palace, a public building that housed the second most important administrator of the colony, was located in the "second" Lower Town, that is to say, the Saint-Nicholas or Palace Quarter. It stood on the banks of the Saint-Charles River. Nearby were the Crown stores and the prison. The only row of houses in the district linked up with the "first" Lower Town at a place called the Canoterie.[6]

Kalm gives us a glimpse of one or more of the characteristics particular to each of these districts. Obviously this picture is not complete. The Swedish traveller forgot to point out that Lower Town included some docks. He did not mention the Cul-de-Sac shipyards in Lower Town, nor those sheltered by the dike in the Palace Quarter. He did, however, remark on the narrowness of the streets in Lower Town compared to those in Upper Town. Still the fact remains that the image that emerged from his observations needs to be further explained and in some cases even qualified.

Neighbourhoods and Streets

Even though the geographic demarcations and thus the physical characteristics of the districts seem easy to define, it is quite a different story when dealing with the various streets, the names of which (and sometimes the route) changed during the 18th century. On the other hand, although Kalm described an interesting landscape overall and in certain cases presented a true picture of the various districts, he nonetheless sketched out only a few characteristics that his visitor's eye had noticed. His too-short stay in the capital did not allow him to become familiar with the land-ownership phenomenon. Moreover, the distribution and public or private use of the land does not seem to have been of interest to him. Finally, Kalm failed to deal with urban facilities set up to ensure the water supply, public health or protection against fire.

What stands out in Kalm's mind concerning Lower Town is the height of the houses and the narrowness of the streets. This situation was dependent upon geography. Wedged between the cliff and the river, this district could only expand south to the far end of Champlain Street. Lower Town ended on this side at the foot of the Queen's battery (on the cliff, south of the Château Saint-Louis), and on the north side at the Canoterie building, which belonged to the priests of the Seminary, located at the junction of the hill of the same name and Saint-Paul Street. Built in the shape of a narrow strip of land measuring scarcely 80 *toises* (150 metres)* at its broadest point, the area measured about 16 000 square *toises* or about 6 hectares.[7] Does this mean that this whole area was suitable for houses or business? No, since we must subtract the space needed for streets and for defensive or harbour installations.

In 1716 Father Thibault listed only six or seven streets; whereas in 1744 Father Jacrau named ten: Champlain, de Meulle, Cul-de-Sac, Sous-le-Fort, de l'Escalier, Saint-Pierre, Notre-Dame (which included part of Place Royale), Côte de la Montagne (the road leading to Upper Town) and Sault-au-Matelot. Father Jacrau did not differentiate between Sault-au-Matelot Street itself and its extension to the north, which the Seminary priests identified in their 1737 "declarations and enumerations" as Saint-Paul Street. It goes without saying that Thibault only included the main streets. The lanes (called "ruelles" or "ruettes") that linked several streets were not mentioned. Between Champlain and Cul-de-Sac streets there were up to eight of these alleys as well as du Porche Street, Nécessaire lane, the dead-end on Notre-Dame Street and Sous-le-Cap lane, which edged its way concealed between the cliff and the back of the houses on Sault-au-Matelot and Saint-Paul streets.

Moreover, it should be pointed out that the Queen's battery was not the only defensive structure meant to protect the harbour and the Cul-de-Sac shipyards; it was supported in this role by the Royale battery at the east end of Sous-le-Fort Street and by the Dauphine battery located immediately to the east of Côte de la Montagne.

Apart from these military installations, the district included some docks: the "New" dock dating from 1747; the Champlain dock; the Cul-de-Sac dock south of the Royale battery; the King's dock located between the Royale and Dauphine batteries, and the Québec and Saint-André docks, which were positioned north of the Dauphine battery.[8] There were no docks in the north-east sector of Lower Town.

These industrial, commercial and military installations took up a significant part of the space available in the area. Since this was the case, should we be surprised at the narrowness of the streets? Still in 1685 Sault-au-Matelot Street was 24 feet wide, this was close to the width of Saint-Pierre Street, which went back to the time of Governor Davaugour (1661-63).[9] Although, based on the criteria of military town planning of the time, these widths correspond to those of secondary streets.[10] We should keep in mind that these standards were set for new settlements that were not subject to geographic constraints such as those imposed on Lower Town. In military circles a variance of 6 feet (that is, from 18 to 24 feet) was accepted; thus the de Meulle section with its 16-foot length was close to the norm.[11] As for Notre-Dame and Sous-le-Fort streets, they measured respectively 18 and 25 feet at the end of the 17th century.

It is true that de l'Escalier Street was only 12 feet wide; however, it was not a road intended for vehicles but for pedestrians. As for the other lanes such as Sous-le-Cap, du Porche or Nécessaire, they were less than 15 feet; and the first was well below the standard with an average of 4.5 feet.[12] However, the main roads met the criteria of military town planners. For the most part, the widths of these streets were close to the standards set by the Academy of Architecture which, in 1700, recommended that public roads be at least 21 feet wide in order to allow two carriages to pass abreast.[13] In short, Kalm's impressions must be qualified: the main streets of Lower Town were not as narrow as they seemed.

In order to find what the habitable area was, we have to subtract the space taken up by the streets from the total area.[14] According to Chaussegros' 1742 plan the habitable area was about 13 500 square *toises* (5.1 hectares). Thus, the network of roads in Lower Town accounted for 15% of the district's surface area.

Knowing the habitable area, it is interesting to find that during the same period, over one-third of the population of the city resided in this district. Although the percentage of the population living in Lower Town fell appreciably during the 18th century (from 60 to 36%), the population density climbed from 270 persons per hectare in 1716 to 359 in 1744, an increase of 33%.[15]

On the other hand, the "second" Lower Town, as Pehr Kalm liked to call it, had only one row of houses on only one street: Saint-Charles. He did not mention Saint-Nicholas Street or the Lacroix and la Digue alleyways. Moreover, he did not write about Sous-le-Coteau (Saint-Vallier)

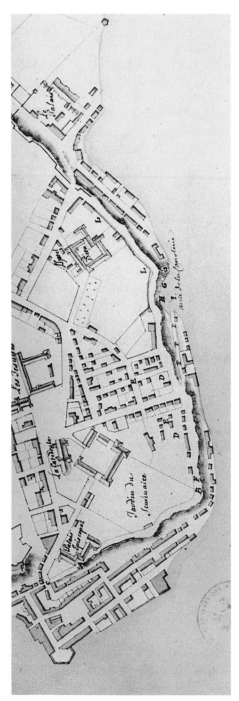

Fig. 3 Map of Québec showing the break between the "two" Lower Towns due to Canoterie cove. This name originated with the canoe shed owned there by the Seminary priests. The cove separated the fief Sault-au-Matelot, property of the Seminary, from the property belonging to the Hospitalières of the Hôtel-Dieu. It was a place where wooden rafts came ashore, and a port of entry for goods. Around 1740 there was also a ship yard there ("H"). *Chaussegros de Léry, 1732. National Archives of Canada, C 15738.*

or Saint-Roch streets, which he considered to be part of the Saint-Roch suburb. This means that the area of the Palace Quarter went from the Canoterie cove in the east to Saint-Roch Street in the west.

The topographic characteristics of the Palace Quarter were similar to those of Lower Town, so that it was called the "second" Lower Town. Caught between the cliff and the estuary of the Saint-Charles River, its surface area was close to that of Lower Town, about 16 650 square *toises* (6.3 hectares). It grew around two centres of attraction: the Intendant's palace, located at the west end of the district, and the shipyards bounded by Chaussegros de Léry's dike and Saint-Roch Street.

Unlike Lower Town, however, the Palace Quarter had little habitable space, not because the network of roads was large (scarcely 735 square *toises*),[16] but rather because the Intendant's palace; the shipyards; the Saint-Nicholas redoubt, which defended the harbour from that side; and the Saint-Roch chapel and redoubt covered nearly 11 000 square *toises* or about two-thirds of the area. The palace (with its structures and gardens) alone occupied 40% of the available space. There was thus a noticeable difference between the "two" Lower Towns in their respective habitable areas. There were only 1.87 hectares left for living space. The way these civil and industrial installations used the land leads to an interesting observation: while the population density was only 78 persons per hectare in 1716, activity in the shipyards quickly led to a fivefold increase in this figure. The Palace Quarter had 352 inhabitants in 1744, a density that was close to that of Lower Town.

As for Upper Town, according to Kalm, its "numerous vegetable gardens give the impression that the town is spread out, even though it does not have that many houses."[17] In fact, the section of Upper Town enclosed by the walls occupied an area of 180 acres (72.85 hectares).[18] In theory, it covered six times the area of Lower Town and the Palace Quarter put together. However, the various religious, administrative and military properties (such as the Château Saint-Louis, the Dauphine and Royale redoubts or even the *cavalier du moulin* and the new barracks), not to mention the network of roads, covered a significant proportion of the surface area. The properties belonging to military and civilian administrations accounted for 3.6 hectares. Convents and other ecclesiastical properties alone occupied 19.6 hectares.[19] The network of roads, which included 31 streets and alleyways around 1744,[20] occupied 4.6 hectares.

Except for Frontenac and du Trésor alleyways, which were 12 and 15 feet wide respectively, all the streets in Upper Town met the town planning standards of the time. The two main streets, Saint-Louis and Saint-Jean, were 36 feet wide. That meant that only 60% of this vast area (about 45 hectares) was left available as living space.[21]

Upper Town had changed considerably since Lahontan's visit at the end of the 17th century. While the space enclosed by Town Adjutant Provost and Constabulary Provost Saint-Simon had a surface area of about 51 hectares as early as 1690; three years later, the Chevalier de Beaucours had reduced it to only 35 hectares. This situation remained unchanged for a good part of the 18th century until Chaussegros de Léry built his ramparts.[22]

Even though it had doubled in area and in spite of the fact that its population had tripled, Upper Town had experienced a 15% drop in its population density: from 59 persons per hectare in 1716 to 50 in 1744. This may be an explanation for Kalm's impression of vastness.

As for the inner and outer suburbs, whereas the first were concentrated on the periphery of the districts and fortifications, for example the Saint-Jean suburb in Upper Town and the Saint-Roch suburb near the Palace Quarter; according to the Church's boundaries,[23] the outer suburb covered the area up to Sillery to the south-west and encompassed the waterside section of the Notre-Dame-des Anges Seigneury along the Saint-Charles River to the north.[24]

Apart from their vast size, the suburbs were characterized by large lots, and a high concentration of undivided religious properties. The Ursulines, for example, owned a property consisting of prairie and pastureland along the Grande Allée that was over 25 hectares in length. Closer to the walls, the Saint-Jean suburb grew by amalgam, while the creation of a "non-aedificandi" area by Chaussegros de Léry in front of his enclosure delayed the subdivision of land undertaken by shoemaker Joachim Girard. Chaussegros also made clear his intention to bring artisans into the Saint-Roch suburb, where he attempted to subdivide the land and control its future use.[25]

TABLE 20

AVERAGE SIZE OF LOTS CEDED
CIRCA 1744
(in French square feet)

Seminary	2091.01
Hôtel-Dieu	2177.00
Manor	2213.86
Jesuits	2379.68
Notre-Dame Parish	3410.55
Joachim Girard	4443.74
Paupers of the Hôtel-Dieu	5733.75
Ursulines	7641.64

The Site Around 1744

Shoemaker Girard's attempt was not unique. Long before him some individuals such as Jean-Baptiste Couillard de Lespinay, subdivided and sold sections of a much larger lot that had been ceded to him by the Seminary of Québec.[26] Not only did the religious communities keep large expanses of land for their own use, but they also owned the largest share of the available habitable area.[27]

Except for lots ceded in the inner suburbs, the minimum surface area of a ceded lot was 2000 square feet (the equivalent of 40 by 50 feet) [Table 20].[28] There was a large difference between the sizes of lots ceded in the first four and the last four landholdings. This difference can be partly explained[29] by the fact that the lots belonging to the Seminary, the Hôtel-Dieu and the Crown were located not only in Upper Town, but also in Lower Town and in the Palace Quarter. As for the Jesuit concessions, they represented an enclave in Upper Town surrounded by the Ursulines' properties and those of the Paupers of the Hôtel-Dieu, the Seminary and Notre-Dame Parish. As well, the lots belonging to the Parish, the Paupers of the Hôtel-Dieu, the Ursulines and even those subdivided by Joachim Girard,[30] all stretched out over the plateau in Upper Town; furthermore, they were located at the west end of the city and even outside.

Undeniably, the physical characteristics of the capital played a fundamental role in the distribution of the property base. On the average, whether located in the fief of Sault-au-Matelot or the King's Reserve, the lots in Lower Town measured 1630 square feet. In the Palace Quarter, they were 2100 feet; in Upper Town, 3500 square feet; and in the inner suburbs they were even larger.

As a consequence of these geographical constraints, the frontage of the lots was adapted to the available space. Thus, the average lot in Lower Town had a 40-foot frontage, one foot more than in the Palace Quarter, which was still five feet less than in Upper Town. As to depth, the lots in the Palace Quarter were shorter than those in Lower Town by almost eight feet and almost 15 feet shorter than those in Upper Town (64.75 feet).

All these figures seem to show a certain conformity in property management, and yet some streets stand out from the anonymity of the statistics. Saint-Pierre Street in Lower Town had habitable areas that were twice as large as the average in the neighbourhood; which means a larger frontage and depth.[31] On Saint-Paul Street, although wider than the average, the lots were squeezed between the riverbank and the cliff.

The residents of Saint-Louis Street in Upper Town had lots that were on the average three times as large as the usual lots in the district. The lots on Sainte-Hélène, du Grison and Buade streets also afforded habitable areas that were larger than the district's average. On the other hand, the dimensions of all the lots falling within the fief of Sault-au-Matelot in Upper Town (Saint-Flavien, Saint-Joseph, Nouvelle, de la Sainte-Famille, Saint-François and Saint-Joachim streets) were below average in size.

The Management of Space

In dealing with concessions and habitable areas, we are inevitably attempting to get a picture not only of how space was "managed," but also of how it was used. The botanist Kalm described many gardens in Upper Town and houses several storeys high in Lower Town. There is no question that the size of the lots available in Upper Town prompted the residents to plant vegetable gardens; whereas in Lower Town the population density and cramped quarters forced the owners to build vertically. Available space and the figures on surface area that illustrate it, reveal a policy of "space management" particular to each of the religious communities and to the government, not only in terms of the lots required for administrative buildings, but also of the lots ceded to individuals.

Convent Properties

The Paupers of the Hôtel-Dieu Property

This piece of land covered almost 6000 square *toises* in Upper Town (2.27 hectares).[32] It was divided into three parts: a small section measuring 150 square *toises*, another measuring 5400 square *toises* and finally, the cemetery, which covered a little over 400 square *toises*. The "corporation" reserved the right to nearly 45% of the entire land for its own buildings, yards, gardens and orchards, which in the 18th century used up nine-tenths of the space. The rest of the ward was divided between the concessions (32%), the Paupers' cemetery, and some streets and alleyways.

As far as the architecture is concerned, it was sober. The main buildings located in the smallest area were side by side with the Hôtel-Dieu properties to the north. The auxiliary buildings were located on the lot bounded on the south and west by Saint-Jean and des Pauvres streets (Côte du Palais), on the north by de l'Église, and on the east by des Morts (de l'Hôpital) lane. All but two of the buildings were made of stone.

The patient facilities occupied a large building that backed onto the Hôtel-Dieu monastery; divided into two wings for receiving male and female patients, this building was 110 feet long. Next to it were the apothecary and a nursing room reserved exclusively for officers of the army. On the other side of de l'Église, the yard and garden area housed a residence for domestic staff, a butcher shop, a storage shed, a charnel house as well as a stable and ice house built of half-timbers. Each of the buildings was one storey high (the French rez-de-chaussée), except for the patient and officer care facilities, which had a mansard-roof attic made of beams covered with slate; the other roofs were made of planks or shingles.

Fig. 4 Québec around 1692, according to the Engineer Robert de Villeneuve. Before this date, most of the communities (excluding Notre-Dame Parish) had lands everywhere, especially in Upper Town. *National Archives of Canada, C 21760.*

Hôtel-Dieu Property

The Hospitalières of the Hôtel-Dieu whose monastery backed onto the patient facilities, owned almost 11 500 square *toises* (4.37 hectares)[33] divided between Upper Town and the Palace Quarter, but most of their properties were located in Upper Town (about 6500 *toises*). The community reserved for itself 50% of this land, and nearly nine-tenths of this half were used for yards, gardens and orchards. The concessions, two-thirds of which were in the Palace Quarter, accounted for 32% of the surface area of the ward; the rest was divided into streets and lots that had not been ceded.

The main buildings, which were all made of stone except for a wooden barn, consisted of two main buildings three storeys high and 170 feet long, one two-storey building and a church. The domestic staff lived in a one-storey stone house. There was also a large 125-foot building that housed a butcher shop, a henhouse, a stable and a dovecote. Another stable, an ice house and a barn completed the complex. All these buildings were roofed over with planks, but some had shingles or slate roofs.

The Jesuits

The Jesuits owned almost 6000 square *toises* (2.25 hectares)[34] within the city limits, the largest part of which (92%) was in Upper Town, south of the Paupers' property. Bounded by Sainte-Anne, des Pauvres and Saint-Jean streets, the land the Jesuits kept for themselves (75% of the concession) was enclosed by a wall. The community built its stone college and church there; but the largest part of the lot contained yards, vegetable and flower gardens, orchards and woods of tall standing timber, which covered about 95% of the area devoted to its works. The rest of the ward had been set aside for concessions.

The church that Pehr Kalm described as "one of the most beautiful in the city" attracted the Swedish visitor's attention thanks to the clock (whose face had large hands) placed at the top of its steeple.[35] Nearby

was a large central building divided into two wings, each over 130 feet long, one rising two storeys and the other, three and even four storeys depending upon the slope of the land. The roofs of the two buildings were made of slate.

The Ursulines

Further to the south-west on the other side of Sainte-Anne Street, the Ursulines' property spread out over 9000 square *toises* (3.4 hectares). As in the other convent properties, a wall surrounded the site of the monastery, which enclosed about one-third of the property. Gardens, orchards and yards covered over 80% of this area. The main buildings were made of masonry and the secondary structures of wood. Among the stone buildings, Pehr Kalm especially noticed the church, whose steeple consisted of a tower with a cupola, topped by an arrow.[36] There was also a main building with two wings, two or three storeys high, inhabited by the nuns; a second one meant for boarding students, and a last one for day students. The secondary structures amounted to a stone stable for horses, a pen, a cowbarn and a shed. Most of the roofs were of planks. The others were made of shingles. Lots that had been ceded and subdivided covered the other two-thirds of the concession.

The Seminary

At the east end of Upper Town, the point of the triangle was taken up by the fief of Sault-au-Matelot which was owned by the Seminary. With an area of 16 200 square *toises* (6.15 hectares),[37] this piece of land spanned Upper and Lower Town, although the largest portion (over three-quarters of it) was in Upper Town. The priests of the Seminary kept only 29% of the land for their own use, which in terms of space translated into an area comparable to those kept by the Jesuits and Ursulines. Here again, only 10% of the surface area inside this enclosure was built on.

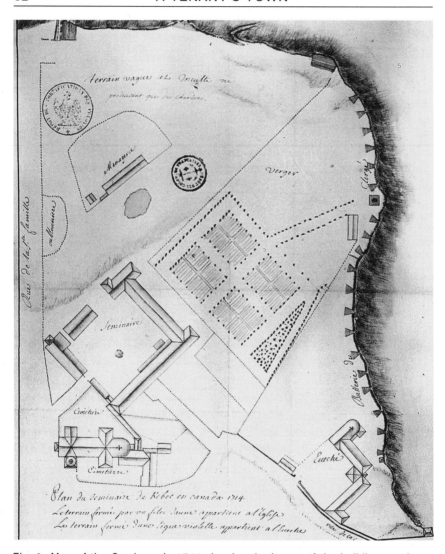

Fig. 6 Map of the Seminary in 1714 showing the layout of the buildings and gardens. It also shows the layout of the Bishopric's lands and part of the land belonging to Notre-Dame Parish. *National Archives of Canada, C-16038.*

The rest of the concession was ceded with part of it kept for the road network.

The Seminary structures, like those of the other communities, were made of stone, except for a shed, and had slate roofs. There was a central building 210 feet long which stood two, three or even four storeys high. A second building called the "little seminary," which had the same dimensions as and was placed at right angles to the first, housed the boarders. A smaller building served as a parlour, while a 120-foot-long structure built on an adjoining lot down below accommodated a menagerie, a butcher shop, a brewery, a barn and a stable.

Notre-Dame Parish

Next door to the Seminary, the Parish of Notre-Dame of Québec administered two parcels of land, Cap-aux-Diamants and Notre-Dame. The parish church stood on the latter. In total, this represented almost 16 000 square *toises* (6 hectares), of which over 90% was ceded or set aside for concessions.[38] Since the church only occupied 169 square *toises*, the rest of the lot, reserved for the use of the Parish. This included a yard and two cemeteries, one of which, on the Seminary side, was known as Saint-Antoine and the other on the Buade Street side, was known as Sainte-Famille: all of this was surrounded by a wall.

The Recollects and the Bishopric

The Recollects only occupied a parcel of land measuring about 4000 square *toises* (1.5 hectares) located at the east end of Saint-Louis Street. It was bounded by Place d'Armes and by des Jardins and Sainte-Anne streets. There again the largest part of the lot was devoted to gardens, orchards and yards. The Recollect Monks' church was characterized by an ornamental rooster perched on the top of the cross on its steeple.[39]

The area occupied by the Bishop's palace, located to the east of the cathedral, was more or less the same as the Recollects' land. The same formula was used there in terms of the layout of the space.

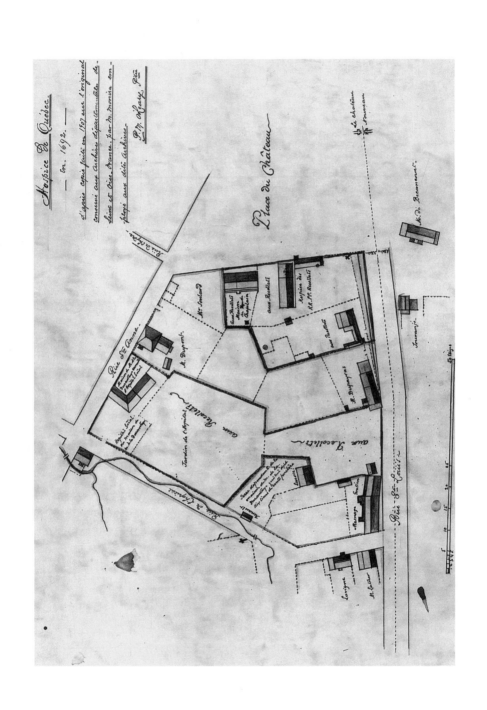

Hospice De Québec.

— En 1692. —

D'après copie faite en 1867 sur l'original
envoiée aux archives départementales du
Loire et Cher, France, par M. Morice en...
Déposé aux dites archives.

P.M. O'Leary, Ptre.

Place du Château

Rue St Anne

Rue Recollet

Aux Recollets

Rue St Louis

Rue de Chapeau

Fig. 7 Map of the Recollects' enclosure, between Place d'Armes and the streets of Saint Louis, de l'Hôpital (des Jardins) and Saint Anne. *Robert de Villeneuve, 1692, P.M. O'Leary copy. National Archives of Canada, NMC 1588.*

Public Properties

The space occupied by public administration about 1745 was mainly concentrated in the site of Fort Saint-Louis and the adjoining Governor's gardens as well as within the fortifications that began to go up that same year. In addition, Upper Town contained the site of the former fortifications of Chevalier de Beaucours, linking the redoubt on the cape to the *cavalier du moulin*; and, in the Palace Quarter, the Intendant's palace. The Governor's garden was nearly 2800 square *toises* (1.06 hectares) while the fort and battery covered nearly 3600 (1.37 hectares).[40]

In the Palace Quarter, the Colonial Administrator's building filled the entire area between Saint-Roch and Saint-Nicolas streets, about 6600 square toises (2.51 hectares). The gardens alone (not counting the various yards) covered almost 2600 square toises (40% of the area).[41] Several buildings were found there, including the King's stores, a prison, various storehouses, barns and sheds. The palace, a two-storey stone structure, was distinguished by its central bell-tower that housed a clock.

While the decoration of cities and fortified towns assumed particular importance in the treatises of engineers and town planners of the 17th and 18th centuries, the message was soon picked up by other attentive ears. Religious communities and lay administrators were inspired by it. It is not surprising to find that there was real concern about landscaping the grounds surrounding convents and public buildings. This was in fact a solution to the "corruption of the air [that] became such an irritating problem in the 18th century." These gardens served to supply pure air, in an attempt to renew the air in the streets, just as fountains contributed to public health by purifying the air and cooling it.[42]

Private Properties

The management of private property differed greatly from that of properties owned by institutions. As to the available space, private indi-

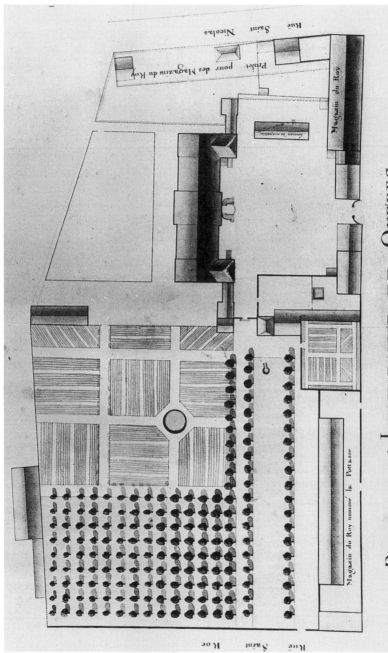

Rue Saint Nicolas

Projet pour des Magazins du Roy

Magazin du Roy

Bureau du magazin

Rue Saint Roc

Magazin du Roy nomme' la Pottasse

PLAN DE L'INTENDANCE DE QUEBEC
Cette Maison Sert aussi de Palais, Elle est Situee hors de la Ville, dans le
Fauxbourg du Palais
1730

Fig. 8 The Colonial Administrator's Palace with its gardens and outbuildings in 1750. *National Archives of Canada, PH/340/Québec/1750.*

viduals used it mostly for living purposes (nearly 90%), whereas the green areas, the gardens and orchards, covered only 2% of the ceded lots. The rest of the space was divided between vacant lots in the city, and prairies and pastures in the inner and outer suburbs.[43] For the most part (90%) the urban lots were not fenced, which differed considerably from the practice of the religious communities. As for the individuals who fenced in their lots, most preferred to use posts rather than the more costly masonry walls. Walls were generally used to enclose the gardens or orchards. Stone fences were used more frequently in Lower Town, especially on Champlain Street. There is no question that, in this case, the masonry walls also offered a measure of protection against the possibility of rocks falling from the cliff.

The way the lots were laid out was due partly to the physical characteristics of the area and the available space. That is why no lots were devoted specifically to horticulture in Lower Town; there were barely any vacant lots there. Also few owners in Lower Town, whether occupants or not, had enough space to cultivate a vegetable garden. Buildings covered slightly over two-thirds of the available surface area.[44] At best, the residents of this district had a yard where they could either store their firewood or keep one or more animals. Some of the least fortunate ones, living in Sault-au-Matelot or de Meulle streets, were literally squeezed between the street and the cliff.

Despite the limited amount of habitable space, the pressures exerted by topography were fewer in the Palace Quarter. All of its residents had yards or vegetable gardens so that the percentage of built-up area was reduced to some 50% of the habitable space.

Upper Town stood out clearly from the two other areas: not only did the built-up percentage fall below one-third of the habitable surface area, but most of the vegetable gardens enumerated were found there (over three-quarters of them). One out of every four houses had a vegetable garden at the back. Still it is difficult to determine how much space was used for horticulture. There is very little data on this subject. For example, merchant Charles Larche devoted one-fifth of his lot (about 7000 square feet) on Saint-Jean Street to horticulture.[45]

Fig. 9 The Intendant's Palace. *Richard Short, 1761. National Archives of Canada, C 360.*

This same Larche also built various secondary wooden buildings on his lot including a tannery, tanning mill, barn, shed, bakehouse and ice house. To this list we should add a stone butcher's shop. All together these structures occupied a surface area of 4100 square feet on the ground; slightly over 10% of the lot.

Although typical of a certain situation in Upper Town, Larche's case is nonetheless exceptional in many ways: on one hand, because of the size of lot ceded (36 000 square feet); and on the other, because of the number of secondary buildings erected on the lot. His lot was equal to ten times the average ceded lot in Upper Town. Moreover, the butcher was part of a minority who built secondary structures on their lots; only slightly over 10% of the grantees constructed sheds, warehouses or other buildings, and this percentage was the same for all the districts. Developing the lots then, amounted to building a house and a yard, with or without a vegetable garden depending upon the district.

The house is the best-known element, because many researchers (especially in Art History) have tried to define its conditions. However, beyond architectural styles or construction techniques, we must determine how the house was "lived in," according to the expression used by French historian Daniel Roche.[46] First of all, an evaluation of its contents is essential.

Around 1744, the house alone covered almost 60% of the lots in Lower Town, 43% in the Palace Quarter and 30% in Upper Town. Stone was the most widely used material (nearly 70%) whereas one out of four houses was made of timbers beam on beam (23%). The remaining 7% or so were divided among half-timbered (having walls of wooden frame work with spaces filled by plaster or masonry)[47] and composite structures (made of stone and wood). Three out of five houses consisted of a single main storey, one-third had another storey and about 5% had more than one upper storey.

Houses never occupied the whole surface area of a lot; the frontage accounted for nearly 80% of the width of a lot in Lower Town and in the Palace Quarter; and only 70% in Upper Town. A passageway usually linked the street to the yard or orchard. This was confirmed by Pehr Kalm. Could this passageway be shared and covered over? Yes, but only in less than one house in ten, and most were in the Palace Quarter, especially on Saint-Charles Street. Also less than one house in 20 shared its

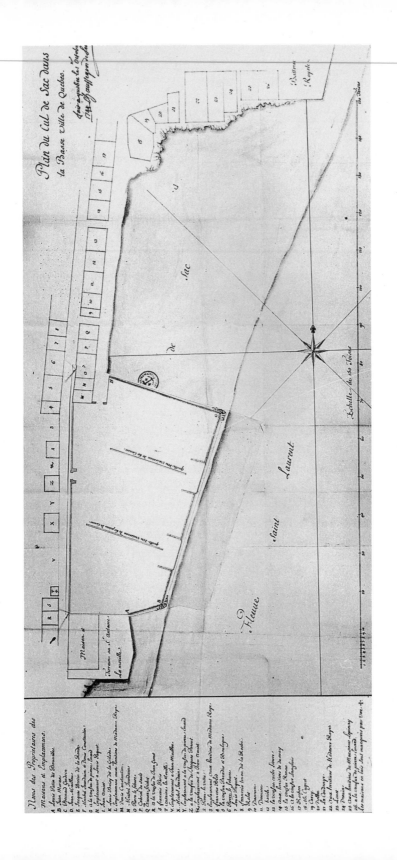

Fig. 10 Compared to the priest's enumeration, this map from 1744 allows us to place de Meulle Street between Sous-le-Fort Street (leading to the Royale Battery) and plot "M." In short, de Meulle Street corresponded to the present-day Petit Champlain Street. Beyond it, to the south, would have been Champlain Street. *Chaussegros de Léry, 1744. National Archives of Canada, C 15729.*

gabled wall. Most of these semi-detached houses were found in Lower Town.

In short, the average house in the three main districts of Québec in Pehr Kalm's time was a detached structure. On average it had 31 feet of frontage in each of the districts (except in the suburbs, where it was four feet less). Depth was 29.33 feet in Lower Town, 26.75 feet in Upper Town, one foot less in the Palace Quarter, and only 21.33 feet in the suburbs. Space was respectively distributed over 2.02, 1.32, 1.36 and 1.0 storey for each of these districts, which corresponds to average habitable areas of 1969, 1290, 1214, and 622 square feet. The largest houses were found in Lower Town where they were more spacious and taller. Houses in Upper Town were slightly larger than those in the Palace Quarter, but not as tall.

Since seven out of ten houses in the whole city were made of stone, one may ask if they were equally distributed within the town. Ninety percent of the houses in Lower Town were made of stone while only 60% of those were in Upper Town and in the Palace Quarter. The houses in the suburbs were mostly made of wood. The stone house offered an habitable area that was three times larger than that of wood houses because stone houses generally had more storeys. Overall, Québec presented a picture of a city built of a resistant material, stone.

We should not be surprised when Pehr Kalm said he was impressed with the merchants' houses in Lower Town, which had three and even four storeys. This was a phenomenon peculiar to Lower Town, which testified to the high density in a neighbourhood where only one-fifth of the houses had only one storey, compared to three-quarters of those in Upper Town.

The landscape in Lower Town changed considerably after it was destroyed by fire in 1682. If we were to define standards for evaluating habitable surfaces, an interesting phenomenon would emerge: the expansion of the housing surface. Toward 1690, intermediate surfaces of 500 to 1000 square feet predominated in Lower Town, while in Upper Town

GRAPH 8

AVERAGE SIZE OF HOUSES
QUÉBEC, 1690 AND 1744

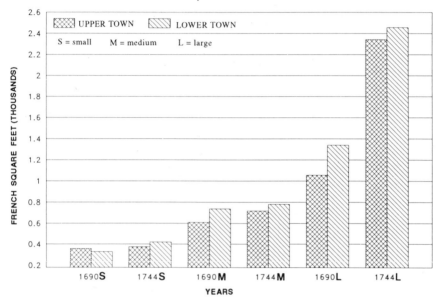

there was a concentration of smaller surfaces (less than 500 feet); these categories represented respectively 50% of the available space.[48] By 1744 small houses had lost ground; they accounted for only 15% of the houses in the inner city. However, they became predominant in the suburbs. The average surface for all categories increased; some slightly while others such as the small houses in Lower Town increased by one-quarter (Graph 8). However, it was the larger houses (over 1000 square feet) that expanded the most both in area and volume. Their area doubled and more importantly, in all the districts, the number of large houses increased to at least 40% of all houses. Even more meaningful is that in Lower Town two large houses out of every three measured over 2500 square feet; while this percentage fell to one out of four in Upper Town and the Palace Quarter.

In Lower Town, the largest houses were on Saint-Pierre Street (3769.5 square feet), where the largest lots were also located. The smallest houses lined Champlain and de Meulle streets. The largest houses in the

Palace Quarter were on Saint-Charles Street (although they were three times smaller than the houses on Saint-Pierre Street) and the smallest were on Saint-Nicolas Street (twice as small). Upper Town offered a contrasting landscape: on Buade Street, Nicolas Jacquin *dit* Philibert owned the largest house in Québec (9828 square feet) and on Nouvelle Street, a few hundred metres away, Philippe Martineau *dit* Saint-Onge, lived in a modest wooden cottage measuring 216 square feet. The smallest houses were found on du Grison Street, while Buade Street had the largest ones. However, we should point out that the size of houses built in the fief of Sault-au-Matelot, although respectable, were well below the average for the neighbourhood.

Thus, the urban landscape in Québec changed radically between Lahontan's and Kalm's visits. Almost entirely concentrated in Lower Town in 1690, the capital's growing population had subsequently settled in the Palace Quarter and in Upper Town. The cramped quarters in the older part of town and the attraction of the shipyards encouraged this geographical and architectural displacement.

Legislation and Urban Facilities

Québec, whose Lower Town was built of wood, recovered slowly and painfully from the catastrophic fire that destroyed about 50 houses in 1682. The fear of a disaster of such scale remained engraved in the memory of the inhabitants, and the fire in Montréal in 1721 was to remind them of it. The shock felt translated into a multitude of regulations, all dictated by this fear. Fire protection laws made up the core of all ordinances and this had a direct impact on the urban landscape. Other regulations dealing, for example, with water or refuse were added along the way. In one way or another they all played a role in fashioning Québec's landscape to various degrees, through regulations respecting paving or street cleaning, public health or shop signs.

Certainly, the best-known ordinance dealing with landscape and urban facilities was that promulgated by Intendant Dupuy in 1727, respecting construction materials. The Intendant advised against the use of wood; he strongly suggested that henceforth construction should be in stone, on two storeys or a minimum of 12 feet in height. Mansard roofs were

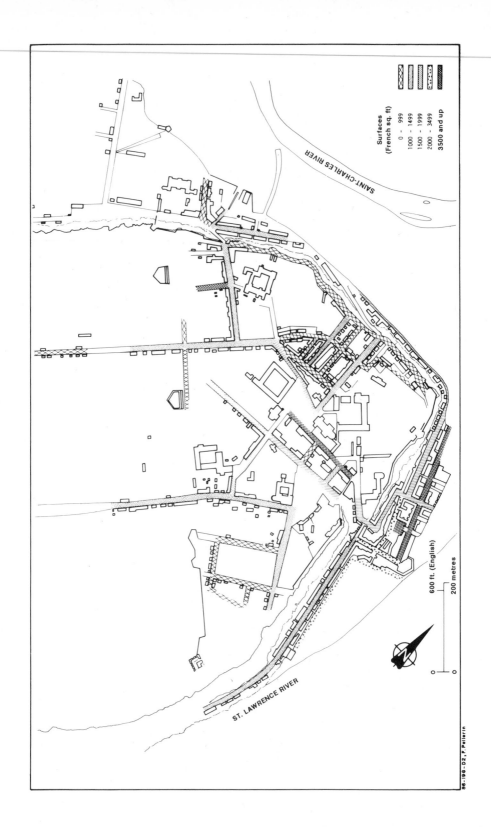

Surfaces
(French sq. ft)

0 – 999
1000 – 1499
1500 – 1999
2000 – 3499
3500 and up

SAINT-CHARLES RIVER

ST. LAWRENCE RIVER

600 ft. (English)

200 metres

86-196-D2, F. Pellerin

Fig. 11 Distribution of houses according to their average habitable area, circa 1740. *Map: F. Pellerin, (86-19G-D2) after a map by Chaussegros de Léry, 1742 (National Archives of Canada, H3/340/Québec/1742/section).*

no longer acceptable. The city must now have ridge roofs and these should be covered not with shingles but with overlapping planks. The floor of the attic or garret was to be separated from the main part of the building by two-inch joints. The chimney was to measure three or four feet and the flue or flues were to be 10 to 15 inches wide, to make chimney cleaning easier. Finally, in the case of semi-detached houses, the common walls must henceforth rise beyond the line of the roof in order to prevent fire from spreading from one to the other.[49]

Although this law may have seemed extreme because of the heavy penalties it carried it cannot, however, be considered as the mainspring behind the transformation of Québec's urban landscape. First of all, we should emphasize that in the preamble to this Act the Intendant recognized that the principle of constructing in stone was already being applied. Moreover, the text itself offers too many ways out[50] to be as demanding as some would have had it. It seems that the Montréal fire, still fresh in the memory of the inhabitants of Québec (and especially of Montréal), was a much stronger incentive to caution. Finally, this ordinance went into force at a time when masons in Québec, too numerous to earn their living in such a fragile market,[51] were heading for Montréal to build fortifications or reconstruct the burned-out city. Beyond this reservation, the fact remains that a fire is one of the catastrophes most feared by both the general public and the authorities.

A whole series of regulations and orders were promulgated in Québec from the end of the 17th century to the middle of the next century. Already in 1689, police regulations required standards similar to those set down by Dupuy for chimneys.[52] A few years before, subsequent to the 1682 fire, the Council reiterated the property owners' obligation to put a ladder on the roofs near the chimneys.[53] In fact Colonial Administrator Bigot passed a similar (almost word for word) ordinance 65 years later.[54] In the meantime this issue was the subject of several calls-to-order. The Intendant or the Superior Council periodically deemed it necessary to remind the citizens, owners as well as tenants, of their obligation to clean their chimneys every month or be fined.[55] Furthermore chimneys were regularly inspected. Again on the subject of architecture, a later text required owners to install "battering rams, machines that have been used successfully in many towns in Old France."[56]

Fire was an omnipresent menace throughout the 18th century; thus one should not be surprised that prevention was the subject of several legal texts. In November 1706, the Colonial Administrator made it illegal for rural immigrants who arrived at night to camp on the riverbanks in Lower Town or light fires to warm themselves while waiting for daybreak.[57] Furthermore, after 1670, the Sovereign Council had made it illegal to "carry any fire at night in the streets of the city unless it was enclosed."[58] Forty years later, during the War of the Spanish Succession, Intendant Raudot prevented English prisoners from assembling after sunset and smoking outside.[59] The Colonial Administrator seemed to believe that fire was a more imminent danger than the enemy!

Smoking as a cause of fire worried administrators to such a point that carpenters and workers at the shipyards were forbidden to smoke while they worked or even approach the site while puffing on their pipes.[60] This can be explained by the presence of wood shavings and sawdust; a spark would soon have set the yard ablaze.[61] This was not evidence of a new fear on the part of the administrators. On the contrary, for over thirty years carpenters and caskmakers had to remove the wood shavings from their shops daily and carry them to the river or else were fined ten livres.[62] Prevention seems to have been carried to bizarre extremes occasionally, but these reflected the situation in the society of that time. For example, a 1721 regulation prevented citizens from firing rifles in the city because discharging the wad may start a fire.[63] Here again this was not new since a similar regulation existed in Governor Labarre's time (1682-85).

In spite of all these texts the inevitable accident could happen. However, limited to isolated houses, fires would now destroy only one or two houses at a time, which nevertheless kept Québec administrators and residents on the alert. Over the years a force of "volunteer firefighters" had been organized. In Montréal, carpenters, masons and roofers were most in demand after fires so these artisans had been "conscripted" into two squads. They were to arrive first on the scene of a fire, carrying their axes and buckets or be fined. These two squads of artisans had wooden or leather buckets, axes, shovels, iron hooks or gaffs, and lad-

ders of various lengths as well as hand battering rams. All this equipment was scattered in the various city districts and stored by religious
communities who safeguarded it. The inventory was updated periodically. Although these squads could do the job, in some situations
other residents and artisans also had to go to the scene of the fire,
equipped with an axe or a bucket.[64]

Although the organization described was in Montréal, there was a parallel one in Québec. Thus, after 1689, police regulations charged carpenters and cabinetmakers "to go to the fire, axe in hand, to use it if
needed."[65] Subsequently, the Council looked after having leather buckets made, the cost of which would be paid in accordance with the number of chimneys[66] by home owners in Québec, or shared half and half by
tenants and owners.[67] As in Montréal, the equipment was scattered
through the various neighbourhoods and entrusted for safekeeping to the
religious communities such as the Jesuits in Upper Town; or to public
buildings such as the Château Saint-Louis in Upper Town, and the Intendant's Palace in the Palace Quarter, and to certain individuals such as
François Hazeur in Lower Town or François Aubert.[68] As was the case
in Montréal, one person was put in charge of looking after the equipment. Since he had first looked after this task on a volunteer basis, in
1736, caskmaker Louis Paquet became the first official clerk of a na-
scent fire prevention department. This job made him a public servant
and thus he was exempt from some small taxes and duties.[69] Finally, it
seems that Québec's equipment was quite similar to Montréal's
pumps,[70] hooks, axes, buckets, tongs, shovels or other tools; so that, all
in all, the residents of the capital had nothing to envy Montréal as far as
fire protection was concerned.

If the fear of fire encouraged administrators to put in place regulations that led to certain modifications on the city's architecture and
urban facilities, it should be added that the buckets were not good for
anything without water! One can expect that the St. Lawrence or the
Saint-Charles rivers could have supplied water at an astronomical rate,
but it must be pointed out that, at best, these two immense reservoirs
could only serve the two Lower Towns. Official texts dealing with fires
remain silent as to the need for water. And yet there were fountains and
public wells in all Québec neighbourhoods in the 18th century. In Lower
Town, there was the Champlain Fountain on the street of the same

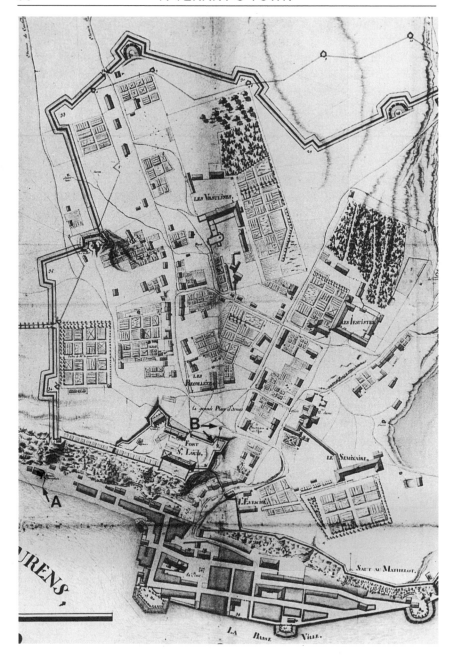

Fig. 12 Champlain's Fountain (A), on the street of the same name, was located at the foot of the cliff beneath the fortifications of Upper Town. A careful look at the map reveals the presence of two wells (B), one in the enclosure of the Château Saint-Louis and the other on Place d'Armes. Moreover, an engraving by Richard Short (Fig. 5) shows Levasseur's covered well in the same square. *Robert de Villeneuve, 1692. National Archives of Canada, C 17764.*

name, and in the Palace Quarter there was the King's Fountain on Saint-Nicolas Street; these two fountains already existed by the end of the 17th century. Upper Town had a well that was drilled by engineer Levasseur de Neré on Place d'Armes during the last years of the 17th century.[71] We can also add the executioner's fountain, located at the west end of Saint-Jean Street on the Hôtel-Dieu land.[72] This fountain supplied water to the Paupers' property and the entire Hôtel-Dieu complex by means of a pipe. To complement these two public fountains, a creek ran through Upper Town from Saint-Louis Street to the back of the Hôtel-Dieu, a course which, from south to north, ran along Saint-Louis Street, branched off at the Ursulines' land, descended des Jardins Street, and followed the Côte de la Fabrique as far as the Hôtel-Dieu.

To the public network, we must add the fountains, wells, ponds and basins of the institutions which could in supply needed water in an emergency.[73] Furthermore, many private houses had wells; judging from the clauses in the leasing contracts this was considered to be a desirable amenity. Thus that public enemy par excellence, fire, led to substantial modifications in the urban landscape, in terms of both architecture and urban facilities. Most of the time we know about these transformations through legislative texts. It was not only fire that led to important laws; on this subject, we must recognize the contribution of personal cleanliness and public health.

Personal cleanliness called for the presence of outside latrines or indoor lavatories. According to the *Coutume de Paris*, the law prescribed that all property owners should have sufficient latrines and privies,[74] although it is true that real conditions were quite different. In Québec, even though most of the houses had such sanitary facilities, some owners did not see fit to install them, and their waste ended up on the street. In order to prevent the spread of disease and to eliminate odours, the Sovereign Council in its police regulations of 1706 enjoined guilty

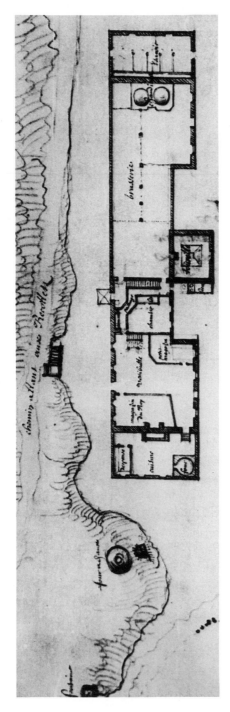

Fig. 13 Talon's Brewery in 1686, later transformed into the Colonial Administrator's Palace. At the extreme left is the King's Fountain. Numerous allusions to this source of drinking water during the 18th century confirm its existence. *Anonymous, 1686. National Archives of Canada, C 50292.*

owners to remedy the situation within one year or be fined 20 *livres*; the same fine would apply to house builders who henceforth built without providing latrines. In order to ensure compliance with the regulations, every building in the city was visited.[75] But such legislation inevitably gave rise to opposition! About twenty citizens claimed that it was practically impossible for them to construct latrines; most of them lived in Lower Town, including notary Louis Chambalon, Gabriel Daveine the shoemaker, surgeon Jourdain Lajus and navigator Jacques Guion Fresnay to mention just a few. After the inquiry, the Council ordered five of these owners to build latrines and exempted 17, provided that they not dispose of their excrement by taking it out to the street; otherwise, they would be fined.[76] No one knows whether the fines put an end to this strange habit!

The Council legislated not only on latrines but also on the whole question of public health: emptying one's chamberpot out the window onto the public way meant that the effluvium of contents would spread through the channels over several hundred metres! But the emanations that tickled the nostrils of the inhabitants of Québec did not come only from human waste. Other odiferous sources must not be forgotten, such as animal manure or liquid or other waste from the butchers' stalls or the refuse that carters unloaded into that vast open-air garbage dump, the St. Lawrence River.

As early as 1689, police regulations ordered that streets in Lower Town should be paved over their full width with sewers in the middle.[77] A pious wish that had hardly any effect since ten years later the same regulation was the subject of a new proclamation,[78] which again failed to have any concrete results. The streets of Québec remained dirty and muddy throughout the period since they basically consisted of beaten earth. Yet here and there channels and sewers, sometimes underground and most often as part of open-air installations, criss-crossed the main streets. We need only remember the case of the widow Dumont, who was sentenced to collect the water that ran off her land, and lead it through a pipe to an underground wooden channel passing under des Pauvres Street in Upper Town.[79] A similar sewer served Saint-François, Saint-Flavien and Saint-Joachim streets.[80] In Lower Town, a difference of opinion between merchants Fornel and Lagorgendière revealed the existence of a pipeline linking Place Royale to the riverbank. Regardless

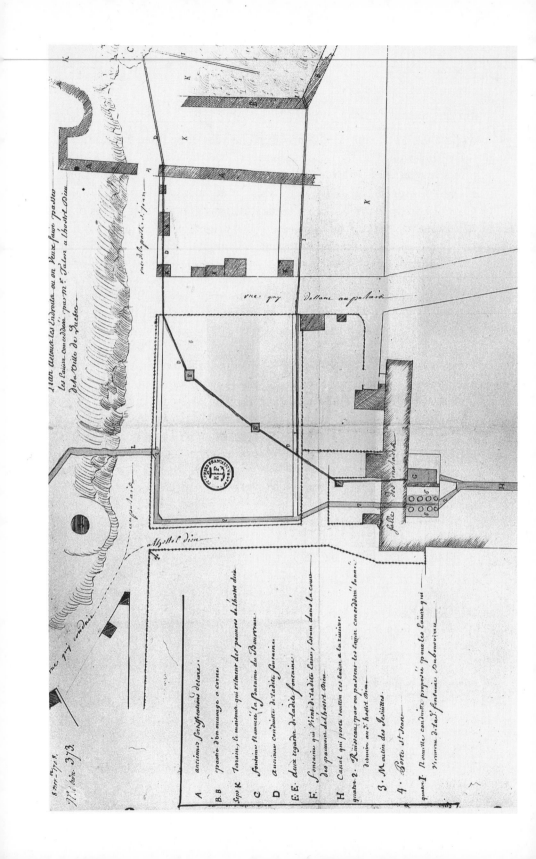

Fig. 14 The water supply system of the Hôtel-Dieu. Conduit (D) takes water from the "du Bourreau" [Hangman] Fountain (C), thus named because the executioner lived nearby in one of the redoubts of the old 1690 fortifications. *Anonymous, 1708. National Archives of Canada, C 15787.*

of the neighbourhood a network of sewers ran through it. How could it be otherwise, given the particular physical characteristics of the city? Nonetheless, it is likely that some streets after torrential rains were quagmires where mud, stagnant water and a juicy hodgepodge of living and dead animals piled up.

The lack of public-mindedness on the part of the citizens forced Colonial Administrator Bigot to enact a regulation respecting street cleaning. "Manure, mud and refuse" was to be piled up along the lots and not spread out in the middle of the streets, and every Saturday the residents of Lower Town would carry them down to the river; while those in Upper Town would take it to quarries outside the city.[81] This ordinance applied to all seasons except winter. Since the refuse collection services were not offered in the winter, this allowed the citizens of Québec to give free reign to their strange habit of disposing of refuse by spreading it on the public ways. This practice always led to some problems, not only olfactory but practical ones when spring came. Manure and other refuse prevented the ice from melting, which made the children happy since they could slide and skate,[82] but which on the other hand caused serious problems, especially to people who tried to climb up the slopes.[83]

Judging by the number of regulations, one of the banes of Québec society seems to have been wandering animals, especially pigs. Since the houses and the yards were not enclosed by fences, it was difficult for owners to keep animals on their land. It was not surprising to meet Mr. So-and-So's cow or to see a pig wallowing in one of the quagmires in the street. The Councillors finally prohibited citizens from raising pigs in Lower Town, from Sault-au-Matelot to Cul-de-Sac. Elsewhere, they had to keep their pigs from wandering; otherwise anyone could catch and kill them.[84] Judging by the frequency of calls to order,[85] it seems that pigs were indeed part of the landscape!

Butcher shops and their stalls were also the subject of particular laws. The Sovereign Council set the number of butchers allowed and their

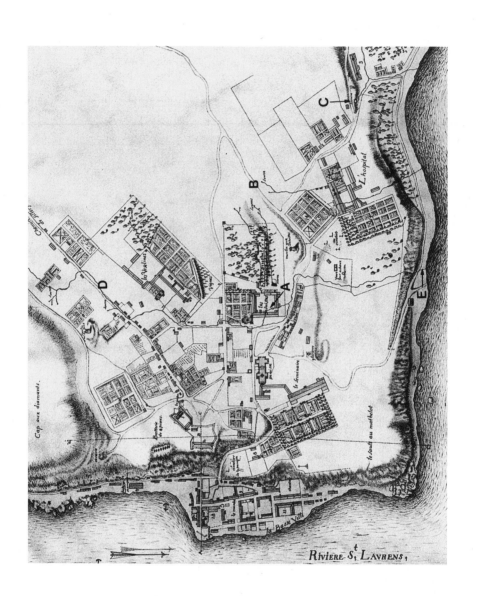

Riviere S.t Lavrens,

Fig. 15 Location of the Jesuit's (A) and du Bourreau (B) fountains as well as the King's Fountain (C) on Saint Nicholas Street. One can also see the brook (D) twisting down from the heights of the Plains of Abraham, passing through the Ursulines' property and des Jardins Street, up to Canoterie cove, where it fed the Richardière Mill (E) before emptying into the Saint Charles River. *Robert de Villeneuve, 1685. National Archives of Canada*, C 15797.

hours of operation. The number of stalls was limited to four "in the most convenient places" and they were allowed to sell their products on Tuesdays and Saturdays. The meat was to be hung on hooks. No butcher could kill and quarter an animal before the Provost inspected the meat. In theory no uninspected meat could be sold to the public. Obviously the butchering business implied owning live animals and presupposed accumulations of manure; on the other hand, it was unpleasant for immediate neighbours to be exposed to the blood of the animals and the odours emanating from the cutting wastes. Therefore butchers were ordered to remove and take down to the river at low tide any manure and waste from livestock that had been slaughtered and to "wash away the blood and refuse" in order to eliminate any odour in their slaughterhouses and in the immediate surroundings.[86]

Butcher stalls lead us to the subject of the market itself. It was also held twice a week, on Tuesdays and Fridays. In order to allow everyone to display their wares and give consumers an opportunity to avoid the bad weather, the assembly of citizens proposed the construction of an enclosed market on the site of the market in Lower Town.[87] However, there is no documentary evidence that this structure was ever built. It was obvious though that no goods were to be sold on the steps of the church in Lower Town, especially during religious services.[88] Of all sales people, fishmongers were the most closely watched. Not only could they not sell on the riverbank (except for eels) but they had to be "sufficiently" far away from any houses or be fined, although the distance was not clearly specified.[89] The urban landscape therfore offered not only a visual experience, but also an olfactory one!

These two senses were certainly active thanks to the way refuse, table and other wastes were cleared away. Pehr Kalm noted that Lower Town was built on a promontory of rubbish. Although this situation astonished the visitor, it was quite another story for the residents of Lower Town who, since the end of the 17th century, saw the refuse collector's tip-cart go by once a week to deposit waste on the riverbank from spring to fall.[90] Furthermore, depending upon the mood of the Councillors and the chief officers of justice, numerous other carters added construction rubble, manure or other refuse. An ordinance dated April 1710 made it mandatory for citizens to take all "garbage, refuse and demolition rubble" to the site owned by Aubert de Lachenaie.[91] However, some people soon found ways to get around this and dump their loads on the riverbank. Therefore Intendant Raudot had to intervene a few months later, probably as the result of pressure from Louis Prat, who was a merchant and harbour captain.[92] Subsequently, the administrators began pussy-footing around: at one time construction rubble was used to fill in the quagmires in the streets and slopes;[93] while at other times, as the result of a considerable expansion in trade, the harbour captain invited carters to expand the harbour facilities in Lower Town.[94] Those who broke the law could evidently be fined.[95] Around 1750, everyone agreed that henceforth the rubbish was to be discarded at the north end of Saint-Pierre Street where "ships did not land too often."[96]

Although Lower Town had to be filled in, care also had to be taken not to take away what was already there! Thus, the Colonial Administrator decided to prohibit carters from collecting sand along the banks of the Saint-Charles River to make mortar. Allard, a carter, was fined 20 *livres* for defying this regulation.[97]

This overview of urban legislation leads us to a different understanding from that of Kalm respecting the urban landscape in Québec in the 18th century. The many abuses by citizens meant that most sectors of activity had to be policed. We could add some interesting legal texts meant for young people as well as adults. Young people were prohibited from throwing stones from the top of the cliff onto the houses below.[98] It is true that these laws obviously were meant for youths, but no one can say for sure whether the law against stealing fruit from gardens was meant solely for them.[99] Gardens seem to have been a preferred spot for certain adults who were looking for excitement.... The Colonial Administrator was obliged several times to prohibit the hunting of turtledoves and other birds.[100] However, the picket fences around them were not enough to keep the most daring hunters out.

*****

This tour of the capital's urban landscape has brought out some of the characteristics of its neighbourhoods in terms of the use of space. On this subject, Pehr Kalm's impressions and descriptions seem to have been accurate. Civil and religious administrators surrounded themselves with greenery; on the other hand, the individual citizens, especially those in the two Lower Towns did not have enough space to do so. Only the residents of Upper Town had enough room to plant vegetable gardens. The use of space by individuals most often boiled down to building a house and laying out a yard; the lot was not fenced in, and only rarely had secondary buildings such as stables, sheds or ice houses.

If Kalm found that Lower Town was overcrowded and its streets were very narrow, this was mainly due to the height of the houses; since according to military criteria of the time the width of the streets was satisfactory, although they were narrower than in Upper Town. In the harbour district, Lower Town attracted merchants in large numbers so that tall buildings housed population concentrations that were as high as those in some cities in France such as Rouen. The same population density was found in the Palace Quarter. However, Upper Town was apparently the exception since its population density dropped. This was due to the increase in habitable area brought about by the construction of fortifications by Chaussegros de Léry in 1745.

These population densities obviously meant that citizens feared the disastrous consequences of a major fire, such as the one in 1682. In order to minimize the risk of fire, an impressive number of municipal regulations were put in place by various Colonial Administrators and the Council that administered the capital. However, Intendant Dupuy's regulations respecting house construction cannot be cited as being a crucial factor in the major changes that took place in the urban landscape. By 1744, 70% of the structures were made of stone, but this trend as the Intendant noted in his preamble had already started. Perhaps we should see this as a push in the right direction for masons in the capital? ... Whatever the case may be each neighbourhood had the facilities necessary for fighting fires.

Both the Intendant and the Councillors were worried about fire, but they were also worried about the quality of the air, because the urban landscape of the capital in the 18th century was not exclusively visual but also olfactory. Although European citizens discussed air as a source of pollution, they rarely talked about the question of water.

Taking into account the fact that the municipal refuse collector dumped rubbish into that immense open-air garbage dump, the St. Lawrence River, it was surprising to read in the Swedish botanist's journal that Québec residents drew their drinking water directly from the river. This statement is even more surprising when we consider that at Québec the St. Lawrence is slightly salty and that every neighbourhood had its own public fountain. On this subject, what the public administrators said and what they did were two different things; nevertheless, they succeeded in staying afloat thanks to the tide....

CHAPTER 4

A TENANT'S TOWN

The population density in Lower Town and the Palace Quarter at the end of the 1730s inevitably implies some crowding in housing conditions. The limited space available to residents for house construction necessarily leads to an examination of renting as a means of solving the problem. This question of housing becomes "a necessary adjunct to any demographic study of a city."[1]

It makes it possible to tackle, sometimes just skim over, some aspects of daily life and to identify certain attitudes, not only on the part of the landlords but also of the tenants in their search for a home. It also makes it possible to identify the owners of rental properties, to map the distribution of this type of housing and to analyze the nature of the landlord-tenant relationships.

Did periods of so-called economic prosperity favour the development of popular districts as measured by parameters such as available space, and the type and cost of rental housing? Did crowding vary in pace with local events or with the overall economic situation in the colony? Did the State have sufficient space for its storage needs? These questions lead directly to an examination of real estate.

Landlords and Tenants

A housing study compares the mobility of the population and the occupation of space as dictated by economic and social conditions that to a large extent themselves determine whether one's home is owned or rented.

The first important stage will be to determine how many houses there were in Québec in the 18th century and identify who owned them. The

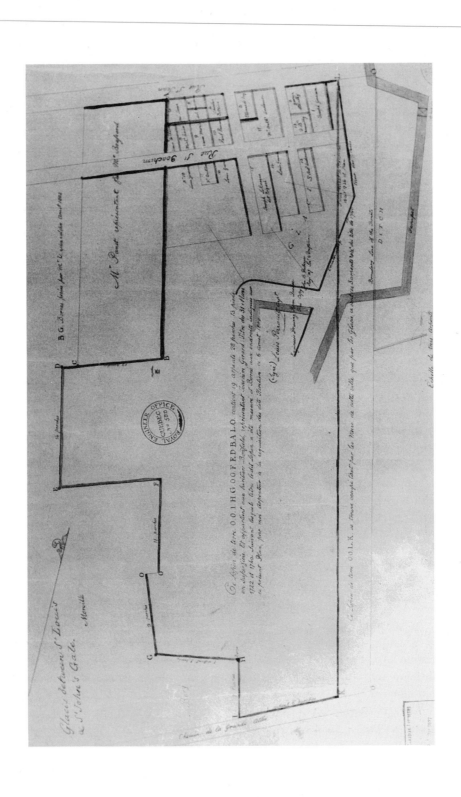

Fig. 16 The dark line marks the boundaries of Joachim Girard's lands located outside the fortifications. Chaussegros de Léry's enclosure (1745) and its glacis covered almost all of Girard's land. *Anonymous original, 1802, Canadian Parks Service, Québec.*

1688 census showed that there were 1407 persons (divided among 230 households according to the 1681 census) living in 207 houses and cabins. According to a 1740 plan there were about 600 houses for 4603 residents.[2] But according to the various "declarations and enumerations" carried out between 1733 and 1744, there were 422 buildings registered with the Colonial Administrator.[3] These buildings were shared by 328 separate owners, including about 40 successions. A comparison of this number with the number of heads of household counted by Father Jacrau in 1744 (1058), shows that 31% of the heads of households in Québec owned their homes. This proportion was 90% at the end of the 17th century.

It is true that the "declarations and enumerations" are incomplete; on the other hand, Father Jacrau's census is also incomplete. If we include, in proportion, the owners of missing buildings we get an additional 139 owners, which means that the maximum proportion of owners was 44%. About 1740 then, Québec had a minimum of 31% and a maximum of 44% of home owners.[4] The situation in Québec was quite different from that in Montréal (70%),[5] but was close to that of various French cities such as Rouen (20%).[6]

However, as in both Montréal and Rouen, the ownership concentration index was low as only 20% of the owners owned more than one house, 16% owned two, 3% owned three, 1% owned four and one individual, the architect and builder Jean Maillou, owned nine lots and houses, of which six were in Lower Town, especially on Sault-au-Matelot Street. The number of lots and houses owned should not be used as an absolute measure as this factor should be weighted by the surface area reported. Most of the people enumerated had comparable areas. Only two names stand out: Maillou again, for his properties on Saint-Louis Street, and the shoemaker Joachim Girard, who owned two houses and a huge lot located directly to the west of the Saint-Jean Gate. Girard started to subdivide his land, but his speculative endeavours were halted by the construction of the fortifications in 1745.

TABLE 21
OWNERS BY SECTOR OF ACTIVITY, 1690-1759

| Total | Services | Business | Artisan | Unskilled | |
				Widows	Others
840	183 (22 %)	177 (21 %)	277 (33 %)	203 (24 %)	0 (0 %)

Although it is more than reasonable to find an architect-builder among the owners, how about a shoemaker? Was he an exception? In short who owned the land? From 1690 until the end of the French régime, people belonging to more than 60 trades and professions owned a house in Québec, from architects to voyageurs, from tinsmiths to goldsmiths. Because of this, it is possible to group owners by sector of activity: service, business, artisan and journeymen or labourers.

The last group can be forgotten straight off as almost no journeymen or labourers owned their homes[7] (Table 21[8]). Artisans and small businessmen working in processing accounted for one-third of all owners.

The service and business sectors both provide the same number of owners, around 21%. There was a fourth group of owners who, considered separately, was quite large: widows. They accounted for 24% of the owners who rented their houses in whole or in part, which means that this was an important social phenomenon in Québec society in the 18th century. Lack of resources forced widows to subdivide their houses, keeping only a room for themselves, as did Pierre Nolan's widow Catherine Houart or Guillaume Nicholas' widow Marie Marendeau.[9] Poverty might partially explain the trend toward remarrying on the part of widows in the capital.[10]

As far as the professions of tenants are concerned (Table 22[11]), most of them came from the business sector, followed closely by the artisan sector. These two groups include almost 75% of all tenants. Service people rented in barely 20% of all cases. Labourers chose renting; but did they really have a choice? Widows rarely rented.

An estimate by sector of activity can be drawn from these two tables (21 and 22): within the service group, 52% owned one or more houses. They and widows were the only two groups where owners were in the

TABLE 22
TENANTS BY SECTOR OF ACTIVITY, 1690-1759

| Total | Services | Business | Artisan | Unskilled | |
				Widows	Others
962	167 (17 %)	366 (38 %)	348 (36 %)	58 (6 %)	23 (2 %)

majority. Among business people the proportion drops to 32%, while 44% of owners worked in the artisan sector.[12]

Considering the trades and professions included in each of these sectors of activity, within the service group, 70% of the Councillors and 60% of the notaries were landowners. On the other hand, the proportion of surgeons who were tenants was 53%, despite the activities of one of them, Gervais Beaudoin, who rented a few of his properties (16 leases). Army officers followed the same trend as a majority (51%) were tenants.

In the business sector 88% of the innkeepers were tenants.[13] Carters, butchers and bakers accounted for 85%, 75% and 75% of tenants, respectively. Sixty percent of the merchants and wholesalers were tenants.

In the artisan sector, most construction workers were owners: 59% were masons, 63% carpenters and 53% framers. Fifty-four percent of the ironworkers (blacksmiths, locksmiths, and edge-tool makers) rented their home as did 74% of the workers in the leather industry (shoemakers, tanners, harness-makers). Seventy-five percent of the people working in the clothing trades (hat-makers, dressmakers, tailors, dyers, weavers) were leaseholders as were 69% of those in the other wood industries (cabinetmakers, sculptors, coopers, turners).

In summary, during the 18th century, Québec became a city of tenants, because the population increased more rapidly than housing construction. In such a situation the residents had to share existing houses, which led to the subdivision of houses and renting. The resident-house ratio rose from 6.79 in 1688 to 7.67 in 1739-40. But this coefficient arises from the assumption that all houses were multiple dwellings, which was not the case. If the numbers are standardized to reflect this reality, we will inevitably become aware of the overcrowding in certain areas and streets. There was only one solution for this situation: an in-

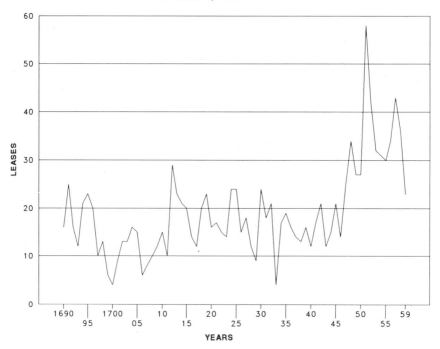

GRAPH 9
ANNUAL DISTRIBUTION OF LEASES
QUÉBEC, 1690-1759

crease in the habitable areas of rental houses as shown in Graph 8. Renting became customary.

The Geography of Tenancy

Everything was for rent in Québec in the 18th century, from a bit of land to a house, to a heating stove, to a loom. In which neighbourhoods and even on what streets were the rental buildings located? By determining this a better qualification of the trades of these tenants, taking into account the possible local effects of their place of work, will be attained.

TABLE 23
TYPES OF RENTAL BY PERIOD

Type	1690-1706	1707-1716	1717-1726	1727-1736	1737-1744	1745-1754	1755-1759	Total	%
Houses	142	104	84	81	70	155	70	706	52.8
Houses and shops	14	6	4	5	9	14	9	61	4.56
Boarding houses	10	5	8	7	2	6	1	39	2.92
Total	166	115	96	93	81	175	80	806	63.0
% of housing	20.6	14.3	11.9	11.5	10.0	21.7	9.9		
Apartments	52	30	58	48	26	97	66	377	28.24
Apartments and shops	6	4	6	3	4	11	10	44	3.29
Total	58	34	64	51	30	108	76	421	32.9
% of housing	13.7	8.0	15.2	12.1	7.1	25.6	18.0		
Rooms	5	3	7	9	5	15	7	51	3.82
% of housing	9.8	5.9	13.7	17.6	9.8	29.4	13.7		
Shops	6	3	10	4	2	8	2	35	2.62
Warehouses	2	3	0	0	0	0	0	5	0.37
Lands	1	4	3	1	2	5	1	17	1.27
Total	238	162	180	158	120	311	166	1335	
%	17.82	12.13	13.48	11.83	9.27	23.29	12.43		

There is a strong relationship between the size of the population, as established previously, and the frequency of tenancy as expressed in Graph 9. Between 1690 and 1706, the number of rentals dropped; it started to rise in 1707, and then dropped again at the end of the War of the Spanish Succession (after 1713). During the 1720s it rose, especially in 1724-25 and between 1729 and 1732, thus reflecting the "prosperity" brought about by the resurgence in maritime trade. But Québec's large shipyards and businesses did not see a major increase in activity until 1745, and this was not without repercussions on renting patterns. Briefly, the rental phenomenon reflects two realities: normal growth in the urban population and the influx of immigrants attracted by the capital's temporary economic boom.[14]

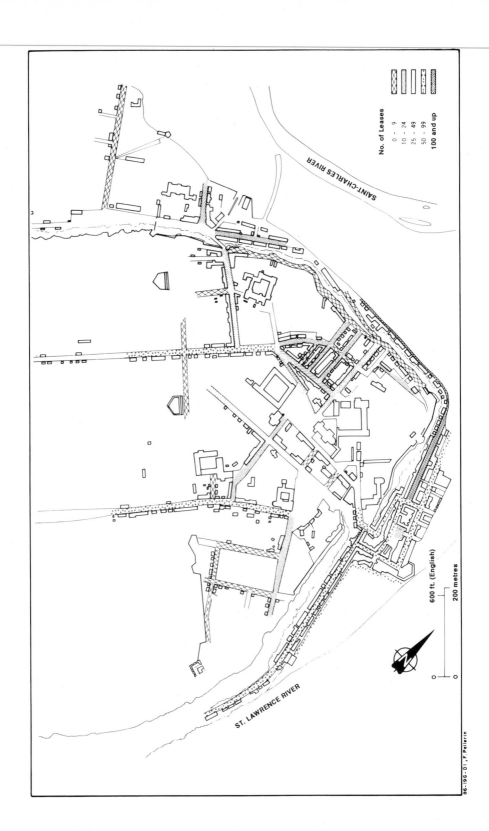

No. of Leases

0 - 9
10 - 24
25 - 49
50 - 99
100 and up

SAINT-CHARLES RIVER

ST. LAWRENCE RIVER

600 ft. (English)

200 metres

86-196-D1, F. Pellerin

Fig. 17 Distribution of rented houses in Québec, for the whole period, after compiling the leases. Compare with Fig. 11. *Map: F. Pellerin, after a map of Chausse- gros de Léry, 1724. (National Archives of Canada, H3/340/Québec/1742/section).*

Most of the time tenants (95%) were looking for a place to live; they very rarely looked for a store or a warehouse alone, and even less often for a lot or garden. In some cases, however, the dwelling doubled as a place of work (a little under one time in ten). Most rentals (63%) were in houses and buildings, apartments took up another third, and rooms the last 4% (Table 23).

These proportions did not remain constant throughout the French régime; house rentals dropped significantly starting in the 1720s, with a parallel increase in apartment and room rentals. This phenomenon meant that the citizens of the capital became more crowded, as the resident- house ratio discussed earlier suggests. House construction did not keep up with the growth in the population. On the other hand, it must be kept in mind that room rental remained a popular expedient for new arrivals during periods of economic boom as almost half the rooms rented can be traced to 1727-36 and 1745-54. Subletting seemed to be a marginal characteristic, barely 8% of the registered leases. However, 68% of the sublets recorded before 1745 took place during difficult economic peri- ods.

Whether or not this migration phenomenon was particularly local still remains to be seen. Most rentals during the entire period were in build- ings or parts of buildings located in Lower Town (54%), compared with 38% in Upper Town and 6% in the Palace Quarter. It was only after the 1740s that most rentals moved to Upper Town; Upper and Lower Towns had split the rental market evenly during the previous ten years. This can be explained by the space available in each of the districts, and by the size of the houses in Lower Town. Only a larger number of houses allowed Upper Town to increase its share of the market, while the ratio of houses to apartments was very similar between the two neighbour- hoods. Again, we have to take into account the stagnation in house con- struction in Lower Town.

There is some correlation between the size of the houses and the num- ber of leases (Figure 17). Houses on Champlain Street are the exception to this rule. Here, there were many rental properties and renting was frequent despite the modest size of the properties. But it must be kept in mind that one-quarter of the leases for dwellings on this street were signed after the construction of the naval shipyards in 1744-46. The same circumstances occurred in Saint-Charles Street in the Palace Quarter.

The correlation between the location of the rental property and the place of work is even stronger. This is evident if we analyze the trades and professions. A survey of the 20 main rental streets in the capital during the 18th century shows that most of those who worked in the service sector, mainly military officers and bureaucrats, were found on three streets in Upper Town: Buade, des Pauvres and Saint-Louis. Even though, for a time, the colony's chief engineer lived on Buade Street (at least until Chaussegros de Léry established a permanent residence on de la Sainte-Famille), various bureaucrats who worked in the Intendant's Palace lived on des Pauvres Street. Army officers, sergeants, and married sergeants and soldiers, who gravitated around the Château Saint-Louis and its garrison, often found lodgings on Saint-Louis Street. This phenomenon attracted other trades, as the presence of soldiers inevitably leads to the establishment of taverns and inns. No fewer than 14 separate tavern-keepers and publicans signed leases on Saint-Louis Street between 1693 and 1755.

Seven streets in Lower Town were characterized by the commercial interests of their rental clientele, compared to only two in Upper Town. These are Cul-de-Sac, de Meulle, Sous-le-Fort, Notre-Dame, Saint-Pierre and Sault-au-Matelot streets and Place Royale; only de la Fabrique and Sainte-Famille in Upper Town showed the same characteristics. While tavern-keepers lived cheek by jowl with sailors (or vice versa!) on Cul-de-Sac, de Meulle Street was a popular street in many ways. No particular group monopolized the largest share of its rental market; however, this street had a certain reputation at the end of the 17th century: depending upon which side of the door a traveller entered from, he might find himself in heaven ... or in hell!!![15] Was this the case throughout this period? The question seems indiscreet! While Sous-le-Fort Street claimed the title as the emporium of shops, both colonial and foreign, it still had to enter into heated competition with the shopkeepers on Notre-Dame and Saint-Pierre streets and Place Royale. Chandlers were found mostly on Sault-au-Matelot, along with the inevitable wholesale merchants. In addition, several tavern-keepers and new bakers, for whom the provision of biscuits to sailors was without a doubt one of their most important markets, were also found there. In Upper Town, a few merchants and bakers were found along de la Fabrique, and many bakers on de la Sainte-Famille.

Eight streets housed mostly salaried employees and small "businessmen" in the artisan sector: Champlain, de l'Escalier and de la Montagne streets in Lower Town; on des Carrières, Saint-Jean, Saint-Joseph and Sainte-Anne streets in Upper Town; and on Saint-Nicolas Street in the Palace Quarter. Carpenters and naval carpenters lived beside coopers and smiths on Champlain Street, along with some sailors. It should be kept in mind, however, that the development of the shipyards coincided with the arrival of some of these workmen.[16] Without the rental activities of Beaudoin the surgeon, the case of de l'Escalier Street would have passed unnoticed; from 1732 to 1758, he rented a forge nine times! However, an attentive observer would have to add that Beaudoin rented it even more often, if the one he rented on de la Montagne Street is the same one! On de la Montagne Street there were among the many artisans several locksmiths, tool-makers, goldsmiths, leather craftsmen and garment workers. While most of the streets in Upper Town drew a well-defined clientele, Saint-Jean Street drew several artisans and construction workers, at least in a certain section. In the Palace Quarter, the Intendant's Palace and the naval yard attracted many bureaucrats and naval construction workers.

In summary, the workplace may influence the choice of a place of residence to a great extent. The bakers on Sault-au-Matelot Street were attracted by the docks as the pulley-maker on Saint-Nicolas Street was attracted by the shipyard. And if this criterion works for artisans and suppliers, it may also explain the strong concentration of merchant's shops on Place Royale. This was the answer to a crucial problem, that of transshipment and transportation.[17]

A house or store located in Lower Town would draw wholesalers or tradesmen involved in shipping activities. This strong demand no doubt influenced landlords to build larger houses, knowing quite well that this demand would drive up rental prices. Was this a speculative reflex or a simple economic calculation aimed at a kind of self-financing? As it has already been established that few landlords owned more than one house,

A TENANT'S TOWN

TABLE 24
RENTAL PRICES BY DISTRICT, 1690-1759
(in *livres*)

Decade	Houses			Apartments			Rooms		
	L. T.	U. T.	P.Q.	L. T.	U. T.	P.Q.	L. T.	U. T.	P.Q.
1690-1699	211.64	87.77	57.08	126.99	57.75	45.00	40.50		37.50
1700-1709	171.16	161.25	37.50	93.82	96.87		37.50		
1710-1719	260.04	134.77	37.50	209.34	87.89	70.31	65.00		
1720-1729	380.42	136.08	85.00	175.04	84.73	59.00	96.83	51.20	33.00
1730-1739	333.67	131.56	160.83	170.25	83.84	69.50	93.33	58.00	
1740-1749	369.02	141.26	179.18	182.25	72.97	95.00	50.00	43.75	
1750-1759	762.78	302.52	332.39	302.61	166.38	231.60	107.50	85.00	89.33

the second hypothesis must be favoured. In this way, a landlord could hope to cover at least his maintenance expenses if not to pay off his mortgage.

Still in a market economy with a "restricted" market, this situation could not fail to have some effect on the prices asked. But can we conclude that a "subtle bargaining between landlords and tenants" existed, while "circumstances modulated the faithfulness of the tenants?"[18] Obviously the amount of space rented is the determining factor for the price charged. Renting a room is cheaper than renting an apartment or a house. During this period, in the same area, an apartment would cost twice as much as a room and half as much as a house (Table 24).

Other than the space factor, neighbourhood was a significant criterion if we take into account its attractiveness to future tenants. Because of the business there and obviously the port, Lower Town was the most expensive area to live in throughout the French régime, regardless of the type of housing rented. There is no question that the limited potential for expansion in the habitable area of the district also created pressure to keep prices high. This is clearly seen when higher housing costs in the Palace Quarter than in Upper Town are experienced after 1730, when the naval shipyards opened.

Thus in the two districts where population density was highest, the price of housing was also highest. It is interesting to also point out that despite its large lots and many gardens, Upper Town was not as attrac-

TABLE 25

NUMBER OF ROOMS INHABITED, BY DISTRICT, 1690-1759

	Lower Town	Upper Town	Palace
Owners	4.190	3.260	2.650
Tenants	2.330	1.810	1.500
Ratio	0.556	0.552	0.566
% Reserved Space	64.300	64.300	63.800

tive to tenants either in terms of number or of quality. The fact that it was farther away was undoubtedly a primary factor. In short, Québec citizens looked for neither large spaces nor for greenery.

Relationships Between Landlords and Tenants

A tenant about to sign a lease would hear the notary reading him a description of the premises he would be living in, followed by several clauses concerning the methods of payment, breaking the lease and the compensations he would have to pay.

To say that the tenant would have less space than a live-in landlord would be a truism. In general, a live-in landlord would keep two-thirds of the habitable space regardless of the neighbourhood (Table 25).[19] This rental area would be laid out vertically and not horizontally, contrary to the French or at least Parisian custom.[20] Occasionally people even lived under the eaves as both leases and succession inventories show. This is one of the aspects of the social economy of housing in Québec in the 18th century.

Let us now proceed to the question of leases. In periods of high immigration (or growth), landlords were reluctant to sign long-term leases, hoping to profit from the inevitable rise in prices when demand exceeded supply. A comparison of Graphs 10 and 11 shows the opposite relationship that exists between variations in the duration of the leases and rental prices.[21] While tenants signed long-term leases during periods when rents were dropping, those same tenants would only be able to get a short-term lease when prices were rising, which was also to the ad-

GRAPH 10
HOUSE RENTAL PRICES
QUÉBEC, 1690-1759

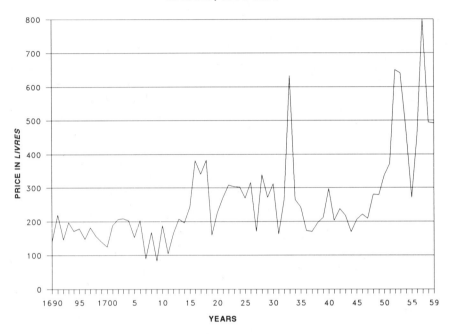

vantage of the landlord. In brief there was in Québec a "subtle bargaining between landlords and tenants."

But does this mean that in periods of rising rents tenants moved more often? Only an analysis of length of residence would make it possible to answer this question adequately. A generally accepted postulate states that small businessmen and wholesalers look for some stability in order to keep their clients. They represent a group of tenants who are at the mercy of rising rents. Lease renewals only accounted for 15% of the cases. However, three times out of four they involved merchants (45%) and artisans (30%). The initial image that arises is one of stability. However, only one wholesaler in five would rent the same building again, which represents a very high mobility index. This proportion drops by several points for artisans and those working in the service sector. But all this would depend upon the neighbourhood where the house

GRAPH 11
AVERAGE LENGTH OF LEASES
QUÉBEC, 1690-1759

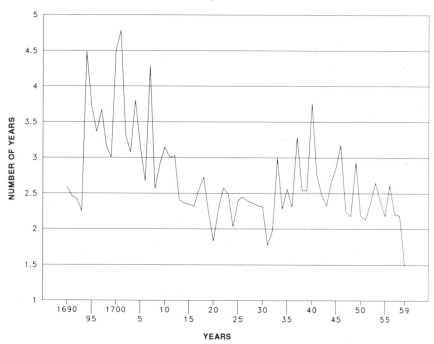

was located. Bakers, tavern-keepers and wholesalers certainly would tend to stay for longer periods than small-business owners or artisans, but this commitment was for a shorter period when it involved renewing a lease in Upper Town (Table 26).[22] Constancy had some limitations.

While wig-maker Florent Michaud kept his house on Notre-Dame Street for 20 years, he was among the exceptions. It is certainly possible to find other similar examples such as the bailiff Joseph Prieur, and later his widow, who lived in their house on Sault-au-Matelot Street for 18 years; or the tailor Guillaume Fabas who did the same. However, there are not many such examples. Of the seven cases found, all but one were located in Lower Town, and all owned stores.[23]

Most tenants signed only one or at most two leases for the same dwelling. While the *Coutume de Paris* set the maximum duration of a

TABLE 26

LEASES AND RENEWALS, BY PROFESSION AND STREET, 1690-1759

| Street | Leases/Profession | | | | | | Renewals/Profession | | | | | | Average Length of Renewals | | | | |
| | | | | | Unskilled | | | | | | Unskilled | | | | | Unskilled | |
	Number	Services	Business	Artisan	Widows	Others	Number	Services	Business	Artisan	Widows	Others	Services	Business	Artisan	Widows	Others
Upper Town																	
Buade	18	10	5	2	1		4	1	2	1			1.5s	1.0	1.0		
Carrières	16	5	2	8		1	0										
Fabrique	19	2	9	7	1		2	1	1				3.0	1.0			
Pauvres	29	15	5	7	1	1	1	1					3.0				
Saint-Jean	62	9	18	29	3	3	3		2	1				1.5	1.0		
Saint-Joseph	18	5	4	8	1		1		1					1.0			
Saint-Louis	60	23	22	9	4	2	6	2	3	1			1.75	3.0	2.0		
Sainte-Anne	17	4	4	8	1		3	1	1	1			5.0	3.0	2.0		
Sainte-Famille	16	3	8	4	1		1		1					3.0			
Lower Town																	
Champlain	44	4	11	21	6	2	5	1	2	1	1		3.0	2.0	1.0	1.0	
Cul-de-Sac	74	17	34	14	8	1	20	8	6	3	3	1	3.5	3.66	2.8	1.8	
De Meulle	24	1	11	11	1		4	1	2	1			1.2	6.0	1.0		
Escalier	21	1	3	17			6			6					3.0		
Montagne	68	8	10	48	2		9	1		7	1		3.0		3.3	3.0	
Notre-Dame	47	5	28	11	3		13	2	5	5	1		3.0	5.0	3.8	3.0	
Place Royale	16	2	10	4			2		1	1				5.0	1.0		
Saint-Pierre	75	12	44	11	7	1	12		10	1	1			3.66	3.0	1.0	
Sault-au-Matelot	94	9	44	28	9	4	17		11	3	2	1		3.9	3.66	3.0	1.0
Sous-le-Fort	59	3	32	21	3		9		6	3				4.0	2.0		
Palace Quarter																	
Saint-Nicolas	19	2	4	13			2			2					2.0		
Saint-Charles	14	7	1	5	1												
Total	796	140	308	281	52	15	120	19	54	37	9	1					

TABLE 27
AVERAGE LENGTH OF LEASES,
1690-1759

Lodging	Years
Dwelling	3.5
House	2.86
House and Shop	2.77
Apartment	2.1
Apartment and shop	2.38
Room	1.57
Shop	2.22
Warehouse	1.58
Land	3.72

lease at nine years, except for ground rents, economic circumstances could change things so that the legal limits were only rarely applied. Renting a house or building, however, symbolizes greater tenant stability than renting an apartment or a room (Table 27). Tenants generally stayed in the same location for three to six years. Constancy was subordinated to mobility....

As a general rule, landlords and tenants appeared in front of the notary together to sign the lease. Of the landlords living outside the city, who accounted for 10% of the total, only one in four used a power of attorney. Slightly over half of the landlords who lived in Québec owned property in Lower Town.[24] Length, payment and occupation clauses were usually agreed upon at this stage. While prices varied quite a bit depending upon the space rented, the circumstances, the neighbourhood and even the street, three out of every four landlords asked for payment every three months[25] (Table 28).

Furthermore, Quebeckers in the 18th century showed a marked preference for moving in the spring, especially on 1 May, which the Colonial Administrator Bigot confirmed in his ordinance dated 20 April 1750 (Graph 12). The end of a long and difficult winter or the coming of spring and renewal seemed to push people to move to a new home. Generally this occurred quickly with an average of 15 days elapsed between the signing of the lease and moving in.

TABLE 28
DISTRIBUTION OF PAYMENT METHODS BY DECADE

Method	1690-1699	1700-1709	1710-1719	1720-1729	1730-1739	1740-1749	1750-1759	Total
Unknown	8	8	23	17	10	9	11	86
Annually	12	8	9	12	12	12	15	80
Bimonthly	0	0	1	0	0	0	0	1
In advance	0	0	0	1	2	1	5	9
Monthly	2	0	2	4	3	0	2	13
Quarterly	110	68	134	109	120	158	302	1001
Semi-annually	30	20	16	19	15	18	20	138
Trimesterly	0	2	2	2	0	0	1	7
Total	162	106	187	164	162	198	356	1335

Sometimes it was the secondary clauses such as permission to use cooking ovens or to draw water from a well that attracted the tenants. One-third of the landlords made a bread oven available to their tenants;[26] but only one landlord in 10 mentioned water in the lease, and half of these are after 1750. While these clauses pleased the tenants, others irritated them.

Suspicious landlords could ask for the full rent or at least for three months in advance,[27] but this happened rarely (in barely 13% of the leases). Tenants seemed to have kept their commitments faithfully since only 3% of the leases were subject to an official cancellation, and subletting[28] was also a marginal practice. Furthermore, any intention of breaking the lease usually had to be announced three months in advance; in fact, in accordance with the method of payment.

Landlords added various binding restrictions and charges to their leases. It was only after the 1730s that the various "municipal" charges that the tenant had to pay were included in the leases. As a general rule, these included sweeping the chimney monthly, cleaning their section of the street in winter and paying various taxes (for fire buckets and other things).

On the other hand, most of the time the tenants had to provide a copy of the lease to the landlord and carry out minor repairs such as replacing window panes or put up building partitions, which the tenant had the right to later dismantle and keep, or even give to the owner. On very rare occasions, tenants had to provide "a good and sufficient guarantor living in this city."[29] In order to guarantee payment of the rent, they also had to furnish the house with "usable furnishings" that could be seized in case of non-payment of rent.[30]

As far as this aspect of landlord-tenant relations is concerned, based on an examination of provostship cases, it does not seem that it was the origin of much friction between the two groups.[31] Certainly all societies have some problem individuals; Québec in the 18th century was not an exception. Landlords do not seem to have been very inclined to seize their tenants' goods. However, one name stands out in the few references on this subject, that of Jacques Armand *dit* Maison de Bois, a pewterer, who faced seizure for non-payment of rent twice in three years.[32] While rare, such failure for whatever reason would seem to represent the most common source of friction between landlords and tenants, and owners often preferred to evict tenants rather than try to recover the amounts owed.

Eviction could also be caused by "breach of contract," for example, failure for a tavern-keeper or publican to comply with a specific clause. Moreover, these two occupations do not seem to have been very popular with landlords. A landlord may implicitly allow his tenant to sell alcohol for take-out, while prohibiting him from serving it on the premises.[33] In other cases, a clause formally prevented the tenant from keeping a public house[34] or even subletting the premises to a publican.[35]

These clauses were sometimes waived though. So when Claude-Charles Dutisné, a lieutenant (and by definition a highly mobile citizen), was undoubtedly called to defend another post, he had to sublet his house, the lease of which apparently prevented him from subletting to tavern-keepers. In this case, one must pay particular attention to the immediate surroundings. The landlord, Louis Normand Labrière, also owned the adjoining house, which was already rented to another tavern-keeper, Laurent Normandin *dit* Sauvage. With this interdiction, the toolmaker Labrière undoubtedly wanted to protect Normandin's market[36] and his two buildings at the same time! Dutisné nevertheless subletted the premises to François Janny, a tavern owner![37] Was this exception granted because of the quality of the tenant who still remained responsible? This possibility is of course plausible.

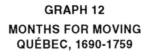

GRAPH 12

MONTHS FOR MOVING

QUÉBEC, 1690-1759

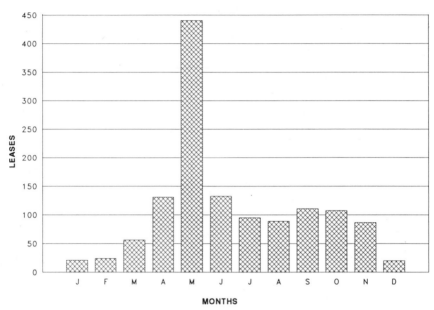

Another restriction was also placed on tenants having to do with animals including chickens, pigs, cows and their manure. While some landlords placed restrictions on keeping chickens on the rented premises,[38]
some tenants still kept chicken coops as succession inventories show.
Some landlords formally forbade keeping animals in the courtyard, the
basement and even the ... attic.[39] Others set a period of time (from six
weeks to three months) during which the tenants could keep animals,
while placing restrictions on pigs[40] or other sources of foul smells such
as fish oils;[41] but there were few landlords with delicate senses of
smell.

Landlords applied other restrictions on their tenants that were of a
seasonal nature: these involved the use of wood and bleach. It seems
that washing was done outside, given the restrictions on doing it inside;
however, we do not know how the tenants managed in the winter. And
since it is necessary to heat the house in winter, most leases show that

the landlord would allocate a space in the courtyard, basement or attic for storing wood. However, it was formally forbidden to hew or chop wood indoors. No mention is made of charcoal.

Occasionally landlords introduced specific clauses respecting a particular lifestyle. While the landlord on Saint-Pierre Street who allowed his tenant to place flowerpots on the balcony is one of the rare ones; what can we say about Noël Collet and the widow Morisseau, who expressly forbade their tenants to disturb their peace by dancing in their rented apartment?[42] Sometimes, renting part of the house improved the lot of people who felt lonely or too old to keep house. Jacques Moran Senior allowed journeymen Laurent Tareau and Phillippe Beaudin to occupy his house on Sault-au-Matelot Street for one year each, on the condition that they keep him, feed him, and clean and mend his clothing.[43] As for the widow who wanted her tenant, a shoemaker, to provide her with bread, and render her various small services such as breakfast in bed, the two parties cancelled the lease before it came into effect.[44]

In short, whether or not they lived in their own buildings, landlords could add various clauses to the contract that bound their tenant or tenants. However, leases became almost standardized in Québec during the 18th century. Renting a building or part of a building became a common practice for both landlords and tenants. At this point we must examine the reasons for such a situation.

Purchasing a Property

While the widow found it profitable to rent part or all of her house for some financial gains that would allow her to meet her obligations, the tenant also benefited. Table 22 has already shown that representatives of the business sector, and small businessmen and salaried craftsmen (artisan sector) accounted for three-quarters of all tenants. On the other hand, while the market met the needs of the tenants throughout this period, why risk buying or building a house? The problem of real estate ownership remains unsolved. The following paragraphs do not claim to be exhaustive; at best, they examine some of this enigma and suggest some hypotheses. This problem touches upon several aspects, from the

initial purchase of the land to the construction of the house, through the
financing of both the land and the house.[45]

The purchase price of land as shown in the documents was rarely
above 600 *livres*. This amount varied, however, as a function of the area
ceded or sold. In order to evaluate the cost of land, we must determine
the sale price per square foot. In the Saint-Roch suburb, for example,
Henri Hiché sold his land at a price of 3 *sols* 4 *deniers* to 4 *sols* per
square foot.[46] Nevertheless, we should point out that the prices asked by
various owners fluctuated greatly. While the Paupers of the Hôtel-Dieu
sold their land in Upper Town suburbs for 3*d.* per square foot; in Upper
Town, the lots were slightly more (and often much more) expensive. For
example, the concessions to Noël Collet and Jean Guenet went for
10*s.*9*d.* per square foot.[47] On average, however, the prices asked by the
Paupers were lower than those asked by Hiché; that is, 6*d.* per square
foot.

The lots sold by the Hospitalières of the Hôtel-Dieu in Upper Town,
while few, nevertheless sold at a good price, but the Hospitalières sold a
great deal of land in the Palace Quarter; on Saint-Charles Street, the
prices varied from 2*s.*6*d.* to 5*s.*6*d.*[48] The Jesuits' prices in Upper Town
were between 2*s.*7*d.* and 5*s.*3*d.* per square foot; in the Palace Quarter
they were much the same.[49]

The Ursulines sold their lots at lower prices, from 2*s.* to 2*s.*10*d.* per
square foot.[50] The Seminary, the most important seller, sold its lots in
the fief of Sault-au-Matelot in Upper Town for between 2*s.* and 11*d.* per
square foot, and that in Lower Town for between 1*d.* and 10*d.* per
square foot.[51] The Notre-Dame Parish asked between 1*s.*3*d.* and 2*s.*9*d.*
per square foot for its land on Cap-aux-Diamants; while its Notre-Dame
land sold for between 1*d.* and 3*d.*[52]

These price fluctuations do not take into account the date when the
land was sold. This may explain in part the variations in a given area, as
prices are always based on the growth or movement of the population.

We should, however, point out that one sale was the subject of a notarized contract with two clauses; on one hand, the sale itself and on the
other, the provisions of a "mortgage," which at the time was a loan earning an annual interest of 5%. Usually the principal, for example 400 *livres*
earning interest at 5% that is, 20 *livres* per year, was paid in predetermined instalments of 100 or 200 *livres* or in a single payment. The

buyer would pay the interest annually, but would not pay off the principal if he only paid the interest. "Double" contracts were common practice during the 18th century.[53]

In the Saint-Roch suburb in the 1750s, sale contracts added a double interest, but this practice was neither new nor unique to property developers like Hiché. Religious communities had for a long time charged a "ground rent." This was seen as a second "mortgage" that encumbered the property sold, and this mortgage was not redeemable meaning that the purchaser only pays the interest and, as a result, the original owners of the land maintain property rights. In brief, this practice is equivalent to renting the land in perpetuity rather than selling it outright.

Let us take the concrete case of cabinet-maker Joseph Gallais *dit* Lafleur, who on 1 July 1696 purchased a 2208 square-foot property with a house on Saint-Joseph Street in Upper Town from the Seminary. The purchase price was 1000 *livres*; thus, 50 *livres* in interest per year. The contract specified that the purchaser could pay back 900 *livres* of the principal, the other 100 *livres* (5 *livres* in interest) going toward the ground rent and consequently not redeemable. On 17 October 1705 Joseph Gallais was forced to return his land to the Seminary; in nine years he had paid 495 *livres* in interest, and paid only 131 *livres* of principal; that is, 14.5%.[54]

It is true that this was land with a building; nevertheless, the example is valid. In terms of cases dealing with land only, the shoemaker Joachim Girard provides many examples. He sold a 680-square-foot lot to Joseph Bédard for 160 *livres*. Of this amount 140 *livres* were redeemable at an interest rate of 7 *livres* per year (5%) payable to Girard, and one *livre* in interest had to be sent annually to the Paupers of the Hôtel-Dieu who owned the land. In fact, 16 of the 19 properties sold by Joachim Girard were subject to these double rates.

Almost all the religious institutions used double rates, even though it was an archaic and even illegal practice, according to the 1441 and 1553 Ordinances. There was one way for the owner to circumvent the law: there was an "exception in favour of the first rents created after the quit-rent [real estate tax] that do not exceed one-third of the value of the property."[55] The above examples fit these descriptions. But did all sales include these two types of rates? The example of Joachim Girard's properties partially answers this question. Barely 15% of the lands ceded by the communities were subject to such "double taxes."

But these rates, single or double, are only one aspect of real estate. A contract must be signed with a contractor in order to have a house built. While it has already been established that most houses in Québec were made of stone, and that the average surface area of the houses increased during the 18th century, it seems that the cost of houses also rose during this period despite a drop in the cost of labour.[56] It is difficult to separate land costs from material and labour costs. We would be better served taking into account the total value of a house, which in principle includes the cost of the land.

From various acts gleaned from a random analysis, but concerning all the neighbourhoods of the city, we know that costs were higher in Lower Town than in Upper Town. The real-estate purchasing movement varies little from that of the rental market; one being dependent upon the other. The price of a house in Lower Town between 1690 and 1749 could vary between 900[57] and 7000 *livres*,[58] and even reach as high as 10 500 *livres* during the period of high inflation in 1719.[59] Prices were comparable in Upper Town.[60]

It quickly becomes obvious that these figures do not take into account the dimensions, materials, or even the street on which the house was located. They only show that an average price of 4000 *livres* anywhere in Québec would not seem to be too much.[61] But this amount had to be financed. People who could pay the purchase price in full were as rare then as they are now. Buyers needed a source of financing. Whether this was a businessman, a parent or someone else does not matter; what is important are the modalities of the "obligation." As in the case of ground rent, the obligation represented by the mortgage followed the same course: an annual amount covering the 5% interest (which means 200 *livres* per year on a 4000-*livre* debt) that does not reduce the principal, as this is paid out in predetermined equal payments.

By this calculation, the residents of Québec did not have the means to finance the purchase of an existing house or the construction of a new one. For this reason renting a house or part of it became a popular solution with recent immigrants who, uncertain of their immediate future, hesitated to plunge into the real estate market.

On the other hand, to become the owner of a house did not seem to be very profitable. The example of the Lavallière succession is a revealing one. Heirs to a duplex on Buade Street, the three parties agreed to rent it. From 1724 to 1731, a seven-year period, the building brought in 2361 *livres*. This was, however, gross income, from which the costs of maintenance and repairs had to be subtracted; which amounted to 369 *livres* 16 *sols* over the same period or 15.66% of income. This means that each side brought in 94 *livres* 16 *sols* per year.

Obviously this amount only partially and indirectly reflects the importance of rental income. Multiplied by three this income if it came to a single owner would be significant; but, taking identified standards into account, this was for a large house. This figure is only representative as a function of the purchase or sale price of a house, the only criterion that makes it possible to evaluate the return. The heirs sold this property for 7495 *livres*; in this context, renting represented a return on capital of 4.5% per year. Since maintenance costs must be deducted this return drops to 3.8%.[62]

While this is only one example, it is possible to generalize. It must be kept in mind that documents of this sort are rare. However, a similar study carried out on a larger scale on the Rouen rental market led to similar observations: the building offered a gross return of 4.6% annually. Once the costs are eliminated it provided a return on capital of about 4%.[63] In a market as restricted as the real estate market in the capital, this return did not encourage eventual owners to speculate; as a result, four owners out of five had only one building. Furthermore, this rate of return is lower than what a creditor would earn from a loan. While merchants and wholesalers in Rouen, a port city, preferred to invest in business where the benefits were greater, why should the situation be otherwise in Québec?

*****

During the 18th century, Québec became a city of tenants. It was only among bureaucrats and officers that a majority owned houses; those in the business, artisan and journeyman sectors were primarily tenants. As in the case of socio-professional distribution, all the neighbourhoods had houses for rent, although the two Lower Towns were the preferred areas; proximity to the workplace reinforced this geographic distribution around rentals and rental density reinforced the prices.

Landlord-tenant relationships seemed cordial, despite the fact that stability was not one of the characteristics of the tenants; prices and economic conditions often forced them to move. This mobility within the city should be placed in parallel with house construction and the type of rental found: the population grew more rapidly than the number of houses, meaning that the resident-house ratio increased throughout the 18th century. At the same time, the average size of the houses increased, while the rental market became more and more oriented toward apartment rentals.

Renting a building in whole or in part represented a commitment of limited duration that often translated into signing one or at most two successive leases with the same landlord. This situation reinforces the impression of mobility that arises from the demographic analysis. Uncertain of their future, those newly arrived in the urban environment hesitate to plunge into the real estate game; on one hand, they have to be sure of having enough income or share of the market; and on the other, they have to find a source of financing. Furthermore since housing speculation earned low returns merchants and wholesalers shy away from it. But maybe they were forced to do so. This was one of the ways in which Quebeckers in the first half of the 18th century showed their uncertainty about the future.

PART 3

CONSUMPTION AND PRODUCTION

We could have called this third section "Fortunes or Misfortunes" after the delightful expression D. Roche used to indicate that "a large share of the town's population is tightly bound by dependence relationships."[1] The play on words, however, reflects a very different context than that of Québec. Nevertheless the result, which is to say dependence within a production relationship, does not seem as far-fetched. While Roche's analysis was restricted to the domestics and wage-earners of Paris, there is room to extend it to include most of Québec urban society in the 18th century.

Analyzing production inevitably implies analyzing consumption. The domestic environment, whether inside or outside the home, or even inside the pantry, translates into a specific language of consumption whose source is only found in production. Instead of re-creating this entire chain, our approach is to place the Québec actors in this initial background. In the 18th century, Quebeckers no longer dreamed of going to the Indies — the Indies came to them! Québec became an international crossroads; the city lived at the pace of the tides and of trade. Workers, artisans and businessmen fell into it, officers and public servants profited from it....

CHAPTER 5

THE DOMESTIC ENVIRONMENT

Tenants were in the majority in 18th-century Québec; this situation implies certain realities that have repercussions on both the material and cultural levels. Tenants, who are mobile by definition, do not accumulate excessive amounts of belongings; on the other hand, they do not ignore current tastes. Out of the inventories of belongings of deceased persons,[1] one could derive a whole thesis of consumption from which some characteristics of the urban lifestyle arise as corollaries.

Outside the House: Stables and Cowsheds

The study of the urban landscape has already brought to light two characteristics of the 18th-century capital: on one hand, the particular topographic configuration of the city does not allow gardening except in Upper Town, so that self-sufficiency in market produce is only possible for a minority; on the other hand, only one dwelling in ten included outbuildings such as barns, stables, cowsheds, etc.

This situation is reflected in the goods owned by 18th-century Quebeckers. While the authorities at the beginning of the century were "scandalized" to see the spontaneous adoption of horses, which had until then been a symbol of prestige for officers,[2] as a mode of transportation in the countryside, they must have been quite pleased with the sobriety of the citizens of Québec in this respect. All honour ... to all lords, we might say! The horse, that noble conquest of man's, did not become at all popular in Québec. A question of price? Perhaps, at the end of the 17th century, a horse cost a little over one hundred *livres*,[3] but certainly not during the following century when they were worth one-third to one-fourth of that price.[4]

TABLE 29
TYPES OF GROUND TRANSPORTATION, 1690-1749

Decade	Invent.	Horse	Calèche	Sleigh	Cart	Tip-cart	Sled	Snowshoe
1690-1699	43	3	0	0	1	1	0	0
1700-1709	95	12	4	3	4	5	4	9
1710-1719	122	9	2	4	6	2	3	12
1720-1729	125	10	4	7	8	1	1	3
1730-1739	132	9	7	7	4	0	3	3
1740-1749	181	18	7	15	11	3	3	8
Total	698	61	24	36	34	12	14	35
%		8.74	3.43	5.16	4.87	1.72	2.00	5.01

However, whether we examine the end of the 17th century or the middle of the next, the proportion of horse owners does not vary significantly: on average, it is under 10%. This situation reflects the realities of housing: there were few opportunities to house animals, store their food, or park vehicles such as calèches, sleighs, buggies or carts (Table 29). In short, 18th-century Quebeckers travelled on foot both summer and winter, at least when distances were not too great. And if they had to carry heavy objects like water or logs they could always harness dogs.[5] While they were a little less cumbersome, dog-carts were no more frequent than horse and wagons. Thus, it is hardly surprising that Intendant Bigot gave priority to pedestrians in the streets of Québec; at that, he was only repeating the ordinance put in place by his predecessor, J. Raudot at the beginning of the century.[6] If people had to travel to the suburbs or if they were pressed for time, there were cart-drivers who were the taxi drivers of the time.

In 1749, it cost six *sols* to travel within Lower Town, and four more if the carter went from Lower Town as far as the Jesuits' house in Upper Town. If he had to go farther, to the Saint-Jean suburb for example, the charge was 14 *sols*. From the Intendant's palace, the cost was six *sols* to the Saint-Roch suburb, nine to the Jesuits', and 12 to go to the suburbs of Lower Town. In short the territory was zoned. The fee for regional transportation was set by the trip. These fees only applied to people, there was a separate price list for goods.[7]

But who owned horses other than carters? Nearly one in two residents of the suburbs owned one, although it is not possible to accord them professions other than the general term of "habitant" or small-scale farmer. Among the city-dwellers, Councillors, bureaucrats, surgeons and officers were the main groups who owned horses; these servants of the State and the public had to move around frequently. The second category of horse owners includes merchants and wholesalers, and some retailers — bakers and butchers — who profited from the transshipment of their goods on arrival and departure. The last group includes mainly construction workers such as carpenters, framers and architects. Thus, Hilaire Bernard de Larivière had to move about frequently in his position as land surveyor. In sum, while owning a horse and carriage or cart could in some cases meet real and practical needs within the context of 18th-century Québec, ownership of a horse was mainly a symbolic measure, to the extent that it reflected a status. Due to the concentration it implies, the urban environment easily frees the citizens from the need to own their own means of transportation.

The limited space available to them and the problems of pasturing and supply of forage forced Quebeckers to use the pastures of the religious communities, to which they paid rent.[8] The same problem affected those who kept animals other than chickens; swine and cattle owners largely outnumbered horse owners: double and triple, respectively (Table 30).[9] Thus, it is not surprising to find various ordinances on the subject of pigs escaping into the streets and onto the walls of the city. With the exception of residents of the suburbs, three out of four of whom owned animals, animal owners were present in many areas: slightly more than one household in three in the Palace Quarter, slightly fewer in Upper Town, and less than one out of four in Lower Town. Cows were more popular than pigs. Being more sedentary than pigs, the lack of a fence around the house did not incite them to wander off to nibble on a daisy or a bit of hay. Furthermore cows produce milk, an essential nutrient, and may end up in the cookpot on occasion.

Steers were less popular. There is reason to believe that, apart from those that wound up on the butcher's block, most were used as work animals as more than half the steers inventoried belonged to households in the suburbs. As far as hens, chickens, turkeys, geese, pigeons and other birds go, we believe that their life expectancies were short: a year at

TABLE 30
TYPES OF ANIMALS OWNED, 1690-1749

Decade	Invent.	Pigs		Cows		Steers		Chickens		Sheep	
		No.	%	No.	%	No.	%	No.	%	No.	%
1690-1699	43	6	13.95	8	18.6	4	9.3	4	9.3	1	2.3
1700-1709	95	23	24.42	23	29.5	14	14.7	12	12.6	2	2.1
1710-1719	122	26	21.31	34	27.9	9	7.4	7	5.7	7	5.7
1720-1729	125	20	16.00	26	20.8	5	4.0	6	4.8	4	3.2
1730-1739	132	17	12.88	14	10.6	3	2.3	2	1.5	1	0.7
1740-1749	181	35	19.34	44	24.3	3	1.6	10	5.5	2	1.1
Total	698	127	18.19	154	22.06	38	5.44	41	5.87	17	2.43

most since egg-laying slowed down during the winter. Sheep were not as widespread as elsewhere in the colony, due to their late introduction for use as livestock.[10]

Taking available space into account, these animals were rarely numerous. They were found in courtyards, sometimes in pastures in Upper Town or even in house basements or, in the case of chickens, in the attic.[11] This phenomenon, however, led the authorities to put in place regulations dealing with the removal of dung.

Other than butchers and tanners, most owners of domestic animals were not Councillors, officials or merchants, but rather artisans in construction, ironworking, clothing and wood. Owning animals in 18th-century Québec was an answer to circumstances: some form of self-sufficiency was sought. The notable drop in the number of animal owners between 1720 and 1740 was not due to the increase in animal prices, but to the general situation in the capital, with high immigration and exceptional mobility as the result. Thus, this low representation of animal owners leads us to assume a greater dependence on butchers for supplies of meat.

From the Yard to the Larder

But the space allotted to animals in Upper Town at least did not encroach upon garden plots. Quebeckers grew many market products in their small gardens, and many trees provided them with fruit in season. By this means, it becomes possible to penetrate the pantries of 18th-century Quebeckers and so understand them better, without having to invite ourselves to dinner.[12]

In addition to vegetables, 18th-century citizens grew seasoning vegetables, herbs and fruits. If we use the pre-established distinction between vegetables; that is, leguminous vegetables, root vegetables, leaf vegetables, seasoning vegetables and finally fruit vegetables, it would seem that Québec pantries were similar to those at the Hôtel-Dieu Hospital in Québec.

Only lentils are absent from the leguminous vegetables; the climate and soil made growing them difficult, and no merchants sold them.[13] On the other hand, fresh or dried green peas could be found alongside beans and kidney beans. Root vegetables were limited to beets, carrots and turnips, the first two being very rare at the Hôtel-Dieu Hospital. Salsify, parsnips and potatoes were generally unknown or ignored.[14]

Four species of leaf vegetables were found: celery; cabbage, by far the most popular; garden cabbage, and asparagus.[15] No mention is made of cauliflower, lettuce (the latter seems to have been very popular according to Pehr Kalm), chicory or endive, all of which are consumed fresh, and so would be absent from inventories.

The seasoning vegetables inventoried included those on the Hôtel-Dieu Hospital table: shallots, onions (red or braided) and leeks. And to make history a little more savoury, François Chasle's peppers in 1747[16] should also be included. Finally, only cucumbers show up among the local fruit vegetables; however, during the 18th century two imports should be added to the list: olives and artichokes. While olives appear to have been more popular, Jean Crespin's[17] salted artichokes were considered a more exotic and refined taste, and were rarer as a result. Councillor Jean François Martin Delino's[18] dried mushrooms should be added to this list.

With some exceptions, the vegetables inventoried were found on the tables of most families, after having grown in market gardens in the city or suburbs. Imported products were rare and only appeared late in the 18th century.

All the cereals mentioned, except for rice, were produced locally. Wheat and wheat flour occupy the place of honour, Laurentian society being a wheat society, and Quebeckers, eaters of bread. Thus, it is not surprising to see that three inventories in ten mention the presence of wheat or wheat flour. This situation goes along with that of housing: recall that one-third of the landlords made an oven available to their tenants for baking their bread.[19]

However, not all tenants could bake their own bread; many had to purchase it from bakers in the city. These were regulated by the public administration, and offered three types of bread: pure white flour bread, whole-meal bread without bran and whole-meal bread with bran. This third type of bread probably disappeared during the 18th century as no later ordinances mention it.

Obviously, the activities of bakers cannot be considered in isolation from agricultural conditions; bad harvests inevitably led the Superior Council, the Colonial Administrators and the Provost to intervene. As often as these three powers made regulations and ordinances on the price of bread, bakers found ways around them, by cheating on weight, by using lower quality ingredients, or by creating an artificial shortage of one or more of the products.[20] But the greatest difficulties were probably faced by those who didn't have ovens and were at the bakers' mercy.

Frustration reached its peak in 1714, when the wives of Québec workmen showed up at a meeting of the Council to complain about the quality of the bread sold by the bakers. Asked to give his opinion, Councillor and Doctor Michel Sarrazin said that "eating such poor bread inevitably causes pestilential illnesses in people that can infect the air and communicate themselves to the more comfortable people in the colony."[21] A medical and humanitarian speech, which nevertheless cannot hide its prejudices....

This exceptional situation arose out of the difficulties of policing the bakers in the city according to the Prosecutor General and the Councillors. In addition to regulating prices, the Council ordered that bread be weighed at the time of purchase.[22] This was not much more effective since, according to the Prosecutor General himself, there was collusion

TABLE 31

REGULATED BREAD PRICES

(in *deniers*)

Year	White	Whole-Meal	Brown
1692	24	22.5	15
1700	30	22.5	18
1707	18	11.35	
1710	25.75	13.75	
1731	21.75	16.0	
1737	22	16.125	
1742	24	20.0	

between the city's four bakers. In 1710, a fifth was given permission to set up in Québec:[23] did this stop the abuse? Starting in 1707 merchants also enjoyed the right to bake and sell biscuits,[24] and it would seem that the bakery business gained some stability. However, during the 18th century, every bad harvest led to worry about the bakers, who always wished to export the more lucrative flour or biscuits, but were still called upon to sell bread to citizens.

Bread prices tended to drop during the 18th century[25] (Table 31),[26] doubtless as a result of the general increase in wheat production. However, it must be noted that price differences between products remained steady throughout the 18th century, so that whole-meal bread sold for roughly 20% less than white bread, and bran bread sold for 25% less than the second category and 40% less than white. In summary, bread, being a diet staple, was regulated by the authorities so that the population could purchase it at reasonable prices.

Rye, buckwheat and barley were used little at the Hôtel-Dieu Hospital[27] and are completely absent from the inventories, which confirms the primacy of wheat in an urban environment such as Québec. However, in the third decade of the 18th century, merchants began selling a new product made from wheat: starch.[28] Best known for its use in laundry starch can also be used to brew beer.

While barley and oats could substitute for wheat during shortages, Quebeckers definitely preferred oats; in normal times this cereal was primarily used as animal fodder, as was bran. Corn was primarily found in domestic kitchens rather than at the Hôtel-Dieu Hospital. Rice, the only imported item in its category, was regularly present, especially at the end of the 17th century. In sum, the cereals sold to the public were very similar to those fed to sick people at the Hôtel-Dieu Hospital.

According to the inventories, fish consumption revolved primarily around the eternal triangle of eel, cod and salmon. Eel was the most popular species, closely followed by cod. Quebeckers, unlike the nuns of the Hôtel-Dieu Hospital, preferred the latter dried rather than salted.[29] Salmon was eaten both salted and smoked, but was primarily found at the end of the 17th century and after 1730. Fresh-water fish and molluscs are both absent with one exception: François Chasles' pickled oysters. The absence of oysters is stunning, given not only their importance as a food but also their "industrial" use later in the century.[30] It is true that fresh-water fish and molluscs were generally eaten fresh, which explains their absence from inventories; a similar explanation applies to crayfish, which Kalm reports not as endangered but as rare due to their excessive exploitation.[31]

The only things left to add to this list are anchovies and sardines from the Mediterranean, the first being more popular than the second, but both remained marginal, probably due to the fact that they only appeared on the tables of rich merchants. However, these fish and crustaceans were not the only species eaten in Québec. Some Quebeckers loved brill and turbot, and adored sturgeon, preferring it to cod. Finally turtles, which went well in soup,[32] should not be forgotten.

The inventories offer little or no information on dairy products, since milk and eggs are eaten fresh and are usually left "for subsistence." The size of the urban dairy herd and the near-total absence of goats lead to the conclusion that citizens fed their children cow's milk. Hen eggs only appear seven times and yet they were popular.[33] Doubtless as a result of storage difficulties, cream cheeses disappear completely from the inventories; while Gruyères and Dutch cheeses start to appear at the end of the 17th century, local cheeses were first mentioned only in the second decade of the 18th century.

Butter was the most widely listed of all oils and fats in the kitchens of Québec households. Tallow and lard follow far behind but before olive oil. Nut oils do not seem to have been very popular due to their high price. However, it should be mentioned that tallow was not only used in the kitchen; it was also used to make candles. Once again, the products sold to Quebeckers seem much the same as those present on the Hôtel-Dieu Hospital table.

Québec cooks had several spices and herbs available to them, the best known of which are salt, pepper, nutmeg, cloves and cinnamon. While salt was primarily used as a preservative, it was also used as a cooking spice.[34] While the description of pepper is vague most of the time, some documents mention that it was white.[35]

Kalm mentions that thyme and marjoram grew plentifully all around Québec,[36] but the notaries dismissed or ignored fine herbs, except in two inventories where fennel[37] and bay leaves[38] are found. However, the spices in Surgeon Lieutenant Jourdain Lajus' pharmacopoeia, most notably sage, known for its therapeutic properties; marjoram, and wild thyme, should be included. These three herbs can enhance the flavour of some dishes and can also grow in Québec. Of the imported spices, Lajus used ginger, saffron and juniper berries.[39] This is the only mention of these spices, and they arise in a specific context; these spices were not in common use in 18th-century French cooking. One last very popular spice should be added to this list: anise seed, which was used primarily in confectionery.

Among the frequently used condiments on Québec tables, we should include first the salted herbs that are ideal seasonings for soups, the basic element of the meals.[40] Imported mustard does not seem to have been popular, but the wild mustard, plentiful in the area,[41] was used in some food since mustard pots figure among the dishes. Garlic is only mentioned once;[42] on the other hand, capers formed part of several meals cooked in the kitchens of merchants such as Claude Pauperet or François Chasle.

Capers, like other foreign products, only came to Québec in vinegar solutions. While these commodities did not appear on every table, vinegar was likely to appear in the family kitchen, especially in the fall during pickling season. It is mentioned in close to 7% of all inventories.

Based on the number of observations, Quebeckers did not eat too much sugar, candies or sweetened pastries. Raw or bleached brown sugar seems to have been the most popular; it is found in just over 7% of all inventories. It is followed by molasses, chocolate and maple sugar, which according to Kalm, was the only sugar eaten by rural people.[43] While clerks and notaries make only a few mentions of sugar before the end of the 17th century,[44] toward the middle of the next century some fortunate people could gorge themselves on Narbonne honey, sugar candy[45] or royal sugar,[46] in addition to syrups, such as lemon syrup.[47]

Preserves made from local fruit were the predominant kind of jams. Some more comfortable hosts could offer their guests candied lemon peels. This practice was rare, however, since most hosts offered nuts of all sorts or fruits instead.

Almonds of all sorts were popular, whether in the shell, dried, slivered or sugar-coated. Almonds were occasionally powdered for use in pastries.[48] Nuts from France seem to have been less popular than those from Wales. Filberts and hazelnuts complete the circle.

Raisins took first place among the imported fruits. Figs and lemons shared second, but their appearance on the table would seem to have been limited and especially unstable: they are found at the end of the 17th century, but not seen again until the 1730s. Finally, goldsmith Paul Lambert *dit* Saint-Paul, demonstrated his exotic tastes by offering coconut to his guests.[49]

Prunes were even more popular than raisins, but they presented a problem; the clerks only rarely specified whether they were of the imported or domestic variety. Apples were mentioned most often among the domestic fruits. Pears were rare; only Aubert de Lachenaie it seems could get them; they came from Montréal. The clerks ignore gourds, melons and berries in the inventories, even though berries and small fruits were abundant.[50] Both the most astute and the more fortunate found the means to conserve them, not only in jams but in spirits.

What did Quebeckers in the 18th century drink? To be sure, water came from the neighbourhood public fountain or from household wells. Children could count on cow's milk. Red wines are most common among the drinks sold by merchants and taverns.[51] Spirits and tafia complete the list of alcoholic beverages. No mention of beer is made despite the fact that there were two breweries in the city in the 18th century. Coffee seems to have become popular during the 1730s, while tea only appears twice. Finally, the essence of licorice appears for a short period at the end of the 17th century.[52]

While it is not a food, but rather a habit that marks the end of a meal, tobacco did not play a very large role in 18th-century customs. Still clerks regularly registered the presence of this "necessary evil" throughout the 18th century. However, few people used tobacco; only 8% of the inventories include tobacco, although it should be specified that this was domestic tobacco not that imported from Brazil, Saint Vincent or Spain. The danger was not from smoking, but rather from ... snuff, a habit that became common among the comfortable classes in Québec in the 18th century, and included both men and women.[53] Ginseng was a very popular item for consumption in 18th-century France,[54] primarily due to its "medicinal" properties. Its export was a source of significant revenue. Because of clever or improper marketing, this product only appears twice in the documentation.

Of all the elements of a meal, only meat really escapes the inventories. To be sure salt pork is found in large quantities: one inventory in five mentions it. This would lead to the belief that the meat diet was restricted to pork. The fact that almost half the inventories were carried out between 1 November and 30 April certainly influences this situation. Salted beef was not popular in the colony. Should we see in this a diet that adapted to the seasons and conservation methods?

Since salt pork keeps well during the fall and winter, beef would be on the menu during the spring and summer. As few people other than butchers and some merchants had icehouses, one must assume that 18th-century Quebeckers did their shopping from day to day, at least on market days, which is to say Tuesdays and Saturdays.[55] But the season never prevents the purchase of beef; rather, the liturgical calendar imposes these restrictions.

Throughout the 18th century, butchers like bakers were covered by regulations,[56] except in certain periods when the administrators were believers in the free market, especially during the period of instability in 1718 and 1719. There were two price platforms for beef depending upon the time of year; Easter to the end of June and from 1 July to Lent.[57] Generally beef was cheaper than salted pork, especially in periods of crisis because the former was subject to a price set by the administration (Table 32).[58]

Based on its price, beef was more accessible in the winter than salt pork. What remains to be seen is whether the quantities produced could meet the needs, at least according to the estimates of the Lieutenant-General of the Provostship, who set the number of carcasses offered for

TABLE 32

PRICE OF MEATS PER POUND

(in *sols/deniers*)

Year	Beef		Butter	Veal		Mutton
	Easter-June	July-Lent		Easter-July	July-Lent	
1692	3 / 9	3 / 0				
1694	3 / 9	3 / 0	6 / 0	3 / 9	4 / 0	
1706	3 / 0	3 / 0	3 / 0	2 / 4	3 / 0	
1710	3 / 4	2 / 8	14 / 0			
1718	6 / 6	6 / 0	14 / 6			
1719	9 / 0	7 / 6	7 / 6			
1730	4 / 0	3 / 0	4 / 0			
1731-44		3 / 6	4 / 0			
1745		4 / 0	4 / 6			
1748	4 / 6	4 / 0	12 / 6	5 / 0	5 / 0	4 / 0
1749	4 / 6	4 / 0				
1750	4 / 0	3 / 6		5 / 0	5 / 0	4 / 0

sale weekly. In 1717, butchers Bellerose, Dolbec and Larchevêque agreed "to offer one animal each per week to the public"[59] for a total civilian population of 2300 people. The following year Joseph Cadet alone agreed to offer as many animals. In 1719 this number increased to five.[60] The beef craze was such that in 1745 the Lieutenant of the Provostship asked the capital's 12 butchers to collectively slaughter 25 animals per week to meet the demands of a population of about 5400 people.[61] In the fall of 1757, Father Récher notes that Québec's butchers slaughtered 80 to 90 animals per week to feed 7300 people.[62] Whoever ignored the law was liable to a fine; this was the fate of Jean-Baptiste Chapeau, Pierre Dorion and Pierre Renaud *dit* Canard, all three found guilty for not having slaughtered their allotted number of animals.[63] The consumption of beef by Québec citizens grew considerably over the course of the 18th century. Assuming a weight of about 500 pounds for a young animal, which leaves only 200 pounds on the block,[64] this represents a daily sale of 23.7 grams per capita in 1717, given a five-day week. This proportion rose to an average of 211.5 grams in 1757. While the population increased by roughly 218% during this period, the amount of beef offered for sale increased at roughly four times that rate (792%).

Unfortunately, the regulations do not contain information for each kind of the meat sold by butchers. However, we can accept the hierarchy suggested by an analysis of food at the Hôtel-Dieu Hospital; beef first, pork a distant second, followed by veal, fowl and finally mutton.[65] This classification seems to arise from the market. Veal was more expensive than beef: it cost almost 50% more per pound at the end of the 17th century,[66] a difference that stabilized at about 15% at the beginning of the 18th century,[67] and dropped to 10% in 1749.[68]

The ordinances are mute in regards to fowl, except to tell us that they were offered on the free market as was pork, so that Québec citizens could buy them from other residents as well as from butchers.[69] This healthy competition, to use Intendant Raudot's term, undoubtedly allowed low prices to be maintained throughout the 18th century, so that fowl became more important on the Hôtel-Dieu Hospital menu.[70] Lamb was only sporadically popular; it seems to have been considered as a beef substitute, "the residents prefer raising Sheep than Cattle" when fodder prices were high.[71]

Game animals seem to have been rare, except among some merchants, who found beaver[72] or muskrat kidneys a delicacy.[73] As far as game birds go, while inventories and leases occasionally mention the presence of a pigeon coop[74] and ordinances sometimes mention that the residents had taken up hunting in the city itself, they were only seen on the occasional menu. Hunting does not appear to have been a wide-spread activity despite the fact that, according to the Militia Act, each citizen aged 16 or older must in principle own a gun. However, in our inventories we found slightly under one gun per five people, which reflects the conclusions of a study on the militia.[75] On the other hand, according to Intendant Hocquart,[76] the area around the capital was "hunted out."

An analysis of bones corroborates this aspect of Québec food: three-quarters of the products consumed were domestic, and one-quarter of the "wild" products came from fisheries. Therefore game only accounted for a small part of the diet. This analysis also confirms the hierarchy of various meat as seen at the Hôtel-Dieu Hospital, the only difference being that fowl is found in slightly lower quantities in the diet.[77] Bird bones were primarily from passenger pigeons (77%), while chickens only accounted for 14%. Was fowl reserved for sick and convalescing people or was this a simple question of taste or availability?

This short overview of the 18th-century Québec larder shows three things. First, it confirms that the basic foodstuffs available on the menu of the nuns of the Hôtel-Dieu Hospital closely corresponds to the daily meals of most citizens. Secondly, the State's occasional intervention in the two key areas, bakers and butchers, confirms the essential role played by these two professions in the food area. It also emphasizes their very different respective evolutions, taking into account the laws of the market: while beef prices remained substantially the same (in crisis periods) throughout the 18th century and even increased slightly, bread prices dropped, except during bad harvests. Should we see this as a sign of a drop in the popularity of "panade" accompanied by a stronger increase in the popularity of beef in the diet? A double explanation must be considered in the case of bread: first, wheat production increased considerably so that prices did not rise extravagantly; second, bakers lost part of their market due to home production. These two factors explain the drop in the price of the best quality bread. Beef could not escape the control of the butchers, except for the small portion of the population with skill at butchery, and its consumption increased dramatically. Thus despite regulations, these two vital food sectors evolved differently during times of crisis in the 18th century. As a third consideration, a double phenomenon that emerges from the analysis of succession inventories should be examined. On one hand fresh foods are absent. On the other hand the clerks found imported goods such as capers, artichokes and mushrooms among the possessions of the better off, which leads to a legitimate question of whether the documents project a false image of the daily life of the lower classes? An analysis of house interiors will make it possible to partially answer this question.

Inside the House: A Choice Between Luxury, the Latest Fashion or a Functional Decor

This is not an analysis of all the material possessions of the various socio-professional groups of 18th-century Québec. While many archaeological studies have already shown that pottery had gradually begun to replace tin during the 1740s,[78] analysis of succession inventories confirms this trend among the better off. On the other hand furniture, except for the occasional mahogany armoire, is much the same from one house to the next; only the number of armoires, commodes and tables changes so that this information is not necessarily an indication of "luxury" decor. But what does decor actually consist of? Can the term "luxury" upon whose definition researchers cannot agree, be applied to the realities of 18th-century Québec? In order to cast new light on this question, we chose to isolate three components of interior decoration, the first two of which have immediate usefulness: lighting, heating and wall decoration.

The socio-professional groups are classified according to the usual distribution of activities: services, business, artisan and unskilled. Services include Councillors, army officers and non-commissioned officers, public administrators and members of the liberal professions such as surgeons, in addition to clerks and other lower functionaries. All the evidence shows that there was a certain degree of hierarchy among this group; a Councillor and an army sergeant would not have lived in the same type of decor. A subdivision allows notaries, surgeons, clerks and troop sergeants to be classed together, making Councillors, officers and administrators a separate category. The same distinction applies to the business sector, where merchants and wholesalers form one group, and members of the food (butchers, bakers, tavern-owners) and transportation sectors form two other subdivisions. The artisan sector includes construction workers (masons, carpenters and framers), metal workers (blacksmiths, tinsmiths, locksmiths, gunsmiths), the leather (tanners, shoemakers), clothing (tailors, wig-makers) and wood-working trades (coopers, chandlers). Unskilled labourers include workmen and domestics.

In addition to curtains and tapestries, wall decoration includes frames and mirrors. Curtains include both those for windows and those for doors. Tapestries include both single Bergamots, the most popular by far, and hangings. While considered to be decorations, these pieces of fabric were nonetheless practical objects in an environment where cold reigns for five months of the year. In the same way that curtains block the cold that comes through the windows, tapestries help combat the dampness seeping from stone walls.[79]

TABLE 33
WALL DECORATIONS: CURTAINS AND TAPESTRIES

Decade	Inventories	Curtains							Tapestries
		Bergamot	Trade*	Serge	Indian	Cotton	Linen	Other	
1690-1699	43	2	1	1	0	4	3	2	17
1700-1709	95	9	3	2	0	1	7	5	22
1710-1719	122	5	4	7	2	1	9	10	26
1720-1729	125	3	9	15	5	3	15	12	30
1730-1739	132	3	6	13	7	11	20	11	37
1740-1749	181	3	8	28	10	9	24	19	47
Total	698	25	31	66	24	29	78	59	179
%		3.6	4.4	9.4	3.4	4.1	11.2	8.4	25.6

* Cloth made for the fur trade, but prized by some people

TABLE 34
OWNERS OF CURTAINS AND TAPESTRIES

Groups	Number	Curtains		Tapestries	
		Number	%	Number	%
Services					
Officers	94	53	56.4	59	62.8
Public Servants	44	17	38.6	18	40.9
	138	70	50.7	77	55.8
Business					
Merchants	75	40	53.3	42	56.0
Food	22	0		1	4.5
Transportation	31	6	19.3	2	6.4
	128	46	35.9	45	35.1
Artisan					
Construction	62	7	11.3	8	12.9
Iron	30	7	23.3	8	26.7
Leather	16	1	6.2	1	6.2
Clothing	19	4	21.1	2	10.5
Wood	18	2	11.1	1	5.5
	145	21	14.5	20	13.8
Labourers	8				
Unknown	258	35	13.6	28	10.8
Total	677	172	25.4	170	25.1

TABLE 35
WALL DECORATIONS: FRAMES AND MIRRORS

Decade	Frames					Mirrors				Invent.
	Portraits	Pictures	Images	Maps	Clocks	Small	Medium	Large	Unknown	
1690-1699	1	5	2	1	2	18	10	5	2	43
1700-1709	6	2	7	1	3	42	4	6	13	95
1710-1719	7	6	10	1	10	41	6	7	27	122
1720-1729	12	9	1	3	13	52	6	16	31	125
1730-1739	17	15	6	2	10	51	6	10	47	132
1740-1749	13	21	7	2	15	88	9	12	53	181
Total	56	58	33	10	53	292	41	56	173	698
%	8.0	8.3	4.7	1.4	7.6	41.8	5.9	8.0	24.8	

According to Table 34, 172 households or 25.4% of the houses had curtains. Tapestries were as popular, being found in 25.6% of the houses (Table 33). The most popular choice among those who owned curtains were "linens" (with no other specifications) or woolly fabrics such as serge. Note, however, that there was a major change in tastes, particularly in fabrics, during the 1720s. While Bergamot tapestries remained popular, curtains of this type became less and less common. Serge and linen held the high ground, timidly approached by cotton and calico, the latter being a block-printed cotton fabric. Lengths of fabric with catalogue numbers first started appearing in the merchants' stock during this decade.[80] In short, due to innovations on the part of textile manufacturers, tastes began to change during the 18th century. While the tapestry sector bottomed out, the curtain sector grew.

However, these two types of decoration remained the prerogative of a minority. Table 34 clearly shows that curtains and tapestries were the decor of choice of the first three socio-professional groups:[81] Councillors, officers and high-level administrators, followed by merchants and wholesalers, as well as public servants, notaries, surgeons, clerks and troop sergeants. Artisans followed far behind, even though we should emphasize the importance that workers in the metal trades gave to these ornaments.

Frames included both profane (portraits, pictures, images, maps and clocks) and religious objects (images of saints or Biblical figures, crucifixes and holy-water basins). Mirrors, according to the clerks, were small, medium and large. Table 35 shows that four households out of

TABLE 36

SIZE OF MIRRORS, 1690-1749
(in French square inches)

Size	1690-1699	1700-1709	1710-1719	1720-1729	1730-1739	1740-1749	Total
Unknown	32	69	107	110	68	106	492
0-49	8	12	5	0	17	17	59
50-99	0	5	3	2	9	8	27
100-249	1	4	5	4	7	21	42
250-499	2	4	1	7	21	23	58
500-999	0	1	1	2	9	5	18
1000 or +	0	0	0	0	1	1	2
Total	11	26	15	15	64	75	206

five owned a mirror, regardless of its size. Framed pictures appeared on the walls of houses in Québec much more rarely than mirrors, but beginning in the 1720s portraits, framed pictures and clocks[82] gained increasing importance. A similar progression occurs with mirrors, which grew over the course of the 18th century, notwithstanding the qualifications of the clerks (Table 36). After 1720, 84% had a surface area larger than 100 square inches. This is due to the French artisans in Saint-Gobain increasing their production and especially their construction methods, a reality to which the clerks had to adapt; mirrors capture, refract and amplify light....[83] They also capture and reflect the image. Thus reality and appearance merge.

The owners of these objects tended to be in the same three socio-professional groups as those who owned curtains and tapestries. Merchants seem to have been more partial to mirrors than Councillors and officers. Perhaps this group was more vain? ... especially when it is considered that merchants most often looked at themselves in mirrors with a surface area of more than 100 square inches. Their vanity, however, fainted as seven out of ten Councillors, administrators and officers or their companions dressed in front of mirrors larger than 250 square inches. One group stands out: representatives of the clothing industry owned mirrors most often; they needed them for their work (Table 37).

TABLE 37
OWNERS OF FRAMES, MIRRORS AND RELIGIOUS OBJECTS

Groups	Invent.	Frames		Mirrors		Religious obj.	
		Number	%	Number	%	Number	%
Services							
Officers	94	41	43.6	68	72.3	33	35.1
Public Servants	44	17	38.6	31	70.4	10	22.7
	138	58	42.0	99	71.7	43	31.1
Business							
Merchants	75	40	53.3	57	76.0	29	38.7
Food	22	5	22.7	14	63.6	2	9.1
Transportation	31	4	12.9	19	61.3	1	3.2
	128	49	38.3	90	70.3	32	25.0
Artisan							
Construction	62	10	16.1	37	59.7	5	8.1
Iron	30	8	26.7	22	73.3	6	20.0
Leather	16	5	31.2	10	62.5	2	12.5
Clothing	19	4	21.1	16	84.2	3	15.8
Wood	18	3	16.7	13	72.2	1	5.5
	145	30	20.7	98	67.6	17	11.7
Labourers	8						
Unknown	258	51	19.8	126	48.8	35	13.6
Total	677	188	27.8	413	61.0	127	18.7

In terms of frames, if religious pictures, crucifixes and holy water fonts are considered separately, the following image appears: 1) these two types of devotional images are the prerogative of a minority, despite the fact that hanging images of saints or biblical scenes on the wall gained in popularity during the 18th century (Table 38); 2) once again merchants, officers and public servants dominate the list, although blacksmiths are close behind (Table 37). It should be specified that in three cases out of five the owners of these objects were over 50 years old. As people aged, the more they professed their faith, which indicates an attitude or a philosophy of life (or perhaps towards death?) more than a question of taste or money. On the other hand younger people tended

TABLE 38
RELIGIOUS DECORATIONS

Decade	Religious paintings		Crucifixes		Inventories
	Number	%	Number	%	
1690-1699	2	4.6	5	11.6	43
1700-1709	6	6.3	18	18.9	95
1710-1719	6	4.9	15	12.3	122
1720-1729	9	7.2	12	9.6	125
1730-1739	20	15.1	24	18.2	132
1740-1749	17	9.4	24	13.2	181
Total	60	8.6	98	14.0	698

not to pay much attention to such objects, not because they were impious but because they had to earn their daily bread and meet essential needs. In that context buying a crucifix becomes a luxury.[84]

Luxuries are not only defined in relation to religious decorations. They also include other wall decorations, despite that the prices of some of them dropped during the 18th century. For example, a mirror cost almost 20 *deniers* per square inch at the beginning of the century; but the price dropped to half that 50 years later.[85] While curtain prices stabilized, the range of choices, both of fabric and especially of motifs and colours, grew enormously. It is difficult to assess the purchase price of tapestries as they were often inheritances. Almost one in two owners of tapestries, curtains or frames was over the age of 50.[86] Thus, the most prosperous people in each profession accumulated such things slowly.

Since these are all decorative objects and affected by factors such as cost, taste, age and even inheritance, perhaps it would be better to explore the essential needs of any house, heat and lighting, when trying to assess "luxury." When the cold season lasts for six months and days become shorter in the winter, these two elements become very important in the day-to-day life of Quebeckers.

Table 39 shows that, during the 18th century, the most common source of light was the copper chandelier, followed by lamps, lanterns, flat candleholders and sconces. Contrary to tableware, tin chandeliers and lanterns do not seem to have been as popular as glass ones. The "other" category includes crystal or china chandeliers and

TABLE 39

LIGHTING, 1690-1749

Decade	Invent.	Lamp	Sm. lantern	Copper ch.	Tin ch.	Candleholder	Sconce	Lantern	Other
1690-1699	43	12	0	34	6	4	5	9	0
1700-1709	95	31	4	63	14	18	8	22	7
1710-1719	122	70	2	76	7	16	11	25	11
1720-1729	125	63	6	82	12	30	16	36	14
1730-1739	132	61	10	64	7	17	21	13	14
1740-1749	181	79	20	94	9	31	28	16	14
Total	698	316	42	413	55	116	89	121	60

various sources of short-life light. In brief, tallow candles seem to have been the main light source in Québec.

However, copper chandeliers lost their relative importance during this period and lanterns lost ground in the eyes of the public starting in the 1730s. The population of Québec had a taste for new types of lights such as sconces and flat candleholders with handles starting in 1720. Lamp use does not seem to have followed the same course as whale oil: known at the end of the 17th century, these lamps became very popular in the years 1710 to 1720, dropped slightly in popularity, but still appear in use by the middle of the century.[87] Lamp oil, on the other hand, enjoyed less popularity judging from its mention by clerks; this may have been due to the smells or soot it emitted.[88]

According to Tables 39 and 40, it seems that many households in all of the socio-professional categories had two light-sources. Considering only the two main light-sources, copper chandeliers and lamps, it seems that both were found in houses belonging to members of the artisan and business sectors slightly more than one in three, while among officers and Councillors this proportion was one in five (Table 41); on the other hand, the latter preferred flat candleholders, a type of lighting most often found among the family silver (25.5%). Among merchants, chandeliers were found not only alongside lamps (40%), but also flat candleholders (32%).

Lamps were more interesting to artisans; it would seem that they were able to adjust to the smells better and preferred the lower prices. The analysis brings out several conclusions about lighting in an urban environment: first, the primacy of candles, although not for all socio-economic groups, since lamps were very popular with artisans. We should

TABLE 40
OWNERS OF LIGHTING DEVICES

Groups	Invent.	Lamp No.	Lamp %	Small lant. No.	Small lant. %	Copper ch. No.	Copper ch. %	Tin ch. No.	Tin ch. %	Candleholder No.	Candleholder %	Sconce No.	Sconce %	Lantern No.	Lantern %	Other No.	Other %
Services																	
Officers	94	24	25.5	9	9.6	63	67.0	9	9.6	23	24.5	35	37.2	26	27.7	19	20.2
Public Servants	44	19	43.2	5	11.4	33	75.0	6	13.6	14	31.8	9	20.4	13	29.5	4	9.1
	138	43	31.1	14	10.1	96	69.6	15	10.9	37	26.8	44	31.9	39	28.3	23	16.7
Business																	
Merchants	75	34	45.3	4	5.3	64	85.3	9	12.0	24	32.0	13	17.3	23	30.7	8	10.7
Food	22	9	40.9	0		16	72.7	4	18.2	3	13.6	1	4.5	2	9.1	1	4.5
Transportation	31	15	48.4	1	3.2	15	48.4	3	9.7	2	6.4	1	3.2	4	12.9	1	3.2
	128	58	45.3	5	3.9	95	74.2	16	12.5	29	22.6	15	11.7	29	22.6	10	7.8
Artisan																	
Construction	62	38	61.3	2	3.2	35	56.4	4	6.4	2	3.2	5	8.1	7	11.3	1	1.6
Iron	30	19	63.3	1	3.3	22	73.3	1	3.3	6	20.0	2	6.7	7	23.3	4	13.3
Leather	16	7	43.7	2	12.5	8	50.0	0	—	3	18.7	0	—	2	12.5	0	
Clothing	19	10	52.6	2	10.5	16	84.2	1	5.3	5	26.3	2	10.5	1	5.3	0	
Wood	18	10	55.5	0		11	61.1	0		5	27.8	0		2	11.1	1	5.5
	145	84	57.9	7	4.8	92	63.4	6	4.1	21	14.5	9	6.2	19	13.1	6	4.1
Labourers	8	1	12.5	0		1	12.5	0		1	12.5	0		1	12.5	0	
Unknown	258	123	47.7	14	5.4	121	46.9	17	6.6	25	9.7	20	7.7	32	12.4	19	7.4
Total	677	309	45.6	40	5.9	405	59.8	54	8.0	113	16.7	88	13.0	120	17.7	58	8.6

TABLE 41
OWNERS OF BOTH COPPER CHANDELIERS AND LAMPS

Group	Inventories	Number	%
Services			
Officers	94	20	21.3
Public Servants	44	17	38.6
	138	37	26.8
Business			
Merchants	75	30	40.0
Food	22	7	31.8
Transportation	31	7	22.5
	128	44	34.4
Artisan			
Construction	62	20	32.2
Iron	30	14	46.7
Leather	16	2	12.5
Clothing	19	7	36.8
Wood	18	8	44.4
	145	51	35.1
Labourers	8	0	
Total	419	132	31.5

point out that this was primarily interior lighting; sconces and lanterns, light sources designed to be used outside,[89] are almost completely absent. There is an obvious direct correlation with the architectural environment, since the lack of auxiliary buildings implies that frequent nocturnal trips outside were rare. Does this mean that Quebeckers did not go out once the sun had gone down? Certainly not but the streets would not have been busy. Didn't Pehr Kalm say that Quebeckers got up early?...[90]

But before blowing out the light they certainly took care to throw a few logs in the stove. Heating was a major expense for 18th-century Québec households, since the stove (not including the fuel) represented at least 4% (among merchants) and at most 11% (among the clothing artisans) of the total value of the furnishings in a house (except for stock in the store). Such a difference implies two things: first, the purchase price of a stove was very high which means that, second, not all households owned a stove and either depended upon another source of heat, a fireplace for example, or that they rented.

The more the 18th century progressed, however, the more unusual renting became; heating using a fireplace also became rarer. While at the end of the 17th century only one household in two owned a stove, by the middle of the next century this proportion had risen to four out of five (Table 42). While cast-iron stoves were the most popular, their use was not widespread throughout the city. The table shows that the use of cast-iron stoves did not extend as far as some travellers have claimed; sales bottomed out as an alternative solution became a reality. The use of brick[91] stoves expanded during the first decades of the 18th century: they were less expensive and could better meet the needs of a clientele in serious economic difficulties. Heating pans also appear in this context.

The brick oven's share stagnated quickly, however. A new type of stove appeared on the market during the 18th century: the sheet-metal stove. Lighter than the metal-plate used in brick stoves, its popularity continued to grow. In addition to its lighter weight, it had the advantage of using a new fuel, coal;[92] although we cannot be sure if this was charcoal or mined coal (the former was very popular after the 1759). These three types of heating were the most important, as chimney fire-backs were only found in 1% of the houses.

TABLE 42
DISTRIBUTION OF TYPES OF HEATING DEVICES, 1690-1749

Type	1690-1699	1700-1709	1710-1719	1720-1729	1730-1739	1740-1749	Total
Unknown	22	34	38	25	30	38	187
Iron	15	32	31	37	38	41	194
Hearth	3	2	0	1	0	0	6
Brick	2	11	19	10	7	19	68
Sheet-metal	0	2	2	9	14	25	52
Stove-plate	0	12	22	27	31	27	119
Tripod stove	0	1	0	0	0	0	1
Pot	0	0	5	0	0	0	5
Iron and Hearth	1	1	1	1	0	0	4
Iron and Brick	0	0	2	3	3	6	14
Iron and Stove-plate	0	0	1	5	4	6	16
Iron and Sheet-metal	0	0	1	3	4	11	19
Stove-plate, Sheet-metal & Iron	0	0	0	2	0	1	3
Stove-plate & Sheet-metal	0	0	0	1	0	1	2
Sheet-metal & Brick	0	0	0	1	0	1	2
Iron, Sheet-metal & Brick	0	0	0	0	1	1	2
Sheet-metal & Stove-plate	0	0	0	0	0	4	4
Total	21	61	84	100	102	143	511
Inventories	43	95	122	125	132	181	698
%	48.8	64.2	68.8	80.0	77.3	79.0	73.2

It should also be pointed out that each of these three types of stoves met one of the fundamental requirements of the reality of 18th-century Québec: mobility. Each was easily dismantled and transported when moving. This, at least, is the reality suggested by the description of the iron stove with its "screws and nuts,"[93] the ease of moving the metal plate of a brick stove, and the lightness of the sheet-metal stove. Since this essential home furnishing was expensive, wasn't it better to be able to move it and one's other belongings easily when spring came? Doesn't Kalm say that they "usually moved the stove during the summer?"[94]

But did iron, brick and sheet-metal stoves appeal to the same clientele? According to Table 43,[95] iron stoves were favoured by members of

TABLE 43
OWNERS OF HEATING DEVICES

Groups	Invent.	Iron		Brick		Sheet-metal		Hearths		Pots		Other	
		No.	%	No.	%	No.	%	No.	%	No.	%	No.	%
Services													
Officers	94	56	59.6	17	18.1	15	15.9	1	1.1	1	1.1	0	
Public Servants	44	22	50.0	11	25.0	8	18.2	2	4.5	0		0	
	138	78	56.5	28	20.3	23	16.7	3	2.2	1	0.7	0	
Business													
Merchants	75	46	61.3	16	21.3	8	10.7	1	1.3	0		0	
Food	22	8	36.4	7	31.8	5	22.7	1	4.5	0		0	
Transportation	31	7	22.6	15	48.4	3	9.7	0		0		0	
	128	61	47.6	38	29.7	16	12.5	2	1.6	0		0	
Artisan													
Construction	62	20	32.2	24	38.7	4	6.4	0		2	3.2	0	
Iron	30	14	46.7	11	36.7	2	6.7	0		0		0	
Leather	16	5	31.2	2	12.5	5	31.2	1	6.2	0		0	
Clothing	19	5	26.3	4	21.0	6	31.6	0		0		0	
Wood	18	6	33.3	8	44.4	1	5.5	0		0		0	
	145	50	34.5	49	33.8	18	12.4	1	0.7	2	1.4	0	
Labourers	8	0		2	25.0	0		0		1	12.5	0	
Unknown	258	58	22.5	108	41.9	4	1.5	4	1.5	0		1	0.4
Total	677	247	36.5	225	33.2	61	9.0	10	1.5	4	0.6	1	0.1

the service sector; they were slightly less popular with members of the business sector (except, obviously, with merchants), and even less common in the artisan sector (except among iron-workers). On the other hand, brick stoves were most common with artisans, and much rarer among the services group. Sheet-metal stoves were most often found in the service sector.

Without a doubt this situation was due to the price of these items. Iron stoves imported from Scandinavia or Germany through France cost an average of about 90 *livres*[96] at the end of the 17th century, and about 50 by the middle of the next.[97] On the other hand, brick stoves cost about 17 and 9 *livres* in the same periods respectively, while a sheet-metal stove cost about 15 *livres* around 1743.[98] It is hardly surprising to see that stove casings often broke in several pieces and were then "clamped together"; on the one hand, this shows that the investment was major; on the other, it emphasizes the fragility of the casings due to the low amount of carbon in the imported products. Despite Intendant Hocquart's clear statement that the residents of Québec preferred stoves forged in the Saint-Maurice Forges,[99] these products found very few takers on the Québec market. The cost of a stove made at the Saint-Maurice Forges was twice that of an import. In this context it is not surprising to see that only 7.5% of the iron stoves listed between 1740 and 1749 came from Trois-Rivières.[100]

Price was an important factor in taste. However, how can we explain the popularity of sheet-metal stoves that were slightly more expensive than brick stoves? Table 42, which shows the various types of heating in each house, indicates that auxiliary heating was also used. This began to become popular with citizens during the decade of 1710 to 1719, although modestly, as only 13% of the houses had two or more types of heating devices.

Auxiliary heating was most often found among officers, administrators and merchants (three out of five). While the sheet-metal stove seems to have been most popular with the service group, we should point out that two times out of three this was an auxiliary stove (Table 44). On the other hand, three times out of five sheet-metal stoves were the only type of stove in the business sector. However, the merchants who copied the heating styles of the service sector should be removed from the latter group. In the artisan world, however, three times out of four only a sheet-metal stove was used.

Brick stoves were found one time out of two as the only stove among officers and administrators, and seven times out of ten among the business group (again the merchants were an exception, since they imitated the first group), and eight times out of ten among artisans.

But the type of stove is not a reliable indicator of the number of stoves. Tables 42 and 44 emphasize that a household might own two or three different sources of heating; this is to say that they owned two or three different stoves. What about those who only owned one? The norm was one stove per family, since only 6.7% of households owned more than one. Merchants and officers stand out again, since two out of three people owned more than one stove in their group. Councillor Charles Guillemin owned three iron stoves and Charles-Aubert de Lachenaie owned four. These are, however, exceptions since the average among this well-off group was two stoves per house.

*****

TABLE 44

DISTRIBUTION OF HEATING DEVICES
BY TRADE

Type	Officers	Public Servants	Merchants	Food	Transport.
Iron	37	15	38	6	6
Hearth	0	1	0	1	0
Brick	1	4	3	2	5
Sheet-metal	4	4	3	4	3
Stove-plate	4	5	5	3	9
Tripod Stove	0	0	0	0	0
Pot	1	0	0	0	0
Iron and Hearth	1	1	1	0	0
Iron and Brick	6	1	2	1	0
Iron and Stove-plate	3	1	2	0	0
Sheet-Metal	8	4	1	0	0
Stove-plate, Sheet-metal & Iron	1	0	1	0	0
Stove-plate & Sheet-metal	1	0	0	0	0
Sheet-metal & Brick	1	0	1	0	0
Iron, Sheet-metal & Brick	0	0	1	1	0
Sheet-metal & Stove-plate	0	0	1	0	0
Total	68	36	59	18	23
Inventories	94	44	75	22	31

Type	Construction	Iron	Leather	Clothing	Wood	Labourers	Unknown	Total
Iron	15	11	3	5	4	0	50	190
Hearth	0	0	0	0	0	0	4	6
Brick	11	3	0	3	1	1	32	66
Sheet-metal	3	1	3	6	0	0	20	51
Stove-plate	9	5	1	1	6	1	68	117
Tripod Stove	0	0	0	0	0	0	1	1
Pot	2	0	0	0	0	1	0	4
Iron and Hearth	0	0	1	0	0	0	0	4
Iron and Brick	1	0	0	0	1	0	1	13
Iron and Stove-plate	3	2	0	0	0	0	4	15
Sheet-Metal	1	0	1	0	1	0	3	19
Stove-plate, Sheet-metal & Iron	0	1	0	0	0	0	0	3
Stove-plate & Sheet-metal	0	0	1	0	0	0	0	2
Sheet-metal & Brick	0	0	0	0	0	0	0	2
Iron, Sheet-metal & Brick	0	0	0	0	0	0	0	2
Sheet-metal & Stove-plate	0	0	0	0	0	0	3	4
Total	45	23	10	15	13	3	186	499
Inventories	62	30	16	19	18	8	258	677

This short overview of the interior decoration of Québec houses in the 18th century indicates that most of the population had sober but fashionable decor that was primarily functional. Certainly, the richer merchants and officers stood out from the masses as the result of the number of things they owned, and the uses they made of them, but is this distinction as significant as the interior decoration of the house would have it? While merchants and officers stand out on the consumption level, what happens when we consider production?

The domestic environment places the social actors into a "consumer-oriented" current at three different levels: local, regional and international. In harmony with their urban landscape, Québec residents had few means of transportation other than their legs; horses and other animals seem to have been superfluous; perhaps dogs were enough? This is a sign of an urban lifestyle where concentration reduces distances. The absence of sheds or barns also confirms the analysis of the urban landscape (Chapter 3), as does the relative rarity of animals, pigs and cows in particular. The presence of these four-footed animals, symbolic elements of desired or imposed self-sufficiency, marks the transition between the city and the country.

The presence of a market as a source of food marks the difference between these two areas; it also shows the citizens' dependence upon the farmers' ability to supply them with the necessary and basic elements of their diet, meat and wheat.

But the language of consumption is not limited to these circles. The epicentre of the phenomenon was in Europe. Québec, the North American spearhead of a French colony, imported German stove plates, Indian textiles and French mirrors. The objects sold in the stores of the capital made Québec a veritable international crossroads where men and ideas, tastes and fashions intermingled.

Behind this criss-cross of products, one must attempt to distinguish, apart from the distribution of objects, the progression of materials and techniques. This is what is brought to mind by the new textiles that appeared in Québec's decor, without forgetting the mirrors or the sheet-metal stoves. Obviously, behind each object hides an owner and, more distantly, a producer. From consumption, we will flip to the other side of the coin, production, and examine Québec's social actors in that context.

CHAPTER 6

INSECURITY IN THE MIDST OF PROSPERITY

Québec in the 18th century was a market open to new products, both imported and local. This trend started in the 1720s; that is, during the 30-year peace and once the monetary crisis had been resolved. The analysis of various consumer goods made it possible to evaluate the changing environments of various social groups. Apart from socio-professional differences, this showed a socio-economic cleavage not only from one group to another, but also within each group. An analysis of financial assets can spotlight this cleavage; and this becomes more evident when compared with population growth and consequently, with the working world. In this context, a word surfaced that was ever present in the vocabulary and rhetoric of colonial administrators: competition. This took place at all levels: urban, regional, colonial and European. Within the population the strongest and cleverest people survived and came to the top; the others vegetated and shared the scraps among themselves.

Assets, Fortunes, Balance Sheets and Inflation

The succession inventories may not represent the last word respecting the worldly goods destined to be divided between the children and the survivor of a joint estate.[1] Nevertheless, they gave a good overview of the material goods, especially real estate owned by the deceased with the exclusion of course of those assets bequeathed by the terms of the marriage contract. Since 18th-century Québec was populated mostly by tenants, it becomes still more interesting to find out how people sub-divided their holdings according to both their positions as owners or tenants, and their socio-professional standings.

At the outset, we have to distinguish between these two positions, and evaluate the assets, the fortune and the balance-sheet of each inherit-ance. The assets represented the value of the personal estate; the stocks or tools listed in the inventory of the store or workshop; the currency found, whether bills of exchange, paper money or hard cash; and finally, credit. This first level makes it possible to compare owners and tenants as a function of their socio-professional class. Since real estate could represent a significant part of the inheritance, it also has to be taken into account. Thus a second level, which for our needs will be referred to as wealth or "fortune," was established: the value of the real estate was added to the assets. But the mortgage contracted could be a heavy en-cumbrance on the family budget, so it was important to obtain a balance sheet of the inheritance; that is, the amount remaining after the debts had been subtracted.

Assets, fortunes and balance sheets represent accounting practices based on currency used as legal tender in the colony. Without rewriting the *Documents Relating to Canadian Currency...*[2] or repeating the com-ments made by J. Hamelin[3] or L. Dechêne,[4] we should remember that the official tender was based on the "*livre tournois*," a monetary unit divided into 20 *sols* and 12 *deniers.* Since hard cash was rare in the col-ony, the administrators devised a special scheme: the issuing of playing cards to which were assigned monetary values and which had to be bought back once the King sent funds for the annual budget. In short, because of the misfortunes caused by the war, an operation of substitu-tion in public credit matters became an "institution." The money of Can-ada or of the country circulated in France at 133-⅓% of its official rate; that is, a *livre* in this country's money was only valued at 15 *sols* in French coinage. From a commercial point of view, this monetary prac-tice could in theory only favour exports and put a brake on imports from France which were more expensive.

The overvaluation of Canadian money, however, ended with the close of the 1719 sailing season since the two currencies were quoted at par the following year. For several years previously, the French authorities had been trying to abolish this accounting overvaluation. The colonial administrators, at grips with an ever-increasing public debt, tried to buy back the cards in circulation because the confidence of the population and especially of the merchants had crumbled. These local problems only "added to the financial disorders of France."[5] As soon as the end of the War of the Spanish Succession was announced and the Treaty of Utrecht had been signed, the Marine Council, which had charge of colonial budgets, agreed to buy back the card money at half its face value. Once this was known, the measure inevitably brought about a rise in consumer prices. Québec had a rate of inflation of 139% in 1714,[6] "since it is not certain that our playing card money will be considered legal tender for trade with France."[7] Utter confusion reigned in the capital: although the Council's decision only reached the Colonial Administrator during the summer of 1717, and did not come into force until the end of 1719,[8] as early as August 1717 the merchant Pierre Lefebvre specified in a lease that the currency had been devalued not by 50% but really by 62.5% as the royal declaration stipulated.[9] In January 1718, the notary Lacetière estimated his succession inventories in "the currency of France in accordance with the King's edict."[10] At the same time notaries Dubreuil and Rivet specified that they still continued to use Canada's currency; nevertheless, they pointed out that if a drop in the card money's value should occur, the prices set would also drop from the day the declaration was made public in this country and at the same rate.[11] Although on 16 April 1718, Lacetière was still making estimates in French money "with 25% reduced, according to the ruling"; six days later, he noted a devaluation of 62.5% of the card money.[12] The public ignorance of the rate of exchange continued through 1719 when some transactions were still effected in the straight undevalued card money, and others in card money devalued by 62.5%. However, the most usual formula remained "in whatever money is legal tender."

    In connection with these examples, we should emphasize that Lefebvre and Lacetière may have had access to privileged information, perhaps due to the fact that the two men belonged to the circle surrounding Intendant Bégon. Lacetière, appointed Clerk of the Upper Council, would have had access to this information.[13] However, the market's adjustment to the situation was even more spectacular. Between 1714 and 1717 inflation caused by the monetary crisis and bad harvests rose to 177 points, in 1718 it began to fall with the result that by 1720 it had

GRAPH 13
SILVER PRICES
QUÉBEC, 1690-1749

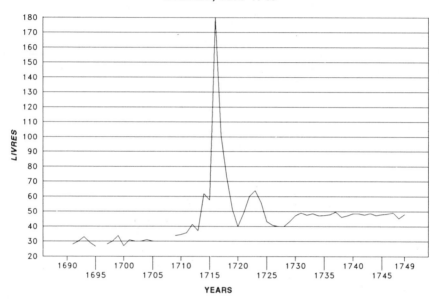

dropped by 113 points. Taking into account devaluation, real inflation during these years was only 2%. However, we must hasten to emphasize that part of the devaluation would never be absorbed, and that almost ten years would pass before there was some stabilization of prices. Thus between 1727 and 1744 inflation was brought under control with the annual rate of inflation averaging 2% a year; this indicates the cost of living doubled in about 36 years. This rate is within several tenths of a percentage point of that noted between 1690 and 1726.

This monetary crisis would have scared the main money lenders of Québec; their confidence shaken, they chose something solid and concrete: silver. Transporters (land carriers, in this case), builders and leather workers were the only ones who invested little or nothing in silver. And the citizens of Québec hoarded in order to invest over 10% of their worldly goods in this type of "insurance." As a result, the price of silver rose by more than 50% during the 1720s (Graph 13).

TABLE 45

DISTRIBUTION OF ASSETS, BEFORE AND AFTER 1727

Value (*livres*)	<1727	%	>1727	%	Total	%
Under 250	41		91		132	
250-499	54		59		113	
	95	28.2	150	45.2	245	36.6
500-999	56		40		96	
1000-2499	62		44		106	
2500-4999	44		39		83	
	106	31.4	83	25.0	189	28.2
5000-9999	32		25		57	
10 000-20 000	20		20		40	
20 000-30 000	10		5		15	
30 000-60 000	15		6		21	
	45	13.3	31	9.3	76	11.4
60 000-100 000	1		3		4	
Over 100 000	2		0		2	
	3	0.9	3	0.9	6	0.9
Inventories	337		332		669	

The monetary crisis unsettled Québec citizens. Coupled with the wars during the previous few years, the period that ended during the 1720s marked 30 years of instability, as much in politics as on the economic or even demographic levels. The juxtaposition of these various data makes it possible to define the stages in Québec's growth since 1690: the last decade of the 17th century began against the backdrop of the first armed clash between Englishmen and Frenchmen in North America (the War of the Augsburg League, 1689-97). Then the War of the Spanish Succession (1702-13) tapped not only the manpower, but especially the financial resources of both Europe and America. Louis XIV, dazzled by the fabulous Spanish riches, must have underestimated his adversaries and overrated his resources. The backlash proved brutal; it was not until 1725-27 that prices stabilized and the economy gained back some strength. "Prosperity" returned then, despite the poor harvests of 1737-44, until a new war (the Austrian Succession, 1740-48) plunged Quebeckers into uncertainty again. Meanwhile, although Québec's civil

TABLE 46

DISTRIBUTION OF DEFLATED ASSETS, BEFORE AND AFTER 1727

Value (*livres*)	<1727	%	>1727	%	Total	%
Under 250	58		107		165	
250-499	57		58		115	
	115	34.1	165	49.7	280	41.8
500-999	61		35		96	
1000-2499	63		44		107	
2500-4999	34		36		70	
	97	28.8	80	24.1	177	26.4
5000-9999	27		23		50	
10 000-20 000	13		16		29	
20 000-30 000	10		5		15	
30 000-60 000	11		7		18	
	34	10.1	28	8.4	62	9.3
60 000-100 000	1		1		2	
Over 100 000	2		0		2	
	3	0.9	1	0.3	4	0.6
Inventories	337		332		669	

population grew from 1800 souls in 1690 to 2200 in 1716, to 5400 in 1744 and to 7300 in 1755, this growth did not proceed in as straight a fashion as it appeared (see Table 3, in Chapter 1). The capital's population grew sporadically alternating between the good and the bad times. To this we must add the economic fluctuations marked by alternating inflationary and deflationary periods (Appendix B). In all, the capital had six phases of growth that revolved around a particular turning-point: before and after 1727. The first period was characterized by a deflationary stage 1692-1706 and two subsequent inflationary stages stirred up by the war and its after-effects. Between 1727 and 1749, Québec underwent two inflationary thrusts and one period of deflation.[14] After 1727, Québec entered a phase more favourable to its expansion, taking into account the limited slow-down on its economic growth caused by the War of the Austrian Succession.

It would be interesting to consider how Québec society reacted to these changes. According to Table 45 Quebeckers had fewer assets after

TABLE 47

DISTRIBUTION OF WEALTH, BEFORE AND AFTER 1727

Value (*livres*)	<1727	%	>1727	%	Total	%
Under 250	28		69		97	
250-499	37		48		85	
	65	19.3	117	35.2	182	27.2
500-999	45		51		96	
1000-2499	71		46		117	
2500-4999	44		35		79	
	115	34.1	81	24.4	196	29.3
5000-9999	49		38		87	
10 000-20 000	21		25		46	
20 000-30 000	12		7		19	
30 000-60 000	22		6		28	
	55	16.3	38	11.4	93	13.9
60 000-100 000	4		5		9	
Over 100 000	4		2		6	
	8	2.4	7	2.1	15	2.2
Inventories	337		332		669	

1727. Although 28% of the inventories mention assets of 500 *livres* or less before this date, this proportion rose to 45% during the following period. All the other asset groups then became smaller, with the exception of those worth 10 000 to 20 000 *livres* and those valued at 60 000 *livres* and more, where the situation remained stable. Even with deducting for inflation which some years reached very high levels,[15] these proportions remained practically the same (Table 46).

Apart from the fact that after 1727 people owned less, these tables show a dividing line, a threshold (perhaps psychological but definitely monetary) below which the acquisition of real estate seemed difficult: the threshold was 500 *livres*. As shown in Table 47 where the value of real estate is included, after 1727, one household in two had a fortune valued at 1000 *livres* or less, while this proportion had previously not reached above one in three, thereby reflecting appreciably the same impoverishment as in the case of the working class.[16] Certainly it can be inferred from a study of these assets that the Quebeckers put much less

TABLE 48
BALANCE SHEET OF ASSETS, BEFORE AND AFTER 1727

Value (*livres*)	<1727	%	>1727	%	Total	%
Under -10 000	1		3		4	
-5000 to -9999	1		2		3	
-2500 to -4999	3		5		8	
-1000 to -2499	6		7		13	
-500 to -999	4		7		11	
-250 to -499	6		6		12	
0 to -249	9		24		33	
	30	8.9	54	16.3	84	12.5
0 to 250	35		65		100	
250 to 499	30		40		70	
	65	19.3	105	31.6	170	25.4
500 to 999	41		38		79	
1000 to 2499	61		36		97	
2500 to 4999	42		28		70	
	103	30.6	64	19.3	167	25.0
5000 to 9999	44		32		76	
10 000 to 20 000	18		22		40	
20 000 to 30 000	16		4		20	
30 000 to 60 000	14		6		20	
	48	14.2	32	9.6	80	11.9
60 000 to 100 000	3		5		8	
Over 100 000	3		2		5	
	6	1.8	7	2.1	13	1.9
Inventories	337		332		669	

importance on their comfort and physical environment in order to devote a larger part of their resources to the acquisition of real estate. Such was not always the case however; the period of peace that was so much longed for did not necessarily bring prosperity to everyone.

The succession balance sheets leave no doubt about that (Table 48). The proportion of households with a negative balance sheet doubled, and this did not take into account the marriage commitments.[17] Those with less than 1000 *livres* of worldly goods accounted for 42%, an increase of 11% when compared with the preceding period. However, indebtedness had hit the better-off as well, since the middle (from 1000 to 5000 *livres*) and upper strata (more than 5000 *livres*) showed a setback of 11% and 8% respectively in their numbers. Only the very rich maintained their rank.

Did indebtedness reach such proportions that Quebeckers could no longer honour the clauses of their marriage contracts? Not at all, since the dowries were based on the husband's property,[18] and the prior right took precedence over any partition of the inheritance. During the 60 years under consideration, the assets of only one inheritance in five did not allow for the fulfilment of the promises pertaining to dowries,[19] and this proportion was even lower when the prior right of withdrawal was involved (13%). However, we should note that this occurred four out of five times after 1727. In short, Québec society on the whole adapted to a new economic reality; the socio-economic pyramid was widening toward the base. The society started to become acquainted with the first hints of impoverishment. Now we must determine how each of the socio-professional groups reacted.

Impoverishment, Credit and Material Goods

That the community became impoverished is an indisputable fact, but does it mean that each of the socio-professional groups reacted in the same manner? In order to measure these reactions, it would be helpful to put the actors in a setting that takes into account the assets, the level of wealth and the succession balance sheets, being careful not to colour it by taking into consideration the acquisition of movable goods (thereby specifying a certain idea of comfort), and the level of indebtedness.

While the inheritance assets did not make it possible to meet the financial obligations undertaken when the marriage contract was drawn up, this situation is even more striking when we consider that, in one case out of two, it involved representatives of the processing sector. According to Table 49, with the exception of the households of officers, Councillors and senior public administrators, the assets of all the socio-professional groups diminished after 1727. By grouping the assets into four categories: under 1000 *livres*; 1000 to 5000; 5000 to 20 000, and 20 000 *livres* and over, we can confirm the widening of the base of

TABLE 49

DISTRIBUTION (%) OF HOUSEHOLDS, BY ASSETS AND SOCIO-PROFESSIONAL GROUP, BEFORE AND AFTER 1727

Socio-Professional Group	Household Assets (livres)												No. of Households	
	0 - 499		500 - 999		1000 - 4999		5000 - 19 999		20 000 - 59 999		60 000 and +			
	<1727	>1727	<1727	>1727	<1727	>1727	<1727	>1727	<1727	>1727	<1727	>1727	<1727	>1727
Services														
Officers	7.1	12.7	9.5		42.9	42.5	28.6	31.9	9.5	10.6	2.4	2.1	42	47
Public Servants	10.7	38.9	25.0	11.1	53.6	33.3	10.7	16.6					28	18
Business														
Merchants		3.4			15.9	37.9	34.1	44.8	45.4	6.9	4.5	6.9	44	29
Food	25.0	40.0		10.0	58.3	30.0	16.7	20.0					12	10
Transportation	33.3	53.8	22.2	7.7	33.3	23.1	11.1	15.4					18	13
Artisan														
Construction	45.7	53.6	22.8	21.4	28.6	21.4	2.8			3.6			35	28
Iron	28.6	44.4	9.5		38.1	55.5	23.8						21	9
Leather	40.0	33.3	20.0	33.3	30.0	33.3	10.0						10	6
Clothing	30.0	55.5		33.3	50.0	11.1	20.0						10	9
Wood	27.3	50.0	27.3	12.5	18.2	37.5	18.2		9.1				11	8
Labourers	100.0	66.6		33.3									2	6
Unknown	44.2	61.1	25.0	14.8	24.0	15.4	6.7	6.7		2.0			104	149

the pyramid with a few exceptions. To be sure, Jean Boucher *dit* Belleville, proved to be an exception among the builders; a contractor for Montréal's fortifications, he would have benefited from the government's generosity. Furthermore, his debts alone amounted to over 34 000 *livres*,[20] a colossal sum in the 18th century. On the other hand, it must be emphasized that all sectors showed signs of impoverishment, especially the clothing industry.

In the world of business, the joint estates of merchants almost disappeared from the circle of those worth 20 000 *livres* or more; while those in the areas of food and transportation fell mainly below the 1000-*livre* threshold. This phenomenon is similar to what happened with the joint estates of minor public servants. Only the households of the officers, senior administrators and Councillors saw their assets grow.

Since we are dealing only with assets, without taking real estate into account, the evaluation of the goods of a joint estate may thus prove to be incorrect. However, adding the real estate does not change the picture that emerged regarding the assets of various joint estates (Table 50). Among administrators and senior officers, more than one survivor in two received a sum of more than 5000 *livres* after the spouse's death. As for the merchants, the joint estates worth more than 5000 *livres*

TABLE 50

DISTRIBUTION (%) OF HOUSEHOLDS, BY WEALTH AND SOCIO-PROFESSIONAL GROUP, BEFORE AND AFTER 1727

Socio-Professional Group	Household Wealth (*livres*)												No. of Households	
	0 - 499		500 - 999		1000 - 4999		5000 - 19 999		20 000 - 59 999		60 000 and +			
	<1727	>1727	<1727	>1727	<1727	>1727	<1727	>1727	<1727	>1727	<1727	>1727	<1727	>1727
Services														
Officers	4.8	8.5	2.4	4.2	33.3	25.5	35.7	44.7	19.0	10.6	4.8	6.4	42	47
Public Servants	10.7	27.8	10.7	16.7	57.1	22.2	21.4	27.8		5.5			28	18
Business														
Merchants		3.4			11.4	37.9	34.1	41.4	43.2	6.9	11.4	10.3	44	29
Food	25.0	40.0		10.0	33.3	20.0	41.7	30.0					12	10
Transportation	33.3	46.1	16.7	15.4	38.9	15.4	11.1	23.1					18	13
Artisan														
Construction	8.6	21.4	20.0	14.3	48.6	42.8	22.8	17.8		3.6			35	28
Iron	14.3	22.2	4.8	11.1	42.8	44.4	14.3	22.2	23.8				21	9
Leather	30.0	33.3	30.0	16.7	30.0	33.3		16.7	10.0				10	6
Clothing	30.0	55.5		33.3	50.0	11.1	20.0						10	9
Wood	18.2	37.5	27.3	12.5	27.3	50.0	9.1		18.2				11	8
Labourers	100.0	66.6		33.3									2	6
Unknown	33.6	50.3	23.1	20.8	30.8	18.1	12.5			2.7			104	149

underwent an appreciable drop of some 30%. The trend toward a decline in fortunes continued and we may assume that the purchase of real estate represented a "luxury" that fewer and fewer joint estates could afford.

Furthermore, the analysis of indebtedness leads to the same conclusion. Now that they were receiving much lower returns on their capital, were Québec households forced to resort to mortgage loans? The levels of indebtedness of each of the groups (Table 51) eloquently shows the close relationship that exists between assets and indebtedness: few households borrowed above the amount that they could post as collateral. In the artisan sector and among the minor public servants, the margin of credit was generally 1000 *livres* or less. This threshold, however, did not apply to merchants or officers.

Yet there was a certain shrinking of the indebtedness, a phenomenon that coincided with the tightening of credit policies by merchants and wholesalers. These people gave less and less credit, with the result that those among them with outstanding loans to the tune of 10% or more of their fortunes became fewer after 1727 (Table 52). It is not surprising to see that the widow Foucault and the widow Legris announced that they would give no credit at all.[21] In short, the period of "inflationary upheaval"

TABLE 51

DISTRIBUTION (%) OF HOUSEHOLDS, BY DEBTS AND SOCIO-PROFESSIONAL GROUP, BEFORE AND AFTER 1727

Socio-Professional Group	Household debts (livres)														No. of Households	
	No debts		0 - 499		500 - 999		1000 - 4999		5000 - 19 999		20 000 - 59 999		60 000 and +			
	<1727	>1727	<1727	>1727	<1727	>1727	<1727	>1727	<1727	>1727	<1727	>1727	<1727	>1727	<1727	>1727
Services																
Officers	40.5	31.9	14.3	14.8	11.9	8.5	23.8	19.2	4.8	21.2	4.8	4.2			42	47
Public Servants	35.7	38.9	35.6	33.3	14.3	16.7	14.3	11.1							28	18
Business																
Merchants	31.8	34.5	13.6	13.7	2.3	17.2	20.4	20.6	20.4	10.3	9.1	3.4	2.3		44	29
Food	25.0	10.0	16.7	30.0	8.3	30.0	41.7	30.0	8.3						12	10
Transportation	33.3	23.2	50.0	38.5	5.5	7.7	5.5	23.1	5.5	7.7					18	13
Artisan																
Construction	11.4	25.0	48.6	40.0	14.3	21.4	25.8	14.3							35	28
Iron	23.8	33.3	52.4	44.4	23.8	11.1				11.1					21	9
Leather	30.0	16.7	60.0	16.7		16.7		33.3		16.7	10				10	6
Clothing	40.0	44.4	40.0	44.4				11.1	20.0						10	9
Wood	36.4	25.0	36.4	50.0	18.2	12.5	9.1	12.5							11	8
Labourers	100.0	33.3		66.6											2	6
Unknown			4.8		2.9		29.8		52.9	100.0	9.6				104	149

TABLE 52

DISTRIBUTION (%) OF HOUSEHOLDS, BY AMOUNT OF CREDIT LOANED OUT AND SOCIO-PROFESSIONAL GROUP, BEFORE & AFTER 1727

Socio-Professional Group	Amount (%) of Credit Loaned from Household Wealth												No. of Households	
	0 - 9		10 - 29		30 - 49		50 - 69		70 - 89		90 - 100			
	<1727	>1727	<1727	>1727	<1727	>1727	<1727	>1727	<1727	>1727	<1727	>1727	<1727	>1727
Services														
Officers	20.0	19.4	44.0	25.0	32.0	30.5	4.0	25.0					25	36
Public Servants	26.3	30.0	47.4	70.0	5.3		10.5		10.5				19	10
Business														
Merchants	2.5	20.0	32.5	28.0	27.5	20.0	25.0	20.0	2.5	8.0	10.0	4.0	40	25
Food		22.2	50.0	33.3	10.0	44.4	30.0		10.0				10	9
Transportation	37.5	50.0	25.0	12.5	25.0	12.5	12.5	25.0					8	8
Artisan														
Construction	55.5	33.3	40.7	55.5	3.7	5.5		5.5					27	18
Iron	50.0	75.0	50.0			25.0							14	4
Leather	40.0	25.0	20.0	50.0				25.0	40.0				5	4
Clothing	42.8		42.8	100.0	14.3								7	5
Wood	50.0	33.3	37.5	33.3	12.5			16.7		16.7			8	6
Labourers						50.0		50.0		50.0			0	2
Unknown	14.0	26.0	38.6	33.3	24.5	19.5	14.0	6.3	3.5	6.3	5.3	2.6	57	123

of the years 1713-19 caused a severe trauma that took the form of a crisis of confidence and inevitably led to monetary losses.

During the 18th century Québec merchants sold progressively cheaper products that penetrated the local, regional and even the colonial markets; once the wars were over, the costs of transportation, freight and insurance dropped. In the same way the merchants' profits dropped. While store stocks were evaluated "in accordance with the usage of this country, at the price which they would have cost in old France, if they had been bought there, with an added value to take into account quality,"[22] it was still true that the French price was really a wholesale price;[23] at no time did the margin of profit added correspond to a net profit.[24] Thus, if this added value had to be reduced, it goes without saying that the net profits of merchants and wholesalers would drop at the same rate.

While the evaluator estimated the gross profit at 50% on the goods stored at Raymond Dubosc's at the end of the 17th century; this amount went down to 20% in 1740 on goods bought from Dugard of Rouen and from Bourgine of La Rochelle,[25] after having reached some 200% in 1717.[26] Between 1722 and 1740 the merchants' gross profit margin stood at 21%, fabrics bringing in less, sometimes half of that.[27]

With profits going down, did Québec merchants look for new markets to make up for the lack of income? According to L. Dechêne, if they let themselves be drawn by the fur trade in Montréal at the end of the 17th century,[28] an examination of the debtors' geographic origins shows no sign of this. Merchants and wholesalers concentrated their activities within an area of 50 kilometres around Québec (Table 53).[29] They progressively withdrew from the area of Trois Rivières, but their presence was a little more evident in the region of Montréal or the lower St. Lawrence. Québec merchants did not retire completely from the western areas or from the fur trade, as witnessed by the activities of merchant Étienne Véron de Grandmesnil[30] or of Charles Guillemin who married the widow of Montréal merchant Jacques Leber.[31] Furthermore the penetration downstream, although it grew during the 18th century, remained just as weak as in the Montréal market; it slowed down as the beluga fishery stopped being a monopoly. Once this industry regained some strength, the region drew the Québec merchants all over again. The geographic origins of the debts show that when they ventured out-

TABLE 53
AREAS OF ACTIVITY OF QUÉBEC MERCHANTS

Period %	Men- tions	Inc.	Québec	Trois- Rivières	Montréal	Lower St. Law.	France	West Indies	Louis- bourg
1691-1711	455	25	244	84	53	39	9	1	0
%		5.5	53.6	18.5	11.6	8.6	2	0.2	
1719-1726	291	5	136	36	92	16	4	1	1
%		1.7	46.7	12.4	31.6	5.5	1.4	0.3	0.3
1732-1749	251	10	141	13	47	30	5	0	5
%		4.0	56.2	5.2	18.7	11.9	2.0		2.0
Total	997	40	521	133	192	85	18	2	6
%		4	52.2	13.3	19.2	8.5	1.8	0.2	0.6

side, the Quebeckers' markets were still located more to the west than to the east.[32] However, as a corollary, we should add that the merchants and wholesalers showed little aggressiveness in finding new markets, except during the difficult years between 1714 and 1726. And it must be pointed out that after 1727, the merchants increasingly hesitated to give credit outside the town, since only one quarter of the "out-of-town" debts were found after that date. Briefly, the merchants and wholesalers of Québec restricted themselves more and more to the urban and regional markets when it was time to extend credit.

Merchants and wholesalers shared the market for commercial and mortgage credit with officers and senior administrators. But it would not be realistic to believe that all these people were shopkeepers: certainly, one household in five lived with the risk of retail trade, but this business background seems to have mainly provided officers and public servants with a way to add to their fixed incomes, eroded by inflation. Moreover, they had started their businesses before 1727, a period during which inflation underwent sudden ups and downs. As for the councillors, they were most often merchants who had kept their businesses; this was the case with Charles Guillemin, Jean Crespin, Jean-François Martin De Lino as well as Martin Chéron.[33] But here again this situation occurred most frequently before 1727. In brief, officers, senior administrators and Councillors who were also shopkeepers became fewer after 1727; however, the number of those whose fortunes were more than 30% based on loans rose appreciably during the 18th century, from one in three to one in two.

These data show not only a tightening of the credit policy but also a splitting up of this market. Merchants preferred profits so that they invested heavily in their stock of goods. Although only one merchant in three devoted 30% or more of his fortune to his business before 1727, this proportion increased to nearly one in two during the 18th century. As for the few officers and public servants who continued in the retail trade, they diminished the value of their stock. Despite a much larger stock, the merchants did less borrowing since their debts seldom were above 5000 *livres* (Table 51).

The suppliers of Québec merchants were mostly from Rochelle; there were over thirty of them including Guillaume Chanjon, the Bourgines (father and son), Veyssière and Pascaud. Then there were those from Bordeaux: Depoix at the beginning of the 18th century and Rouleau in 1720 and 1730. Next in order come those from Paris with Gendron at the head of the line; then those from Rouen, with Robert Dugard and Pierre Lemoine in 1730 and 1740. After 1720 there were some from the West Indies, such as Étienne Leblanc and Lajanière in Martinique and Lemorandais in Guadeloupe. And, from time to time, there were other suppliers from France, such as Jahan from Orléans, Delisle-Collin from Tours or even the Paris and Gautier Company from Marseille.[34]

There were also some minor public servants who had shops, such as notaries Florent Lacetière and Louis Chambalon or the surgeon Gervais Beaudoin Sr. However, few owned a business after 1727, shopkeepers like Chambalon or Beaudoin Sr. were in trade at the end of the 17th and at the beginning of the next century. Minor public servants as were these two men also cut back their loans significantly after 1727. All in all, there was a tightening of consumer credit by the merchants and shopkeepers of Québec in the 18th century.

Could a greater circulation of money explain this tightening? Almost all the socio-professional groups had solid reserves of liquid assets at their disposal; these reserves were even larger after 1727 in all groups with the exception of those in the artisan sectors related to naval construction and the clothing industry (Table 54).

Did these figures really show a wider circulation of money or, on the contrary, a more widespread hoarding of money in reaction to a period of very high inflation and uncertainty about the value of money as legal tender? The analysis of durable goods, particularly silver (Table 55),

TABLE 54

DISTRIBUTION (%) OF HOUSEHOLDS, BY CASH ASSETS AND SOCIO-PROFESSIONAL GROUP, BEFORE AND AFTER 1727

Socio-professional Group	Households		Cash Assets		Average Amount (*livres*)	
	<1727	>1727	<1727	>1727	<1727	>1727
Services						
Officers	42	47	22	23	723.93	1309.85
Public Servants	28	18	12	7	563.83	752.55
Business						
Merchants	44	29	32	19	2618.43	4860.53
Food	12	10	6	5	548.00	831.36
Transportation	18	13	1	5	20.00	289.14
Artisan						
Construction	35	28	6	8	579.25	1542.60
Iron	21	9	11	2	463.25	971.41
Leather	10	6	3	0	554.38	
Clothing	10	9	5	1	1680.52	692.35
Wood	11	8	4	2	3272.18	404.31
Labourers	2	6	0	2		142.91
Unknown	104	149	28	45	405.16	814.70

whose value increased during the 18th century,[35] strongly supported the theory of hoarding. Indeed, neither all the groups nor all the joint estates protected themselves by buying silver; many did not have the means to do this because of the dwindling of their financial resources. However, for some groups such as the officers or minor public servants, ownership of silver could be considered positive "insurance" against all future depreciation, which would explain why on average they invested respectively 20% and 17% of their movable assets in silver.

Others may see this as evidence of a search for comfort, although this idea may be difficult to put in perspective. This hypothesis could perhaps be verified for some groups. Nevertheless an analysis of the

TABLE 55

DISTRIBUTION (%) OF HOUSEHOLDS, BY SILVER ASSETS
AND SOCIO-PROFESSIONAL GROUP, BEFORE AND AFTER 1727

Socio-professional Group	Households		Silver Assets		Value of silver (*livres*)	
	<1727	>1727	<1727	>1727	<1727	>1727
Services						
Officers	42	47	35	38	579.50	685.90
Public Servants	28	18	14	9	220.50	244.50
Business						
Merchants	44	29	32	20	464.20	460.72
Food	12	10	5	5	92.50	219.18
Transportation	18	13	3	6	399.07	110.94
Artisan						
Construction	35	28	9	4	92.45	112.22
Iron	21	9	12	4	197.42	151.16
Leather	10	6	1	3	7.50	121.22
Clothing	10	9	5	5	124.44	52.30
Wood	11	8	5	3	113.41	22.92
Labourers	2	6				
Unknown	104	149	26	49	108.50	247.50

amount of movable goods led to a consideration that was completely different from that of comfort (Table 56) for most of the groups.

A greater inclination to acquire movable goods could be glimpsed among the officers. Before 1727, four households in five had at their disposal fortunes less than half of which consisted of such goods; while after that date in nearly one household in two, the same goods accounted for half and even more of their fortunes. This situation, however, was not so evident among the merchants since they kept such large stocks. For them the acquisition of worldly goods was subordinate to more pressing needs: those of the market.

A notable change in behaviour took place after 1727 among the minor civil servants: two-thirds of the households owned movable goods that

TABLE 56

DISTRIBUTION (%) OF HOUSEHOLDS, BY WEALTH IN MOVABLE GOODS AND SOCIO-PROFESSIONAL GROUP, BEFORE AND AFTER 1727

Socio-professional Group	Portion (%) of Wealth in Movable Goods												No. of Households	
	0 - 9		10 - 29		30 - 49		50 - 69		70 - 89		90 - 100			
	<1727	>1727	<1727	>1727	<1727	>1727	<1727	>1727	<1727	>1727	<1727	>1727	<1727	>1727
Services														
Officers	16.7	12.8	35.7	23.4	26.2	14.9	21.4	48.9					42	47
Public Servants	7.1		25.0	22.2	35.7	5.5	32.1	5.5		16.7		50.0	28	18
Business														
Merchants	50.0	44.8	38.6	31.0	4.5	10.3	6.8					13.8	44	29
Food	16.7		41.7	30.0	33.3	10.0	8.3	10.0		10.0		40.0	12	10
Transportation			22.2	23.1	33.3		16.7			15.4	27.8	61.5	18	13
Artisan														
Construction	14.3	14.3	82.8	42.9	2.8	3.6		10.7		10.7		17.8	35	28
Iron	28.6		71.4	22.2	—	44.4						33.3	21	9
Leather	10.0	33.3	20.0	16.7	20.0		50.0	33.3				16.7	10	6
Clothing		11.1	30.0		10.0		20.0	11.1	10.0	44.4	30.0	33.3	10	9
Wood	9.1	12.5	27.3	25.0		12.5	45.5	25.0			18.2	25.0	11	8
Labourers				40.0			—	40.0			100.0	20.0	2	6
Unknown	10.6	4.7	10.6	14.1	16.3	19.5	31.7	32.9	7.7	4.7	23.1	20.1	104	149

represented 70% or more of their wealth. The situation was the same in the food and transportation categories. After 1727, three out of four of these households devoted more than 70% of their fortunes to durable goods; while the ratio had earlier been one household in four. Among butchers and bakers, the phenomenon was the same, increasing from none to one household in two.

All the trades in the artisan sector underwent the same change in behaviour, and the same 70% norm was found there. Only day-labourers and those whose trade was not known showed a different profile; however, we should emphasize that there were only eight inventories for day-labourers or servants.[36] Among those whose trade was not known, one household in four still put as much importance (70% or more) on its belongings.

In view of such changes, it would be very difficult to believe in a search for more comfort. However, if this situation is placed alongside another, it can illustrate the precariousness of the financial situation of Québec households in the 18th century. In a very large majority of the socio-professional groups, the proportion of households showing a negative inheritance balance sheet doubled after 1727. More precisely, with the exception of several trades and professions, the inheritance balance

TABLE 57

DISTRIBUTION (%) OF SUCCESSION ASSETS BY SOCIO-PROFESSIONAL GROUP, BEFORE AND AFTER 1727

Socio-Professional Group	Succession Assets (*livres*)													
	Negative		0 - 249		250 - 999		1000 - 4999		5000 - 19 999		20 000 - 59 999		60 000 and +	
	<1727	>1727	<1727	>1727	<1727	>1727	<1727	>1727	<1727	>1727	<1727	>1727	<1727	>1727
Services														
Officers	7.1	15.0	2.4	2.1	4.8	8.5	31.0	19.1	33.0	40.4	19.0	8.5	2.4	6.4
Public Servants	10.7	11.1	7.1	22.2	17.9	16.7	50.0	22.2	14.3	22.2		5.5		
Business														
Merchants	2.3	13.8		3.4		6.9	20.4	27.6	31.8	31.0	34.1	6.9	11.4	10.3
Food	8.3	30.0	16.7	20.0	25.0	10.0	16.7	20.0	33.3	20.0				
Transportation	11.1	23.1	11.1	30.8	38.9	23.1	27.8	15.4	11.1	7.7				
Artisan														
Construction	5.7	7.1	5.7	25.0	28.6	17.8	42.8	28.6	17.1	17.8		3.6		
Iron			14.3	22.2	14.3	11.1	33.3	44.1	14.3	11.1	23.8			
Leather	10	50.0	20.0		30.0	33.3	40.0			16.7				
Clothing	10	44.4	30.0	44.4	40.0	11.1	20.0							
Wood		37.5	9.1	12.5	36.4		18.2	50.0						
Labourers			100.0	66.6		33.3								
Unknown	16.3	18.1	16.3	23.5	28.8	34.2	26.9	14.1	11.5	8.0		2.0		

sheet worked out to less than 250 *livres* in one case out of three (Table 57).

During the 18th century as Québec society became poorer, it had to learn to live by new rules. The situation was not confined to Québec; it was the same in Paris[37] and in Bayeux.[38] But there it was only a result, as was the tightening of credit policy, of a deeper cause: the lack of employment and the inevitable competition that this situation produced.

Moving Toward a Different Society: Competition and Production Relationships

All sectors of economic activity were affected by competition, from shopkeepers to the men who made barrels. Only the service group were free from it, and only partially; because the situation was different depending upon whether one was a senior public servant or a notary. In fact, the first remained almost immune despite inflation, while the remuneration of the second was directly dependent upon the population's income. The brisk competition in the working world of Québec in the

18th century led to a re-evaluation of production relationships; the attraction of the New World during the 17th century gave way to disillusionment. While it had been difficult to climb the social ladder in France, it was equally so in the colony. Money, however, did not count for everything....

Forced to absorb a devaluation of their currency as well as a drop in prices, Québec merchants also had to cope with growing competition from foreign merchants. Although the entry of foreign merchants on the domestic market had been limited by regulation before 1717, this control disappeared after that date. Henceforth there would be a free market. Faced with this situation tradespeople had to offer a wider range of merchandise to satisfy their clients. However, since competition was becoming stronger and stronger, each one's share of the market became smaller. Consequently the suppliers hesitated to extend credit to Québec merchants and they, in return, to their clients.

But the foreigners were not the only competition for Québec merchants; during the 1720s, the French business houses and their representatives became established in Québec. The best known would certainly be Mr. Havy and Mr. Lefebvre representing Robert Dugard of Rouen, not to mention Goguet, Mousnier and Veyssière. The competition proved too strong for Quebeckers with the result that in this "overcrowded profession" Frenchmen monopolized the import and export trade, and consequently the largest share of the profits.[39]

Moreover, in 1741, Intendant Hocquart deplored the fact that Québec had nearly 100 merchants although about 50 would have been enough.[40] In this situation Québec merchants again tightened up their credit, thus leaving a door open for officers and senior civil servants to get into the lending market. Since customers are attracted by a wider choice of goods and the best credit conditions, and since Québec merchants could only meet the first of these two conditions, their clients became dissatisfied and took their business to the French shops. Thus between 1730 and 1738, Havy and Lefebvre raised their credit by 3600%.[41] Under the circumstances, the only answer was for Québec merchants to associate themselves with the business houses of La Rochelle or Bordeaux; for example, Charles Guillemin became the agent for the widow Pascaud of La Rochelle.[42] This was how the more fortunate kept going; more astute, they realized there was no hope of competing with overseas people, and that it would be much wiser to join their ranks.

The merchants' plight during the 18th century, and the comments it inspired from the colony's administrators, notably Intendant Hocquart, contrasted strongly with the remarks made by one of his predecessors, Raudot. The latter, on granting a brewing licence to Denis Constantin, could not prevent himself from apologizing for the free competition.[43] It would be only 30 years before the Intendant's comments on political economy would change radically; in 1732, Hocquart even wrote to Maurepas that only public expenditures could rejuvenate the country's economy.[44]

This last statement by Hocquart indicates that the situation had deteriorated not only at the level of retail sales, but also in most other economic sectors. An analysis of wealth indisputably confirms that most households were becoming poorer, particularly those connected with the artisan sector, whose subsectors were badly hit by competition.

Thus, the masons could only rely on house construction, except for the building of the Intendant's palace. The period of the large construction projects, both private and public, was finished and Minister Maurepas refused to ratify the project for the fortifications. After the beginning of the 18th century, the masons preferred to sign a contract with a client rather than to work as employees of the contractors. Finding themselves more and more numerous and with their share of the market shrinking, the masons had no other choice than to lower the wages paid to their apprentices. While at the end of the 17th century, administrators and clients had grumbled about the high cost of manpower, there were no more complaints after 1720.[45] By coincidence Montréal caught on fire and her fortifications had to be rebuilt, so that part of the surplus manpower found work there. The masons who remained in Québec had to put up with a depressed market, helped temporarily and suddenly by a short boom period between 1728 and 1731. These years correspond to the rise in maritime trade and the renewal of naval construction, which momentarily assured the town some prosperity. This climate, however, soon drew to the capital a number of day-labourers and skilled workers, both from the surrounding countryside and from France.[46] Competition became tight again. If construction was not making progress, what was happening in other fields of activity?

In the food category, bakers had to cope not only with competition from individuals who baked their own bread, but also from merchants who hired bakers to make the hardtack intended for the sailors. Competition here proved fierce, and even more so when the State regulated the industry after the failure of the wheat harvest. Although it was a basic element of the diet, the price of bread fell slightly during the 18th century. As far as butchers were concerned, the more than sustained demand on the part of those who ate meat helped triple their numbers between 1717 and 1744; this, at a time when the State was concurrently maintaining a policy of controlled prices. This paradox in relation to the official political economy doctrine of non-interference could only be explained by the "social conscience" of the State, which was trying to maintain acceptable conditions of public health; besides, it placed its reliance on and stood surety for Québec's low rate of inflation between 1727 and 1744.[47]

In land transportation, the carriers could only deplore competition by merchants who oversaw the unloading of the ships and delivered their cargo using their own transportation equipment. On the other hand, we should not forget competition by rural people who came to be carriers in the city during the summer with their horses and wagons. As for maritime transport, competition seemed similar between skippers and sailors, and merchants and officers, who were also ship owners.

The iron workers also met strong competition from products imported by the merchants: sheet metal for stoves, files from Germany or Scandinavia, nails present by the hogshead; almost all the products for everyday use were imported as well as weapons and fire beaters. The blacksmith soon became a repairer of tools and objects, abandoning manufacture except for sheet-metal stoves with which he succeeded in competing with the imports, even though he used imported sheet metal! Neither was it rare to find a blacksmith sometimes making edge-tools, sometimes being a locksmith: he adapted himself to any contingency. Moreover, since locks were almost never listed in the merchants' inventories, we are led to believe that they were not sold ready-made but had to be fabricated when needed. Iron workers also competed to repair the military guns, but the responsibility as King's armourer could be granted to only one of them. At first sight it would seem to have been lucrative to be a goldsmith in Québec since exotic products appeared on the table of one of them, Paul Lambert *dit* Saint-Paul; but this was not the lot of all of them as Pagé *dit* Carcy, Michel Coton and Jean-Baptiste Maisonbasse did not leave many worldly goods. In short, the iron trades were equally subject to competition not only at the level of work but also at the level of products. Had it not been for their participation in naval construction and house building, the iron workers would have known a fate comparable to that of the leather workers.

Among the latter, the figures speak for themselves: in 1700, there were 14 artisans, but 43 were enumerated in the 1740s.[48] Too numerous, they had to share among themselves a market that was too sensitive to European novelties. Caught between overproduction and competition from foreign products, people in the leather industry could only become poorer. This situation shows some similarities with that of those in the clothing industry: hatters, tailors and wigmakers. While the hatters disappeared, abandoning the market to Parisians, the tailors and wigmakers saw their numbers swell and the price of raw materials drop. Consequently, labour costs had to be lowered; and this was not counting competition from the widows who entered the labour force as dressmakers.

Finally, in the wood category: even though there was competition from the French at the end of the 17th century, the coopers and the shipwrights had no local occupational rivalries once the second generation entered the market.[49] When the State decided to open a naval shipyard, the wood working artisans did not benefit from the rise in prices, they only changed employers because Canadian shipowners continued to buy ships from New England.[50] Under these circumstances and despite the growth in demand, the purchase of ships from outside the colony only served to control the expected rise in wages.

Competition even affected some occupations that had seemed to be protected until that time: even though they were dependent upon the administration, surgeons and notaries could nevertheless scarcely make ends meet on the income from their positions; their clientele was becoming poorer. After 1712, as a solution Québec surgeons tried to limit the practice of their profession in the city to surgeons already established there. But the Superior Council refused their request so that the capital continued to be a wide open area where only ships' doctors were "persona non grata."[51] A large number of notaries if not most filled minor administrative jobs as well without counting those who were shopkeepers like Chambalon and Lacetière. Already in 1700 Québec had six notaries.... After all, colonial administrators were strong proponents of the free market....

In short, all sectors from business on down felt the effects of competition during the 18th century. That is, all except one, services. To be a senior public servant or an officer at a time when the rate of inflation was low meant having a first-rate sanctuary; when necessary, a minor public servant despite a modest salary managed to survive during difficult periods (before 1727) by moonlighting. Nevertheless, these State employees enjoyed fixed and guaranteed incomes; their salaries did not fluctuate with the market.

So with competition like that during the 18th century, it is not surprising to find a certain mobility among the population. This mobility showed up on levels that were at the same time geographic, professional and social. Geographic mobility includes moving from a village to a town, or from one town to another. For example, Québec masons moved to Montréal, Trois Rivières and Saint Frédéric;[52] and there was the case of Jean Maillou, who tendered for the construction of Louisbourg.[53] On the other hand, the prosperity during 1727-30 drew these people back again to the urban setting of the capital. Besides, during this brief lucky period, a number of artisans from most sectors of activity returned to Québec in search of a lucky break. In these circumstances, nothing suited better than rental accommodations; besides, most did not have the wherewithal to buy a house.

Yet, the competition that brought about such comings and goings among the workforce, and the effects that this movement brought in its wake, lead us to question the nature of production relationships. The context of the 18th century meant that some artisans who had been small contractors became merely paid workmen. At least this was suggested by the analysis of the number of movable goods compared with the wealth of the households (Table 56). Certainly, the circle of officers and senior public servants included people more inclined to spending, a habit made apparent by a search for a certain level of comfort. We should point out again that these people were paid by the State. On the contrary, the position of small businessmen, transporters and artisans was completely different: competition within various trades could explain why artisans in various sectors of activity were earning less, but it did not explain why almost one-third of these households, after 1727, had no other possessions but the furniture earned by the sweat of their brows. However, the number of shops in these same trades remained relatively stable, dropping by scarcely 5% between the two periods.[54] As a result, a greater number of artisans had to hire themselves out to shopkeepers; this situation evolved normally from one of the basic principles of free-trade capitalism in which the "workers" become increasingly dependent, since the system has robbed them of their means of production.[55]

We can easily believe that Canadians "rejected" employment, preferring to be their own masters; to suggest that this "mentality" was peculiar to Canadian workers and to claim that artisans in France were resigned to continue working as paid labourers is unacceptable. This fallacy, based on the premise that the new world offered greater social and professional mobility, really arose from a misunderstanding of the circumstances, this is mistaking the effect for the cause. An attitude is forged in answer to the circumstances and, in this case, this meant that "if one craft were not satisfactory, one could embrace another skill or, as was often done, exercise more than one trade."[56] In the practice of several of these trades, the condition of a paid worker could appear "degrading," but this meant that the worker did not question the social status quo; besides, since the number of artisans went up by 180% between 1716 and 1745,[57] could a worker afford to question it?

There is no doubt that the artisan and even the minor public servant practised several trades at the same time. The examples of which there are many demonstrate that work was scarce and emphasize the effects of free trade. However, we should not be led to believe that all artisans became wage-earners during the 18th century; that would be falsifying reality. The revealing example of the masons, bears witness to the change in the social order of when the artisan became a wage-earner. While several contractors at the end of the 17th century controlled the largest share of the market and recruited apprentices and helpers, by the turn of the century the workforce in this sector claimed its own share so that the market split up. The masons of the capital looked for construction projects out of town. Armed with the necessary skills some found themselves again in Montréal or elsewhere. Those who remained behind experienced difficulties in financing their enterprises and, when the good years returned, the "exiled" contractors came back to Québec, thus putting pressure on the humble masons who could barely keep body and soul together. Unable to compete with the contractors, the masons saw two avenues open to them: sub-contracting or working for wages. Faced with this situation did the masons have a choice? They could only submit to the will of the contractors; and we should add that the merchants' trustee, Pierre Trottier Desauniers, obtained the contract for the capital's fortifications in 1745 because the contractors did not have sufficient capital at their disposal.

This dependence on capital is even more striking in the case of the maritime forwarding agents who did not have the necessary resources to become boat-owners. So, of all the boats listed in the inventories, the merchant-traders and the Councillors owned as many as did the skippers and pilots, thus leaving the door open to various forms of associations including limited partnerships[58] and wage earners. This was suggested by the distribution of wealth among the carriers, the first "artisans" in the economic recovery of the 18th century. This transformation in production and consequently social ratios affected every sector of society to varying degrees. Québec society changed ... it became urbanized. Again, one must refrain from seeing it as a society in the process of becoming working class. The examples of military duty[59] or taxes for the barracks proved that in an ordered society the privileged are always part of the social landscape.

*****

The analysis of the assets, balance sheets and fortunes of Quebeckers who died between 1690 and 1749 led to the realization that the population had undergone a general impoverishment during the 18th century. The year 1727 marked the return to normal prices, a period of population growth began and prosperity in maritime trade was reborn; all these combined to leave the feeling that private enterprise would be able to pull the capital out of its stagnation; but this did not take into account the mechanisms of the market.

Prosperity drew to the city a number of artisans and day-labourers, with the result that there was an oversupply of workers in most trades.

This situation combined with the absence of guilds and skills favoured free competition in the work market. The same situation was true of the business sector, since merchants and traders had to compete not only with the nobles, senior officials and officers, but also, after 1717, with travelling salesmen; and from the end of the 1720s, with agents of the big business firms of La Rochelle or Bordeaux, which had set up branches in the capital.

Only one sector of activity escaped this direct competition: the service sector. Even then, only the officers and senior public servants who were paid by the State escaped it. Notaries and surgeons, although the creation of their positions was the responsibility of the State, still suffered the effects of this competition, since their clientele were becoming poorer. Certainly, the fixed remuneration for officers and senior public servants proved a handicap when inflation worsened, which was no longer the case after 1727; however, before that date various people had to hold down several jobs or go into business in order to make ends meet.

But as to their wealth, the privileged groups including officers and senior administrators, fell well above the threshold of 500 *livres*. With less than this amount, individuals could rarely buy property. Before 1727, only one household in three was in this position; after that date, the proportion rose to one in two. In this context, we can easily see that Québec became a town of tenants in the first half of the 18th century. This sudden change was not as unexpected as it would seem at first glance. The analysis of the households (Chapter 2) already pointed in this direction. The merchants were no longer the main employers of servants in 1744, instead the officials were; while in 1716 the reverse had been true.

The language used for the objects listed in Québec homes in the first half of the 18th century matches the more down-to-earth description of the belongings of these citizens, and more importantly, crystallizes it. Not only did the artisans and merchants have to compete with each other, but they also had to measure up against foreign goods. The infrastructure of the capital like that of the colony could not resist the foreign markets, despite a few attempts at control such as the making of metal stoves on a small scale.

But beyond competition, the situation in Québec makes it possible to separate the superfluous from the ordinary. In the case of transportation methods, the capital wished to be a town of pedestrians. Furthermore one should not see in the absence of religious decoration a society turning away from Christianity, but rather we should refer to the ideas of the time respecting what was necessary and what was superfluous, and take into account the values of the people at that particular time.

Finally, our prying into the nooks and crannies of these Quebeckers' homes allowed us to stop at their table and notice the frugality of their pantry. The diet of Quebeckers in the first half of the 18th century rested on two basic foods: bread and meat. While some of them learned to bake their own bread, thus creating a new form of competition for the bakers, they were also able to eat four times more beef than in earlier times. This meat, available not only in the summer but all year long, was less expensive than pork.

Québec, the capital and the town, stood out from the rural world around it by offering its new residents a way of life much more vibrant than that of a village. The village may have hummed with activity, but in town the pace quickened. The intensification of the city's activities and urban interrelationships stemmed in large part from the competition felt by labourers, artisans and merchants, a phenomenon found at a much more modest level in the rural environment. In fact, town and village were distinguished from each other by the enforced idleness of some of the town's labour force at various times. And the town spreads its net far and wide....

EPILOGUE

When a connection between demography and economy, housing and town planning is established, we come up with a remarkably homogeneous portrait of Québec. The French capital of North America does not appear to be the gate to Asia sought by the discoverers. The administrators' many ideas for setting up an economic infrastructure that would be dynamic or at least viable, revolving mainly around trade and shipbuilding, ended in partial failure.

The growth in Québec's population during the 18th century followed the same course as economic growth: the years 1706 to 1713, 1727 to 1736, and 1744 to 1755 make it possible to link the two phenomena. In the intervening periods, the city experienced periods of slowdown not only demographically, but also on the micro-economic level, since the slackening in growth was combined with a drop in consumer prices.

The fluctuations in the growth rates and prices are directly related to the demographic behaviour of the inhabitants of Québec. Throughout this whole period, the city did not absorb all the people born there; it only kept three out of four, which meant migration toward the bordering parishes.

Furthermore, two out of three children died before reaching the age of 15; this situation was a very serious handicap for the renewal of the generations. Therefore an important influx of outsiders was necessary to fill the ranks, whether they came from bordering parishes or from the home country. Consequently, three times out of five Québec women married outsiders. Better yet, the pattern in marriages and births shows to what point the lives of the residents of Québec were governed by the sailing season.

But when trade and sea-going activity were slow often some of the "foreigners" returned to their home parishes where they had kept their lands. In short, activity in the harbour encouraged them to stay for a while, but not to make their permanent homes there; this at least, is what the tenancy phenomenon seems to indicate.

The massive arrival of outsiders in the urban landscape of the capital did not happen without problems. In a system of capitalistic trade, they had to get themselves hired; the free competition praised loudly by the administrators at the beginning of the century entered the picture and shaped production relationships. This gave rise to a general impoverishment of the population, except for a privileged few: the richest of the merchant-traders as well as the senior officers and public officials.

In this context access to property was limited; Québec did not have any large land speculators. Four landowners out of five owned only one building and, when the situation led them to look for milder climes, they did not hesitate to rent it out. Thus in the first half of the 18th century, the residents of Québec were mobile, we might even say "volatile"; already, the massive arrival of outsiders was pointing in this direction.

Mobility was seen on two levels: professional and geographic. In the geographic sense, it again had a double aspect: not only did Quebeckers move from the countryside to the city or vice versa, but their loyalty to their landlords rapidly eroded. The shortness of their stay, scarcely less than two lease periods, is eloquent proof of this, not to mention the spareness of their surroundings, whose vital elements such as the stove, were meant to be taken apart and moved.

The simplicity of the surroundings not only answered practical needs. It arose partly from the fact that the population was impoverished because the market was dominated by free competition. From this point of view it is not surprising to note that a framer could become a carpenter or a sculptor; a blacksmith, a toolmaker or locksmith; a mason contractor, a quarryman, stonecutter or simple mason. Each man adapted in his own way to the competition and the circumstances.

We must be careful when talking of the circumstances. They were not always as favourable as some may claim. The pressures on the religious communities to subdivide their lands must be placed in the context of the market: in the city of the 18th century everyone learned to play the game. The Seminary ceded its lots in Sault-au-Matelot at competitive prices; nonetheless, they were smaller and the streets were narrower than in some other areas. This subdivision of real estate, however, made it possible for the Seminary priests to settle part of their debts. While the Colonial Administrators, such as Dupuy and Hocquart, urged the communities to subdivide their lots, we must see in this only a temporary move provoked by a brief economic explosion. Later, this type of pressure became rare and communities had to face a depressed market.

This notion of the real estate market is apparent in the various districts of Québec, where different industrial installations and notably the shipyards built in the Palace Quarter, attracted numerous artisan and day-labourers. Since they had few means of transportation, the workers preferred to live near their places of work. As a consequence the district became over-crowded and population density per hectare reached heights similar to those in certain French cities. In turn, the price of housing increased considerably. The same situation was encountered in Lower Town.

Only Upper Town stands out in terms of population. This was due to two factors: distance from the workplace and architecture. The urban landscape in this district was one of small houses, which were more difficult to subdivide than those in Lower Town. Despite the green spaces found there, environmentalist preoccupations were not part of the city-dwellers' daily concerns.

During the first 50 years of the 18th century, the capital rapidly became urbanized: legislation and urban facilities took shape. Thus began the weekly rounds of the garbage collector in charge of disposing of wood shavings and manure in the river; here again the "green approach" had not yet been invented. However, the administration and the institutions surrounded themselves with greenery and flowers; translated into the 18th century code, that meant that it was necessary to purify the air.

Apart from being interested in the quality of the air, the administration wanted to regulate the layout of the built-up areas. Buildings that were too close together prevented air circulation and also increased the risk of spreading fires. It was thus necessary to build out of stone and erect fireproof walls everywhere they were needed. At the same time, the masons in the capital who were struggling with a faltering market took advantage of this situation.

Actually the administration was motivated by the fear of the catastrophic effects of a fire such as the one in Montréal or the one that had devastated Lower Town in 1682. This was why every district had its squad of "volunteer" firemen, and a public fountain. Since the latter was an excellent source of drinking water, its existence somewhat mars the credibility of the hypothesis that water was taken directly from the river, especially since water was the drink most often accompanying meals.

Despite the refinement that characterized French gastronomy during this period, Quebeckers' meals during the first half of the 18th century were very simple: probably consisting of bread and beef five days a week. Furthermore, these were the only two foods for which the administration regulated the prices. While some residents of Upper Town cultivated vegetable gardens, most of the citizens bought their vegetables at the market.

Some residents, particularly artisans, looked for some self-sufficiency in dairy products, meat and eggs. This desire for autonomy by owning cows, pigs, chickens or other animals reflected the precariousness of some peoples' financial situations. They were certainly not the best: when the administrators wrote to the Court that wheat sold at an excessive price as the result of poor harvests or over-exportation, these were distress signals.

Food was limited to the absolute essentials; thus, it should not surprise us that curtains and wall coverings or decorations, religious or not, were absent from Québec houses in the 18th century. Priorities moved at the same pace as the population!

This is the story that Yves Arguin would have been able to tell us. And because he was one of the traders, Arguin was one of the privileged few. At this point, we may wonder about the prejudices that he may have expressed. Certainly, he would have shown some compassion for the dispossessed, but he probably would have made sure his own interests came first. After all, the principles of trade would hold him to it!

APPENDIX A
THE VALUE OF SUCCESSION INVENTORIES
IN QUÉBEC BETWEEN 1690 AND 1749

For several decades the use of succession inventories has earned both criticism and praise. Sometimes described as "exceptional," sometimes considered as "individual cases," these sources have for some years been the subject of special attention in the historiography of French-speaking Canadians.[1] We could even say that succession inventories are all the rage! We cannot make an exception by neglecting such an interesting source, taking into account urban housing conditions and their repercussions on "fortune." From this point of view, the records of notaries who worked in Québec during the French régime have been subjected to a systematic analysis, document by document.

A single individual could not undertake such an analysis. To go through 60 000 notarized documents and to search succession inventories for the construction of graphs could not be accomplished by one researcher in six months. Only a team[2] could complete this and other related tasks, since inventories were not the only documents listed and indexed; so were marriage contracts and leases. And each transcribed document has to be checked in order to correct the inevitable errors.

Geographic Framework

Since this study deals with Québec from 1690 to 1749, the notaries who practised in the capital or in its immediate vicinity were subjected to analysis. This covered some 30 offices. The parameters of selection for the collection of data taken from inventories were limited to very simple criteria: first, that the person whose inventory was being done had to live in Québec. Even though this did not represent irrefutable proof of "permanent" residence, (but was more probable if the person had movable possessions there or better yet, real estate), this criterion proved to be the most conclusive despite the mobility of the population.

Second, inventories of those people who were "shipwrecked" in Québec during a voyage had to be eliminated. Such cases seemed obvious after simply reading the description of the inventory, since there was no mention of relatives and the inventory had usually been drawn up at the request of the Crown Prosecutor. Finally, duplicates and pieced-together inventories had to be eliminated. The duplicates were actually inventories interrupted as they were being written and completed later. The term "pieced together" refers to an inventory that tried to retrace missing objects listed in an earlier document. This type of document, written often several years after the first, was therefore ignored.

About 1750 succession inventories were traced; of this number, 703 were for residents of Québec and its suburbs.[3] Of these 703 inventories, 81.1% involved various joint estates. The others were divided between inventories of broken marriages (meaning remarried survivors) [11.8%], and those of the two members of the same joint estate (7.1%). Remarriage meant a new division and consequently a new joint estate; therefore, these documents had to be considered separately. In other respects, keeping the two inventories of the same joint estate might seem paradoxical. This can be explained in two ways: on one hand, by the time lapse between the two deaths, averaging 13 years; and on the other, by the lack of any indication of the deceased's trade, which was the case 40% of the time.

But what was represented by the inventories in terms of the number of deaths recorded in Notre-Dame Parish in Québec? First, it must be emphasized that the question of the source's value should not stop at this consideration alone, but should also include several other characteristics such as the trades listed compared with the trades practised in the city,[4] ownership — especially in a rental area like Québec, or even distribution by age groups.

General Outline of the Succession Inventory

These considerations give rise to questions about the deed itself and its principal characteristics. The document was usually prepared in the following manner: after a person's death, the survivor (of a couple) or the legal heirs would request a notary to draw up an inventory of the deceased's worldly goods and property. The notary would go to the latter's home accompanied by an appraiser who would estimate the value of the goods in the inheritance. It should be noted that these goods were rarely identified as being new. In order to authenticate the document, the notary would have it signed not only by the survivor of the joint estate and the heirs, but also by two or three witnesses,[5] usually neighbours of the house under inventory. So that those whose presence was "required" (the witnesses were always men) might not be embarrassed too much, it was sometimes recorded that they made themselves comfortable with a few jugs ... of wine. Perhaps this is one of the reasons why the figures in some inventories were written in a rather unsteady hand!

The document was generally divided into three sections: first, the identification of the deceased; second, the list of the objects most often described in their exact context; then the description of the papers including, apart from liabilities and assets, the deeds pertaining to the purchase or possession of real estate. Sometimes the last two categories were separate. The shortest inventory is four pages and the longest 393.[6] Even though all the documents had to describe and identify the deceased, not all of them contained figures; for one reason or another, 2% of the inventories included no evaluation of goods. Moneys owed to the deceased were mentioned three times out of five, but two times out of three when they represented a liability. As for the status of owner or tenant, the inventory pointed this out about nine times out of ten.

In his identification of the deceased, the notary listed the date, the name of the petitioner and his relationship to the deceased, thus making it possible to determine whether this was a joint estate or that of an unmarried person. Right off, we can say that 95% of the succession inventories were for the estates of married people. The notary continued by indicating (two out of three times) the man's trade (and on a single occasion, the woman's), and the names of minor children or at least their number. Since the surviving spouse usually became the guardian for the minor children, the legal system required that a deputy guardian be appointed. Lacking the names or the number of children, the mention of two legal guardians in the inventory shows that the couple had minor children; and since majority was not reached until the age of 25, this situation was not rare. Only cases of early marriages or inventories of aged persons as well as those of childless couples lack this. It wasn't surprising to find that seven inventories out of ten (of those with joint estates) noted the existence of minor children.

The notary rarely forgot the place of residence (scarcely 8% of the cases). On the other hand, he noted by many almost enigmatic phrases that the appraisal had been done "without taking into account appreciation,"[7] and "since the impossibility of selling the objects because of the uncertainty of the times, means that we are not certain that our paper money would be accepted as legal tender in France."[8] The phrase could also read: "without adding appreciation,"[9] or again "without appreciation being included in the appraisal."[10] The authors Paquet and Wallot have mentioned the existence of appreciation and even pointedly noted that appreciation was equal to 25% of the evaluation, and thus to one-fifth of the total. The added value was significant but was applied only when the evaluated possessions were later sold at auction.[11] Transcripts of several sale records show that the sale could bring in substantially more than the evaluation alone had indicated.[12] Since appreciation, in principle, should have compensated for any under-valuation by the appraiser, we should then conclude that, with or without appreciation, the final price of each of the objects represented the value of the goods or their "true value."[13] Three times out of ten, the notary specified that appreciation had been included.

A last element that can be helpful in tracing the identification of the person, aside from his civil status, was the date of his or her marriage contract, a document normally mentioned along with the deeds and papers. Since the inventory usually marked the end of the union and the marriage contract indicated its beginning, a comparison of these two documents can be very interesting. Although the marriage contract had been very popular during the French régime,[14] we only found evidence of it two times out of three in our inquiry, although a few references may have escaped us, especially for the first years of the study when many unions were solemnized in France or outside the region. Nevertheless, this situation may partly echo the mobility observed among the residents of the capital (Chapter 1).

Although the date of the marriage contract may be used to mark the beginning of the union,[15] the inventory date, to the contrary, did not always correspond with the date of death. The notary omitted two vital items of information in his description of the deceased: the date of death and his or her age at that time. Although he sometimes mentioned the first, the second was almost always missing. To settle this, it was therefore necessary to search the Registry for baptisms, marriages and burials for each of the death dates as well as the age of the deceased when given. We now know the date of death in 73% of the cases, and the age in 63%.

With these facts established it became possible to: check whether the various legal provisions were followed, for example, deadlines in writing up the deed; or pair the age distribution and the criteria of ownership or even the average length of a marriage[16] (lacking a reconstruction of family trees). Better yet, they made it possible to validate or call into question the monetary provisions set out in the marriage contract while weighting them using certain variables, such as the length of the marriage.

There remained a last point to be explained: the data figures and real estate evaluations. The inventories, like most notarized documents, indicated the value of the goods in the currency of the time, in Canadian or foreign currency. All the data used in this study were converted into French currency. On the other hand, it must be noted that real estate evaluations were rarely made: popular at the beginning of the period under consideration, this custom cost the heirs dearly and fell progressively into disuse. Thus only 11.1% of the inventories mentioning properties in town contained their monetary value. Despite this low rate of correlation, it nevertheless was possible to obtain from it an order of magnitude that could be applied to all the properties, regardless of the period.

Respect for Legal Provisions

Claude de Ferrière in his *Commentaire sur la Coutume de la Prévôté et Vicomté de Paris* pointed out that only a succession inventory "made, flawless and closed" could dissolve the joint estate.[17] To be "flawless," the inventory had to carry the signature of two notaries, and it was completed when it was registered with the Provost. Furthermore, the inventory had to be drawn up ("made") in the presence of "capable persons and opposing counsel," so that if the couple had minor children and the surviving parent became their guardian, there also had to be a deputy guardian who became the lawful opposing counsel.

The law did not require the filing of a succession inventory;[18] rather, this came about at the request of an interested party. If no inventory was drawn up, then the joint estate continued to exist and the children could ask for it to be extended or divided. This right applied as well to the children of a second marriage.[19] Every inventory had to be "made, flawless and closed" within 90 days after death; otherwise, the survivor tacitly accepted the existence of the joint estate. When the survivor remarried without having had an inventory drawn up, the estate was divided three ways; if the two parties had children, at the death of one of the two new spouses the joint estate would be divided into four parts. The ultimate aim of this legal exercise was to describe in detail the material possessions, real estate or even the debts of one of the parents, taking into account the provisions established in the marriage contract, thus allowing the widow, in particular, the choice of accepting or renouncing the joint estate depending upon whether the balance sheet was positive or negative.[20] She had 40 days after the settlement of the inventory to deliberate on her choice.[21] In short, the legal provision was only applicable when one of the parties requested the drawing up of an inventory. At this point, our task was to find out how often the population of Québec requested a succession inventory.

Between 1690 and 1749, the priests of Québec as well as the Hôtel-Dieu Hospital and General Hospital nuns, registered 1937 deaths of men and women over 15 years old.[22] This number was divided almost equally between the two sexes; however, it does not include the number of deaths where the age of the deceased was omitted; namely, 653 cases. Although these were very often deaths of newborn babies (perhaps even seven out of ten times), it seemed preferable not to leave them out; this is the reason for including them in Table 58. In order to facilitate the reading of this table, it must be pointed out that the "gross" refers to all deaths including unknowns, and that the "net" leaves out the unknowns.

TABLE 58
DEATHS AND INVENTORIES, 1690-1749

Decade	Deaths							Inventories			Proportion (%)					
	Men		Women		Total						Total		Men		Women	
	Age known	Age ?	Age known	Age ?	Gross*	Net**	Age ?	Men	Women	Total	Gross	Net	Gross	Net	Gross	Net
1690-1699	74+	33	52+	19	178	126	52	29	16	45	25.3	35.7	27.1	39.2	22.5	30.8
1700-1709	153+	26	156+	32	367	309	58	49	46	95	25.9	30.7	27.4	32.0	24.5	29.5
1710-1719	137+	91	127+	66	421	264	157	66	56	122	29.0	46.2	28.9	48.2	29.0	44.1
1720-1729	148+	63	133+	54	398	281	117	73	53	126	31.6	44.8	34.6	49.3	28.3	39.8
1730-1739	190+	57	180+	45	472	370	102	81	51	132	28.0	35.7	32.8	42.6	22.7	28.3
1740-1749	275+	97	312+	70	754	587	167	90	93	183	24.3	31.2	24.2	32.7	24.3	29.8
Total	977+	367	960+	286	2590	1937	653	388	315	703	27.1	36.3	28.9	39.7	25.3	32.8

* includes unknowns
** does not include unknowns

In short, the table shows that the gross proportion was 27.1% and the net was 36.3%. These rates were high, bearing in mind that the same exercise for the same town at the beginning of the 19th century produced a result of only 11.3%, which even compared advantageously with the proportions found by French historians who have studied the same period.[23]

It must be noted that the ten-year distribution presented an unquestionable stability all during this period as the deviation in comparison with the overall mean varied only slightly. As far as the distribution of the sexes is concerned, the men were slightly overrepresented since 55% of the inventories were for them; nevertheless, this is comparable to the general evolution in the capital's population since men made up an absolute majority during the course of the 18th century.[24] An annual breakdown of the distribution was not necessary since the gap between the moment of death and the drawing up of the inventory caused some anomalies so that, in the same year, there could be two and one-third times more inventories than deaths. This was notably the case for 1704, because a smallpox epidemic had caused a major crisis in the death rate during the preceding two years.

Determining the date of death made it possible to establish the time gap between the moment of death and the drawing up of the inventory. Table 59 shows that in more than one in two cases, this gap exceeded the prescribed 90 days. The same table also shows that those who exceeded the 90-day limit were very late in turning to the inventory since

TABLE 59

INTERVAL BETWEEN DEATH AND INVENTORY

Interval	Inventories	%
0 to 3 months	234	45.7
3 to 6 months	53	10.3
6 to 12 months	55	10.7
1 to 2 years	64	12.5
Over 2 years	105	20.5
Total	511	99.7

60% waited more than one year.[25] This long delay could explain why 15% of the spouses had remarried when the inventory was drawn up.

Moreover, the age of the deceased gave a good idea of the distribution of the components of Québec society in the 18th century. Table 60 shows the size of each of the age groups that asked for an inventory. Although our compilation of Québec deaths was drawn up as a function of specific age groups,[26] there was no doubt that the distribution of age

TABLE 60

AGE GROUPS, BOTH SEXES
1690-1749

Age Groups	Number	%	Charbonneau
Under 20 yrs	3	0.67	4.76
20 to 29 yrs	57	12.84	12.67
30 to 39 yrs	110	24.77	13.69
40 to 49 yrs	72	16.22	13.51
50 to 59 yrs	65	14.64	14.82
60 to 69 yrs	62	13.96	16.90
70 to 79 yrs	50	11.26	15.65
80 to 89 yrs	22	4.95	7.50
Over 90 yrs	3	0.67	0.48
Total	444	99.98	

TABLE 61

INTERVAL BETWEEN DEATH AND INVENTORY,
BY AGE GROUPS

Interval	Age Groups									Invent.
	90-99	80-89	70-79	60-69	50-59	40-49	30-39	20-29	15-19	
Same day	0	0	1	1	1	1	0	0	0	4
Under 3 mo.	3	14	31	35	45	33	28	13	2	204
3 to 6 mo.	0	3	5	3	2	6	16	9	0	44
6 to 12 mo.	0	0	6	4	8	6	13	9	0	46
1 to 2 yrs	0	3	1	9	2	6	20	9	0	50
2 to 3 yrs	0	0	1	1	1	4	17	5	0	29
Over 3 yrs	0	2	5	5	6	16	16	12	0	62
Total	3	22	50	58	65	72	110	57	2	439

groups in the inventories nevertheless closely followed the general distribution of the population, with the exception of a few groups. Thus referring to the observations of the demographer H. Charbonneau, it seems that the colony's population died in the same proportions as those in our age groups, except for those between 30 and 39 who accounted for 10% more in the inventories.[27] Thus, the notary was called upon more often to draw up an inventory in the case of sudden and unexpected deaths.

Since a person living in Québec in the 18th century was already old at 60, could there have been a relationship between age at the time of death and the time elapsed before drawing up the inventory? According to Table 61, the heirs or creditors of aged people wished to know the financial state of the joint estate quickly, since 64% of the inventories for persons over 60 were drawn up within the prescribed 90 days. On the other hand, the possessions of those under 40 were subjected to an inventory within the required time in only one out of every four cases. This situation can be partly explained by the fact that the older the deceased, the less chance there was of having a surviving spouse while the situation was reversed for those aged 30-49. Furthermore, the situation can be statistically proven since in one out of every two cases (54.7%) if the deceased was over 60, there was a surviving spouse; while the proportion is four out of five (84.6%) for those between 30 and 49. The age of the deceased cannot explain everything though; many other factors have to be taken into account, such as profession, the length of the marriage, even ownership status, in order to evaluate the alacrity of the heirs.[28]

It was much more difficult to determine the socio-professional distribution of those whose inventories have been traced, since the notaries only mentioned the trade of the deceased or spouse three times out of five. Furthermore, we could not complete our data using those compiled by the priests since they very rarely entered these particulars in the registry unless they happened to concern a person "of good quality," as the expression of the time put it. The only way available to us was an analysis of the professions listed in the two censuses carried out in the 18th century. In this comparison, we have adopted the very practical grouping in four sectors: services, business, artisan and unskilled.[29]

Certainly it would have been proper to check whether this socio-professional representation applied only to the upper echelons in each of the sectors. However, at no time did the inventory make it possible to distinguish between merchant and clerk or between a contractor and a lowly mason. It would be necessary to obtain a career profile for each individual to do this. Jean Boucher *dit* Belleville, although listed as a mason, nevertheless built the fortifications in Montréal, which implies that he was a contractor who hired wage-earners.

We should also emphasize another ambiguity in the socio-professional identification: that of successive jobs. Although it can be established that a framer could also work as a carpenter or even combine the two jobs, only a study of his tools would make it possible to determine which of the trades the deceased really practised. But this was not really the heart of the problem since this trade remains in the artisan sector. Only the question of hierarchy (i.e. employer or employee) remained unanswered.

The situation becomes ever more difficult in the case of a merchant appointed to the Superior or Sovereign Council, making him a potential candidate for two categories: services and business. Since the notary identified him as a Councillor, he became part of the service group notwithstanding the presence of his shop and stock. This identification derives from the description of the notary, who accorded all the privileges of his status to the deceased. This fits in perfectly with the context of the 18th century in the capital in which the privileged people in an

TABLE 62

SOCIO-PROFESSIONAL BREAKDOWN (%)

	Services	Business	Artisan	Unskilled
1716	23.2	30.6	36.0	10.2
1744	15.0	33.5	39.1	12.4
1690-1749	32.3	30.7	35.1	1.8

orderly society were learning to recognize the new rules of a class structure in the process of formation. Examples of this situation are common in Québec, not only for specific things such as military duties or taxation for barracks, but also in everyday things such as marriage contracts.[30]

Table 62 makes it possible to evaluate the relative importance of each sector of activity, by comparing the data gathered in the two censuses with those drawn from the inventories. We find that there was an almost total lack of unskilled labourers and a higher representation of the service sector (almost double). The business and artisan sectors are practically the same. It seems that in spite of the overrepresentation of services to the detriment of unskilled labour, Québec society was accurately reflected in succession inventories. However, this gave us a horizontal section, which had to be completed by an in-depth analysis, something that could not be done on the basis of the inventories.

Table 63 also shows the interval between death and the drawing up of the inventory as observed in the various sectors of activity. Although the spouses of representatives of the services sector requested a notary within the prescribed time limit three times out of five, and those in the business sector a little over one time out of two; in two out of seven cases, artisans or wives of artisans did not show the same haste.

Certainly it would be tempting to put forward the hypothesis that more people in the artisan sector died at a younger age, in most cases leaving survivors to look after the succession inheritance. This explanation would seem valid when we consider that more than 50% of those in the services sector died at the respectable age of 60 or more. However, this hypothesis does not fit the fact that, both in the business and artisan sectors, one person in two was in the 30-49 years group. Although age

TABLE 63
INTERVAL BETWEEN DEATH AND INVENTORY, BY SECTOR OF ACTIVITY

Interval	Services	Business	Artisan	Un-skilled	Total
Same day	2	1	0	1	4
Under 3 months	63	48	31	3	145
3 to 6 months	8	8	16	1	33
6 to 12 months	9	9	18	0	36
1 to 2 years	9	12	19	0	40
2 to 3 years	4	5	9	0	18
Under 3 years	14	9	20	0	43
Total	109	92	113	5	319

and family situation were two important factors in ensuring that a succession inventory would be drawn up, might there not have been a more important variable in a context such as that of the capital in the 18th century?

Real Estate

If the heirs had recourse to the inventory, they did so with the aim of describing not only the material goods but especially the real estate. From a town where most people were owners (85%) at the end of the 17th century, Québec's proportion had dropped to 30%, or at best 44%, by 1740. According to the inventories, there should have been many more owners than tenants in Québec. According to Table 64, owners and tenants would have been in inverse proportions. By including unknowns, presumed to have been tenants, 61% of the succession inventories were for owners; by excluding them, the rate rises to 69.5%.[31] On the whole, the applicants wished to have a notarized description of the properties in a joint estate. This concern could not be neglected when we consider that 22% of the owners had a fortune valued at 1000 *livres* or less, this

TABLE 64

NUMBER OF OWNERS, BY SUCCESSION
INVENTORIES

	Number	%
Owners	369	52.5
Tenants but owners in Québec	23	3.3
Tenants but owners outside city limits	33	4.7
Unknown (Québec) but owners outside city limits	3	0.4
	428	61.0
Tenants	188	26.7
Unknown	87	12.4
	275	39.0
Total	703	

sum being considered the psychological barrier below which few individuals could have access to property. Besides, distributed by age groups, over 62.5% of deceased persons for whose estates an inventory was drawn up were owners, except for those in the 15-29 years age group (Table 65). This situation could easily have happened, taking into account the average length of a marriage was 14.5 years. On the other hand, if we classify the identified owners according to their sector of activity, the breakdown for each of the spheres of activity would have to be adjusted slightly, as shown in Table 66.

This table shows that unskilled workmen did not have the means to buy a house. Yet those who in principle had enough resources, the business people, invested little in real estate. The situation of the merchants and those in the world of commerce was not confined to Québec; it showed up as well in other port cities of the 18th century, especially in Rouen. Merchants and traders placed little importance on their surroundings, preferring to concentrate more on the profits from their commercial investments than in those from real estate.[32]

The presence of real estate as one of the important criteria leading to the need for a succession inventory can not be brushed aside lightly.

TABLE 65
DISTRIBUTION OF OWNERS BY
AGE GROUP

Age (Years)	Owners	Inventories	%
15-19	0	3	
20-29	26	57	45.6
30-39	70	110	63.6
40-49	45	72	62.5
50-59	42	65	64.6
60-69	44	62	71.0
70-79	34	50	68.0
80-89	15	22	68.2
90-99	3	3	100.0
Total	279	444	

TABLE 66
DISTRIBUTION OF OWNERS BY
SECTOR OF ACTIVITY

Services	Business	Artisan	Unskilled
32.7	24.7	41.4	1.1

Since it has already been established that Québec was a city of tenants in the middle of the 18th century, we must now examine what happened to the owner-inventory relationship half a century later. According to the 1818 census, although they had been mainly tenants, the succession inventories at the beginning of the 19th century show that now Québec framers, carpenters and blacksmiths were more often likely to own real estate. And the situation would have been similar in Montréal at the beginning of the 19th century since, between 1792 and 1796, 79% of the inventories were for city owners, and this proportion rose to 91% between 1807 and 1812.[33]

Some may claim that real estate was not even the subject of an evaluation; consequently why should particular attention be paid to it? This question of evaluation can be explained by changes in the capital's position. We should stress that the capital's population was becoming impoverished during the 18th century; thus, to have a property evaluated entailed important expenditures for the likes of a mason, framer, carpenter or blacksmith. And since tenants were in the majority, there was no real need to have the property evaluated; only its mention mattered, since real estate represented an important part of the inheritance.

Two other indices also point in this direction. How can we explain that, for a population that was twice as large after 1727, there was practically the same number of inventories (337 before this date and 332 after)? Certainly, this could be an effect of the general phenomenon of impoverishment, but still.... Even though the proportion of inventories in relation to the number of deaths remained practically the same; this may mean, if not a longer lifespan, at least a greater mobility on the part of the population. And mobility means tenants. So we are back at the starting point!

Finally, we must emphasize the phenomenon of remarried widowers and widows. While in four out of five cases the inventories were for separate estates, in 12% of the rest of cases, one of the survivors had remarried or become widowed anew. Real estate was at stake in 85% of these cases.

Therefore, ownership of real estate must be considered as one of the criteria determining the drafting of a succession inventory in Québec in the 18th century. And this despite the fact that property could not be concealed or moved, which also explains why the notary at times rounded out the figures. This is not the only possible scenario, but it may be the most conclusive.

A Valid Source?

Asking a question entails a reply, but before we do that, the targeted objectives must be outlined. Since the objective was to learn about the urban environment in the 18th century, and determine how much it affected the "fortunes" of the citizens, this source of succession inventories proved to be one of the most important ones.

Although it involved a majority of owners in a town where most people were tenants, this source made it possible to see more clearly what it meant to be an owner in Québec in the 18th century and, as a corollary, to explain how it was that tenants came to be in the majority. This evaluation of ownership (should we say bourgeois?) status could not evidently be based only on a knowledge of personal possessions. Real estate also had to be taken into account in order to be able to draw up a balance sheet for the inheritance.

However, figures on property evaluations were lacking; for the 392 inventories of city property, only 41 contained such details, which nevertheless represents a little over 10%. Still, this sample seems adequate to establish a general proportion of real estate value. The latter was calculated by establishing the value of the assets; that is, the value of the personal belongings added to that of the shop's contents as well as cash on hand and accounts payable; and by defining the proportion of the known real estate values, taking into account the assets. For the period between 1690 and 1749, it is clear that the value of real estate accounted for 38.9% of the "fortune" of a city owner.[34] Furthermore, this proportion of the share assigned to real estate was only 31.5% for merchants and wholesalers who owned their business property. But this relative gap was narrowed when absolutes are taken into consideration. Subsequently, in order to obtain the provisional balance sheet for an inheritance at the moment of death, it was enough to subtract the total of debts owed.

In short, there were three levels of comparison of a joint estate's "fortune," depending upon whether only the personal belongings were considered, which made it possible to concentrate on the study of the tastes of the deceased people, taking into account that no real estate was included. However, this method ignores the primordial aspect of the real estate sector.

In comparing the various levels of wealth; that is, in taking into account the value of real estate, the gaps between different socio-professional groups could be narrowed; it then becomes possible to place the businessmen in a different perspective, since they were not inclined to invest in real estate.

Finally, the third level of comparison derives from the previous one. Owners rarely paid cash for their properties; as a general rule, they resorted to credit in one form or another. That this was an investment was never in doubt, even though regular payments had to be made to discharge the debt. Thus, the provisional balance sheet debited the inheritance with the various debts against the joint estate.

These three levels of analysis make it possible to compare different socio-professional groups in terms of their personal tastes, whether on the basis of the importance accorded to personal belongings, to the dwelling, or even to the effect of indebtedness. But the method has one snag: attributing a proportion in place of real estate value proved a handicap when the owners had very high or very low assets, and when their real estate had not been appraised. This involved the risk of over- or under-evaluating wealth.

An analysis of the worldly goods of the less well-off owners revealed that, with few exceptions, the person who had few assets lived, not in a palace, but rather in a small half-timbered house. The house's value could represent a great deal more than the assets (sometimes up to three times the amount). However, judging by his or her debts, very often this same person had contracted a mortgage equal to the established value (39%, but 31% for merchants) of the fortune, so that the latter could be the same as the mortgage. In short, despite very limited assets, the relative allocation taking the place of the real estate evaluation can be justified and is justifiable, save for a few exceptions.

Only in the cases of high assets can the relative evaluations lead to error. But, since high assets are found mainly among businessmen and they invest less in real estate, the phenomenon of over-evaluation may be less important than we think. Here again, a careful look at the provisional balance sheets makes it possible to control the undue inflation of wealth.

It is important to know that a balance sheet would never be final since real estate owned outside the town (most often simply land and particularly shares in land) was never appraised, except for a few exceptions. Therefore it was not evaluated. We must add another scenario whose questions the inventory cannot answer: there were cases where the widow had started to dispose of or to distribute the tools and equipment of her late husband for the benefit of her children. How many inven-

TABLE 67
ASSETS AND FORTUNE OF YVES ARGUIN
(in *livres*)

Goods	Invent.	Partition Accounts	Diff.
Cash	1042	1042	
Movable Goods	4761		
Merchandise	16275	35305	+14269
Active Debts	25773	17461	− 8312
Real Estate		12520	+12520
Total	47852	66330	+18478

tories of this sort can there be? It is impossible to answer. Besides, perhaps the guardian and the deputy-guardian agreed to go ahead with the
auction of all or part of the deceased's worldly goods, in which case the
proceeds of the sale are added to the kitty. Therefore only a report on
the division of the inheritance can indicate the real balance sheet of the
estate's assets.

Certainly it would have been tempting to consult only the inheritance
records to establish the levels of wealth, but this method would have entailed the inconvenience of relying only on the pairing of 75 inventories
and partitions,[35] these last being drawn up on average eight years after
the death.[36]

As an example, let us compare the data in the inventory and the records of the partition of the inheritance of wholesale merchant Yves Arguin (Table 67). The two documents were drawn up after an interval of
only 18 months. According to the inventory drawn up by notary Gilbert
Boucault de Godefus, the merchant had left assets of 47 852 *livres*,
without including the property mentioned but not evaluated.[37]

According to the account given by François Lemaître Lamorille, however, the inheritance comes to 66 330 *livres*.[38] This difference is due in
large part to the value of the real estate. However, the data in these two
documents differ appreciably. This can be explained by the profits produced by the auction sale of possessions and merchandise, and also by
the elimination of certain bad debts. It must be noted, however, that in

applying the coefficient of real estate value (which in the case of merchants was different from the general mean) to the inventory data, the amount of Arguin's "fortune" was about the same as that shown in the report; in fact, it was higher by 3%.

However, the final accounting of the Arguin estate took place soon after the merchant's death and this was not always the case; sometimes this had to wait until minor children came of age. In the case of wholesale butcher Pierre Duroy, who died in 1723, the partition accounts were done only 20 years later after the death of his widow, Marguerite Levasseur;[39] since the latter did not close her husband's inventory, the joint estate continued to exist and Marguerite Levasseur enjoyed the usufruct of his worldly goods without rendering any account to their children.

At the time of the inventory of the Levasseur estate, the assets were 14 455 *livres*;[40] that is, some 340 *livres* less than noted in the partition. However, since the real estate was not evaluated at the time of the inventory, the estimate of the fortune falls short despite the allocation of a real estate coefficient. The deficit was some 20 000 *livres*. The Duroy case, however, must not be generalized since they were very few who, like Mr. Duroy, owned more than three houses in the city of Québec.[41]

These various figures show that the estates calculated from inventories are most often undervalued. It must also be noted that neither assets from accounts nor the outcome of inventories represent the total to be divided.[42] While liabilities must be deducted from the wealth figures calculated on the basis of the inventories, the result differs from that of the final reckoning for the partition of the estate, since we must not only deduct liabilities, but also the various expenses incurred since the person's death. And the longer the plaintiff waits, the higher the expenses will be. Briefly, despite the fact that it under-evaluates wealth, the succession inventory is a valid source to identify the levels of wealth.

Nevertheless, one must mistrust what is represented by the level of the estate at the time of death. According to comments made by the notaries during the difficult years of 1716 to 1718, the bailiff evaluated the worldly goods according to the principle of "valued as new" from which he subtracted depreciation due to wear and tear. Annual inflation must be taken into account as a result.

*****

This review of sources shows that the succession inventory is a most important source for someone seeking to know about his ancestors' material past. However, we must refer to the inventory with full knowledge of intent and avoid considering it as the ultimate truth. Most petitioners had a definite aim: to list and describe one or more properties; in a town of tenants, this is a significant move. It may partly explain why the notary's figures are somewhat vague. As well, it justifies the large proportion of owners observed in all age groups from 20-29 up to 90-99. It partly cautions against the delay in registering the inventory. But especially it distorts the portrait that we have of the citizens as a whole; it only shows us the more well-to-do.

APPENDIX B
PRICE INDEX FLUCTUATIONS

Working with a 60-year period in order to make certain comparisons between the beginning, middle and end of this time interval has numerous drawbacks, such as the effects of inflation. We could overcome this obstacle by creating a composite price index. Although the terms inflation and deflation were not part of the economic vocabulary of the 18th century, these were nonetheless tangible realities in Québec.

Some thirty years ago, Jean Hamelin eloquently illustrated the inflationary fluctuations that occurred between 1714 and 1719;[1] and all subsequent price data have confirmed this.[2] The fact remains though that Hamelin's study did not deal specifically with this phenomenon; it only emphasized it. So the problem remained unsolved. More recently, J.-P. Wallot and G. Paquet worked on reconstructing consumer price indexes for Montréal and Québec. However, their data were for the end of the 19th century. Their numerous articles demonstrate the usefulness but also the complexity of such an undertaking.[3]

Since these data series did not answer all his questions or meet his expectations, historian F. Ouellet tried again. In collaboration with J. Hamelin and R. Chabot, he reported on several numbered series concerning various consumer products of rural origin. However, contrary to Paquet and Wallot, Ouellet distinguished between urban and rural sale prices. Although some tables in his article[4] deal with the French régime, the column on Québec shows no figures; Ouellet and Hamelin explain that "the data used to prepare the wheat price curve could not be found." Thus, for the French régime, known consumer prices amounted to the two wheat price curves for Québec and Montréal as defined by L. Dechêne and J. Hamelin.[5]

Sources

While Paquet and Wallot, followed by Hamelin and Ouellet, offer the reader price series covering 54 or 70 different products, should we use exclusively the price of wheat to evaluate the cost of living in Québec under the French régime? Or should we refer exclusively to church sources to evaluate these same prices? Right off, the question is worth debating; not that we should challenge Hamelin's interpretation of the situation, but rather bring out slight differences in meaning, and specifically take into account not only local prices such as the price of wheat, but also the prices of imported products such as spices (nutmeg, pepper, salt).

Hamelin admitted that the Seminary's archives lacked information on other grains, and that products such as peas were only found there on a few occasions.[6] Obviously completing these price series using archives from other communities could be an alternative;[7] even then, it first must be possible to have access to them; and secondly, we must be able to establish the level of activity of the seigneuries of these institutions. Finally, and this is particularly true of the Seminary, these institutions had at different periods an urgent need for money. This may have influenced the price at which wheat was sold. In short, this source must be compared with other sources.

Since the weekly market price fluctuations have disappeared from our archival heritage,[8] we have to look for another source likely to contain figures indicating the prices in force in Québec under the French régime. Succession inventories contain this type of information, although the data only rarely deal with perishable goods which, in general, are not included in the valued goods since they are left to the survivors "for subsistence." Thus, onions, carrots, leeks, eggs and chocolate are more often just mentioned than actually evaluated. On the other hand, salted lard, flour, firewood and or salt keep longer so they are often evaluated.

The use of such a source may lead to numerous objections. Researchers Paquet and Wallot discredit it, pointing out that:

The notary ignored a good many of the perishable goods. Several inventories pointed out that the estimate was obtained "with appreciation included." But cereal stocks could fluctuate enormously depending upon the season when the notary took the inventory.

*Furthermore, sometimes stocks included the quantity of supplies
and cereals required and put aside to feed the family until the next
harvest, and for the tithe and rent paid to the seigneur, and these
were evaluated; sometimes the inventory only mentioned gross
quantities or values; sometimes, it accounted for the remainder and
only indicated an unknown quantity meant for these purposes and
not evaluated [translation].[9]*

This criticism of the sources seems to be slightly hasty and even premature since everything depends upon the objective, and above all, the
method used.[10] Paquet and Wallot based their work on a sample broken
down in accordance with the criteria of socio-professional class, limited
to a given area and studied in five-year periods. Dividing the documentation this way inevitably affects the chronological sequence. It also
limits the number of inventories retained since a socio-professional
criterion must be respected.

However, these two researchers warn their colleagues against the seasonal fluctuations in the prices of commodities. This observation seems very
pertinent since the prices of harvest products will vary depending upon the
quality and quantity of the stocks. As to the area covered, in this case the
inventories must be for persons living in Québec or its surrounding area.[11]

The gathering of basic data gave rise to the selection criteria described in Appendix A. In sum, these criteria amount to the following:
systematic gathering of succession inventories of persons residing in
Québec, as identified by the place of residence determined by the notary, from the offices of the clerks of some 30 notaries who practised in
Québec or in its immediate area between 1690 and 1749. This being the
case, the limitation inherent in Paquet's and Wallot's selection method
disappears; we only have to identify clearly the place of residence.

Systematic studies also offer the advantage of identifying only those
urban residents whose goods are evaluated by the clerks and notaries
who also resided in urban communities. For this reason, these people
knew at first hand about the cost of living in Québec since they experienced it. Even better, in the case of merchants, they called on persons in
the same trade, which confers a certain unity to the estimated prices.
This was also the case with artisans' shops.

However, this does not solve the problem of seasonal prices. First of
all, 55% of the inventories consulted were taken during the winter sea-

son (1 November to 30 April). In theory the prices listed must reflect the situation brought about by the harvest (in the case of harvests of local or regional products). On the other hand, the inventories taken in the spring or summer only rarely recorded the existence of goods such as wheat or flour, whereas prices would tend to rise because of the scarcity of the product at that time of year. Since it was impossible to "seasonally adjust" prices, the annual average of the prices observed was used instead. However, the appraisals of the different clerks were surprisingly stable.[12]

The question of appreciation is not an obstacle to evaluating prices since "currency,[...] dishes[...] bills, bonds [...], large fruits, salt, wood and coal" are not subject to the instructions concerning appreciation.[13] In short, consumer goods evaluated in accordance with market prices were exempt. Appreciation only applied to 30% of all the inventories consulted. Furthermore, it only applied to 29% of the inventories taken between November and April, 12.7% of which contained evaluated goods. While this formality applies to an under-evaluated inventory; in theory, adding this "proportion" should produce a figure equivalent to the market price. Whether the appreciation was applied or not, the appraised price hinges on the "current price" or the "fair value" of the item.

Use of Wheat Prices and Their Fluctuations as a Scale

There is a short way to comparing prices taken from succession inventories. It consists of relating them to the price of a *minot* (larger than a bushel, but precise capacity unknown) of wheat obtained by Hamelin. However, this operation remains incomplete because from 1690 to 1749 Hamelin reported only eight observations.[14] Thus, we have to do a comparison of the curves, in order to identify the same fluctuations.

Table 68 shows two things: on one hand, the prices listed in the succession inventories are most often lower than those taken from the Seminary's account books; on the other, it seems that prices from these two sources followed the same upward and downward trends. Finally, we should emphasize that the differences between the two types of prices for these years comes to 8%.

As far as the price curve (Graph 14) is concerned, the curve for the inventories follows the same trends as the one for the Seminary. Thus,

TABLE 68
PRICE OF A MINOT OF WHEAT
(in *sols*)

Year	Inventory Price	Seminary Price	Difference (%)
1690	60.00	86.25	30.00
1692		93.75	
1694	39.93	43.50	8.20
1700	90.00	93.75	4.00
1710	47.47	51.75	8.20
1712	39.30	37.50	-4.80
1715	127.50	120.00	-6.25
1718	150.00	180.00	16.67

GRAPH 14
WHEAT PRICES, BY INVENTORIES
QUÉBEC, 1690-1749

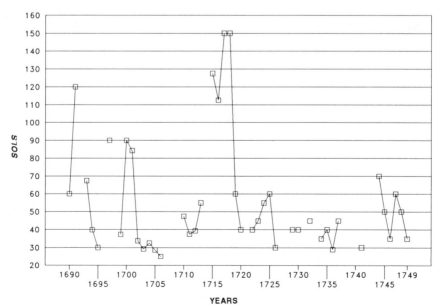

after the pronounced fluctuations during the period from 1690 to 1701 the price of wheat dropped and only started to go up again in 1708-09. Then in 1713 we find the same inflationary spiral. This economic movement began to slow down around 1719 and prices dropped rapidly. They stabilized later but sporadic bad harvests caused abrupt and spontaneous price rises. In short, the fluctuations in the price of wheat, as shown by the notaries and clerks in the inventories, faithfully followed the trends of the urban market.[15]

Products

Having made this observation, we may assume that the other prices listed in the inventories also adjusted to the realities of the marketplace. This is the advantage of the succession inventories: they focus upon many consumer goods. Initially, 31 products were retained;[16] but a low representation for some products led to an early weeding-out. All products whose prices were unknown for more than two-thirds of the period under study were eliminated which left 17 products (Table 69). Among these were not only colonial products but also imports such as silver, pepper, nutmeg, white sugar, candles, olive oil, cloves, vinegar and salt. Pepper, nutmeg and cloves were imported from India via France, but sugar came from the Caribbean. Silver, candles, olive oil, salt and vinegar were imported from France. As for tobacco, while it was domestic,[17] production was not limited exclusively to the immediate Québec area.

This broadened range of products allowed us to evaluate the effect of three situations on the various prices. First, there was the effect of a regional current through goods brought in essentially from the surrounding countryside; second, the effect of France's economy; and finally, that of intercolonial trade. Even though this range of products was found in most households, the lack of data for two-thirds of the years under consideration forced us to limit the range to nine products.

If we retain only those goods for which there are 30 annual price indications (silver, firewood, wheat, butter, salted lard, salt, flour, pepper and candles), the perspective of intercolonial trade moves somewhat into the background. But judging from their frequent annual appearance, the eight eliminated products do not seem to be among those used daily,

or at least needed daily in large quantities. Four of the nine products retained came from France (silver, salt, candles and pepper, which only
passed through in transit); the five others (wood, wheat, flour, butter
and lard) were produced regionally; and three of these (wood, butter and
lard) were not connected to the harvest.

Wheat and Flour

Without dwelling on the details of the products under consideration,
which would take too long to analyze, we should consider individual
trends in the prices of the main commodities. In the case of wheat,
available data made it possible to capture various situations brought
about by years of poor harvests. From 1690 to 1693 wheat was expensive, but in 1694-95 the prices fell dramatically (by almost 50%). They
rose abruptly in 1700-01 and then dropped by about 65% between 1702
and 1706. In short, during these first 16 years, the last decade of the
17th century coincided with numerous poor harvests; while after 1701
there were several good years observed.[18] Flour[19] followed the same
price trends.[20]

The upward trend observed by Hamelin in the Seminary's prices and
by Rousseau with regards to the Hôtel-Dieu Hospital prices was also
evident in the inventories, probably beginning in 1708. The fall in
prices probably began in 1719-20. A point to be noted is that the period
from 1714 to 1718 corresponded not only to a strong inflationary movement, but also to "mediocre" harvests, in the Intendant words.[21]

Since the colony had good harvests from 1719 to 1722, the prices of
wheat and flour fell. The drought of 1723 resulted in higher prices in
1724 and a mediocre harvest helped to keep them high during the following year. Subsequently, prices fell from 1726 to 1736, except for a
slight jump in 1736 after a mediocre harvest led to the fear of a famine;
that same year, there was a particularly deadly epidemic of smallpox. In
1737-38 very bad harvests led to a shortage and even an almost total
lack of supplies in the winter of 1737-38. This translated into a rise in
the price of wheat and flour in 1737, and a regrettable lack of data for
1738!

TABLE 69
ANNUAL PRICES OF VARIOUS COMMODITIES, 1690-1749
(in *livres*)

Year	Silver (mark)	Lard (lb.)	Flour (mt)	Wood (cord)	Wheat (mt)	Butter (lb.)	Salt (mt)	Pepper (lb.)	Candles (lb.)	Tallow (lb.)	Tobacco (lb.)	Peas (mt)	Nutmeg (lb.)	Cloves (lb.)	Rawsug (lb.)
1690	28.00		3.00		3.00							0.37			
1691	30.00			3.19	6.00	0.37						0.37	8.00	8.00	0.47
1692	33.00			3.75			3.00		0.45		0.75	3.00			
1693			3.75	3.19	3.38		2.25		0.39						
1694	29.25	0.30	1.87		2.00	0.34	2.25	1.87	0.94		1.05	1.08	7.50		
1695	26.63			3.56	1.50	0.26	2.62		0.45				7.50	7.50	0.75
1696															
1697	28.13	0.22	4.50	3.00	4.50				0.64		0.67				1.12
1698	30.00			3.47		0.30	2.81		0.37		1.42		10.50	10.50	0.75
1699	33.75		2.06	1.87	1.87				0.35		1.03		5.62	5.62	0.37
1700	27.00		4.50	3.75	4.50	0.41	1.50					3.00			
1701	30.94	0.22	4.42	3.56	4.22	0.36	1.50	1.46	0.37	0.20	0.37	1.87	8.25	9.00	
1702	30.00	0.21			1.69	0.19	1.60	1.12	0.45	0.26			8.25	8.25	0.56
1703	29.95	0.20	1.50	3.47	1.46	0.23	1.71	1.46	0.42	0.36	0.33	1.31	8.81	9.57	
1704	31.17	0.15	1.50	3.38	1.63	0.21	3.00	1.87				1.50	11.25	11.25	
1705	30.00	0.17	1.31	3.00	1.44										
1706	30.00	0.15	1.12		1.25	0.15	3.00	1.87	0.37		1.12	1.12	9.00	9.00	
1707	30.00			3.37											
1708															
1709	33.75	0.13	1.78	3.28		0.23	3.25	2.25		0.22		0.37			
1710	34.50	0.20	2.25	3.75	2.37	0.25	4.13	2.81	0.45	0.37	0.52	3.00	12.00	12.00	0.55
1711	35.70	0.21	2.44	3.19	1.87	0.30	3.38	2.69	0.51	0.34	0.37	1.87	15.00		
1712	41.25	0.23	1.78	4.13	1.97	0.37	3.75								
1713	37.00			3.19	2.75	0.37				0.37					
1714	61.88	0.45	4.69	4.50	6.38	0.62	15.00								
1715	57.45	0.37	6.75	7.50	5.63	0.87	9.60	6.50	1.03	3.00	0.85	4.88		36.00	0.75
1716	180.00		7.13	5.25	7.50	0.75	11.25	7.50	1.12	0.37				7.50	
1717	101.00				7.50	1.50	12.00	6.00	1.12		1.03		50.25	50.25	
1718	72.94	0.72	5.25	5.38	7.50	0.51		3.00		0.75		8.50	50.25		
1719	51.50	0.37	2.58	3.00	3.00	0.38		2.25	0.60	0.50					

TABLE 69 (con't 1)
ANNUAL PRICES OF VARIOUS COMMODITIES, 1690-1749
(in *livres*)

Year	Maple Sug. (lb)	White Sug. (lb)	Rice (lb)	Cinna. (lb)	Prunes (lb)	Eggs (12)	Saltbeef (lb)	Oats (mt)	Bran (mt)	Lamp oil (pot)	Olive oil (lb)	Vineg. (pot)	Eels (100)	Molas. (lb)	Choc. (lb)	Coffee (lb)
1690																
1691				3.00												
1692			0.37													
1693		0.82			0.02											
1694		0.75	0.22	7.50								0.45				
1695			0.19						0.30							
1696										0.75						
1697		0.82									0.67			1.05		
1698			0.22	10.50		0.30	0.22			0.60	0.52	0.56				
1699		0.67	0.17		0.30						0.32					
1700								1.12					6.00			
1701		0.45	0.19		0.11			1.12	0.75	1.12	0.49	0.56	5.25			
1702		0.75		6.00	0.13		0.09	0.82			0.37				1.12	
1703		1.12	0.19	10.50	0.13			0.75	0.43	0.75	0.83	0.66	3.00			3.75
1704	1.69	1.12					0.07	0.75				0.75	3.75			
1705	0.30															
1706	0.19	0.75						0.45				0.75				
1707																
1708																
1709	0.19							0.37	0.65							
1710	0.19	0.53	0.45	12.00				0.75	0.51	0.69	0.84	1.33	7.50		0.75	
1711				15.00				1.31	1.12		0.75	0.37				
1712									1.12			1.50	6.00			
1713										0.75	0.94					
1714																
1715	0.75	1.50						1.87	1.50				15.00	1.50		
1716				7.50		0.75										
1717	0.94	2.25		50.25					1.75			2.62	20.00			
1718							0.26									
1719							0.22							1.50		

TABLE 69 (con't 2)
ANNUAL PRICES OF VARIOUS COMMODITIES, 1690-1749
(in *livres*)

Year	Silver (mark)	Lard (lb.)	Flour (mt)	Wood (cord)	Wheat (mt)	Butter (lb.)	Salt (mt)	Pepper (lb.)	Candles (lb.)	Tallow (lb.)	Tobacco (lb.)	Peas (mt)	Nutmeg (lb.)	Cloves (lb.)	Raw sug. (lb.)
1720	40.00		2.00		2.00										
1721	48.67	0.22	2.00	2.50		0.50	2.00	3.50		0.40	0.50	2.00			
1722	60.00	0.20	2.00	3.00	2.00	0.30	2.50	2.50	0.50	0.75	0.18	2.00			0.40
1723	64.00		2.00	3.00	2.25			1.50		0.30		3.00	14.00		
1724	56.13	0.30	2.50	3.94	2.75	0.27	3.05	1.63	0.60	0.37	0.25		14.33	16.00	0.30
1725	43.13	0.20	2.50	3.50	3.00	0.40	1.50	1.50	0.50	0.37				12.00	
1726	40.88	0.20	1.75	4.25	1.50	0.25	2.75	1.38	0.50		0.20		16.00		
1727	40.00	0.18				0.30	2.00		0.50	0.30		2.00			
1728	40.00	0.15													
1729	43.25	0.31													0.15
1730	47.14	0.20	2.00	4.00	2.00	0.40	1.50		0.50	0.40	0.20				
1731	49.00	0.20		3.00		0.30		1.50	1.00		0.75				
1732	47.50	0.20	2.25	4.00	2.25	0.28	1.94	1.75	0.25			2.00			0.25
1733	48.43	0.29		3.00		0.28	2.50	1.83	0.42	0.25	0.25		8.00	8.00	0.37
1734	47.13	0.25	1.88	2.67	1.75	0.30	1.75	1.33	0.45	0.30		2.50	8.50	9.00	
1735	47.29	0.22	1.50	3.00	2.00	0.30	2.00	1.50	0.50	0.25					
1736	47.86	0.15	1.50	4.00	1.45		2.67			0.25	0.20				0.10
1737	49.71	0.20		3.00	2.25		3.00				0.30				
1738	46.00							1.50	0.37						
1739	47.14	0.15	1.50	3.69		0.20	3.00								
1740	48.50	0.15				0.25		1.30	0.35	0.29	0.12	2.00	6.00		
1741	48.40	0.14			1.50	0.32	2.00			0.30	0.25	2.00			
1742	47.56		2.50	3.50		0.25	1.90			0.30		4.00			
1743	48.67	0.25		3.50		0.15	1.50	1.50	0.60	0.33			5.00	5.00	0.10
1744	47.25	0.28	3.00	3.00	3.50	0.40									
1745	48.00	0.23	2.63		2.50	0.25	1.69	1.25			0.05		8.00	9.00	
1746	48.33	0.34	2.00	4.50	1.75	0.43	4.42	2.50	0.33		0.35		10.00	6.50	
1747	49.31	0.36	2.83	4.67	3.00	0.50	5.38	6.00		0.50	0.30				0.25
1748	45.33	0.63		6.22	2.50		2.00	2.00		0.50					0.38
1749	48.00	0.29		6.71	1.75	0.35	1.75	1.00	0.60	0.36	0.20	3.00	12.00	12.00	0.20

TABLE 69 (con't 3)

ANNUAL PRICES OF VARIOUS COMMODITIES, 1690-1749

(in *livres*)

Year	Maple Sug. (lb)	White Sug. (lb)	Rice (lb)	Cinna. (lb)	Prunes (lb)	Eggs (12)	Saltbeef (lb)	Oats (mt)	Bran (mt)	Lamp oil (pot)	Olive oil (lb)	Vineg. (pot)	Eels (100)	Molas. (lb)	Choc. (lb)	Coffee (lb)
1720	0.40															
1721		1.00								1.00	1.00	1.00				
1722								0.88	0.50	0.60	1.25				1.00	
1723								0.75	0.40			0.75				
1724			0.40	12.50					0.75		0.90		7.50			4.00
1725				12.00												
1726	0.30	0.95			0.26								6.50	0.65		
1727		1.00														
1728																
1729																
1730		0.75	0.40								0.75					
1731	0.25	0.65									0.30				1.00	3.00
1732		0.60									0.88	0.40	4.00			
1733		0.40	0.09	6.50	0.50						0.75					
1734			0.35	8.00				0.50	0.75		0.50		6.00			3.00
1735									0.75	0.75		0.50				2.00
1736									0.75							
1737																
1738								0.75								0.60
1739																
1740											0.50		9.00			0.63
1741		0.25							1.50			0.75	7.00			1.00
1742								1.00		0.63		0.30	6.25	0.50		
1743	0.25				0.50		0.10					0.40	10.00			
1744		0.25								0.80				0.60		
1745			0.16		0.15						0.75				2.00	
1746				7.00		0.18		0.97		0.58		1.75	3.00	1.00		
1747		0.25		7.00				1.50		0.42		1.25			2.00	1.00
1748		0.50									0.75					0.95
1749		0.25	0.20	6.00		0.37			0.25	0.79	0.50	0.63			1.13	1.50

Other bad harvests were observed between 1741 and 1744. This inevitably had an impact on the prices recorded by the clerks; the prices of wheat and flour take into account the situation prevailing at the time the succession inventory was taken. Certainly, the variations only affect average annual prices and not quarterly or monthly prices; but it still remains true that there were strong fluctuations. In this respect they only bear witness to a demand met by production that was too often deficient or uncertain.

Lard

But does this mean that the prices of all the products evolved in a similar fashion, except during the years of "inflationary upheaval?"[22] As far as lard is concerned, while its price dropped from 1703 to 1706, we should emphasize that it only went down by about 20%. Its vertiginous rise began in 1710, two years after the rise in wheat prices; and then plateaued in 1718 at the same time as wheat did. Whereas during the 1720s, lard dropped back to considerably lower prices, production seems to have been lower at the end of this decade and at the beginning of the next one, since prices reached new heights in 1729 and in 1733-34. Was there a production crisis, a crisis due to an excess of exports[23] or one due to some illness? Nothing for the moment makes it possible to say. Furthermore, prices went back to "normal" and only started to go up again in 1743, and then more rapidly between 1746 and 1748.

Thus lard followed almost the same trends as wheat. However, lard prices reacted more slowly to the economic situation since there was a shift of one year between the wheat and lard curves. The only notable exception to the similarities between the two curves was the increases in the price of lard that took place between 1729 and 1734.

Firewood

The data on firewood do not mention the types of wood; moreover, these only rarely appear on the notarized documents for the period under consideration. A cord of wood represented quite a stable expense which was not subject to the whims of harvests or illnesses. Therefore, except for 1699, the price remained between three and four *livres* per cord until 1713. It reached a plateau in 1715 and then fell slowly until 1718. In 1719 and later, the price returned to the level it had been at the end of the 17th century, except for 1724, 1726, 1730, 1732 and 1736, when prices showed an increase of about 33%. Starting in 1746, the price of a cord of wood increased considerably every year; in 1748, it climbed by 33%.

Some of these price increases were due to demographic phenomena, for example, the epidemic of smallpox in 1732 or the mortality crisis in 1748. The others are still unexplained. In spite of these fluctuations a cord of wood remained a relatively stable consumer product throughout the period, except for the two inflationary upsurges of 1714-19 and 1746-48.

Butter

Despite the fact that it is a dairy product, butter prices followed the same trends as wheat prices until 1719. However, they reached a peak in 1717 and then fell abruptly beginning in the following year. Subsequently, butter showed relatively stable prices until 1739, except for three peaks in 1721, 1725 and 1730. It started to rise in 1740 and stabilized in 1743, only to jump again more markedly. All in all, the price of butter fluctuated by periods. For example, although high at the end of the 17th century, it fell during the first decade of the following century; and then, like the other products, started an inflationary upsurge in 1708-09; this phenomenon ended in 1718. The price of butter remained stable for nearly another 20 years. Only the last decade remains unexplained; but since butter contains salt perhaps we should refer to this product in order to find some answers.

In all, local or regional products reacted in accordance with a pace that depended upon certain climatic or demographic currents (internal migration) that influenced the regional situation in a particular fashion. Thus, we have to refer to an evaluation of imported products to be able to "measure" the effect of an external situation on the domestic market.

Salt

Salt was imported from France or occasionally from Labrador, and its price reacted differently from that of regional products. From a modestly high price during the War of the League of Augsburg its value fell starting in 1700 and then rose by about 75% in 1705 as the result of the pressures due to the War of the Spanish Succession. It remained at this level until the end of the war, and until the Navy Treasurer decided during the following year to cut by 50% the value of the Canadian currency.

This decision was a dramatic one since it led to a 300% increase in the price of a *minot* of salt. Salt, an essential element in the conservation process, became almost inaccessible. Over the next three years the price of salt stabilized, but at much higher levels than previously. "Normal" prices did not return until 1719. It was maintained, except for a few jumps between 1736 and 1739, at a level of 2.5 *livres* per *minot* until 1746. In 1746 and 1747 Québec experienced a salt shortage; therefore, the Colonial Administrator sent up to six ships per year to Newfoundland to buy supplies from fishermen.[24] This temporary shortage caused an increase in prices of about 160% the first year. Nevertheless, throughout the period Québec could count upon relatively stable supplies.

In short, imported products, subject to their own situation, reacted differently from local products; but, does this mean that all imported products reacted in the same way as salt?

Candles

The price of a pound of imported candles was surprisingly stable until 1713. Except for 1694 and 1697, the price stayed at eight to nine *sols* per pound. Perhaps this was due to competition from domestic candles, made out of tallow; since, although the price followed the same trend as all the other products from 1714 to 1718, the increase was only 100%. On the other hand, the prices stabilized after 1719 but at a higher level than at the end of the 17th century. There was an increase of about 20% in the price of a pound of candles in the last 30 years. In 1732, there was a large upswing when the cost was twice as much. Thus, candles do not meet the same criteria as salt when the time comes to study the economic situation.

Pepper

Although it was imported from the East Indies, this spice went through France in transit before arriving in the colony. The evolution in its prices was similar to that of its sister product salt. From a relatively high price, almost two *livres* per pound during the last decade of the 17th century, pepper was an interesting purchase at the beginning of the next century, at slightly over one *livre* per pound. Starting in 1704, the difficulties involved in getting supplies due to the war, sent the price back up to the level it had been during the previous war. Subsequently, it continued to climb to reach a plateau of 7.5 *livres* in 1716.

The drop in prices began in 1718, and in 1723 pepper stabilized at about 1.5 *livres* per pound. It was not until the War of the Spanish Succession, when the opponents confronted each other on the battlefield, that one could observe the effects of the situation in the home country on the price of pepper in the colony. In 1746, pepper sold in Québec for twice as much as the previous year and by the following year, it was two and a half times this amount. In short, in the space of two years, the unit price of this spice increased by 380%.

Salt and pepper followed similar trends until the years of high inflation from 1714 to 1719; subsequently the prices of these two spices followed different courses, with the price of pepper showing greater stability. However, the war produced the same inflationary effect on the two products, salt was less affected (only a 218% increase over the two years), perhaps because of the decision by colonial authorities to call upon Labrador's resources.

Imported products must be evaluated taking into account the situation in France, especially the political situation. The periods of war led to a strong upward pressure on prices because it was difficult for ships to navigate on the high seas. The only exception to this rule was candles. This imported product, which was used daily, still had to compete with domestic production. So its price followed a different course from that of spices, which did not have any competition.

Silver

Silver showed the greatest stability of all the products analyzed. It was a highly durable good and this characteristic led to its specific price evolution. Although some might reject this product as being non-representative, not sought-after and thus impossible to evaluate on the basis of popular demand, we should remember that silver was the product most often mentioned in the succession inventories at 40%. Given that these documents referred to almost 30% of the deceased adult population of Québec, we can assume that silver represented an important symbolic acquisition for a good part of Québec's population. The small artisan who owned a silver goblet cared as much about it as Jean Valjean did about his candlesticks in *Les Miserables*.

In a context where Canada's fictitious currency was subject to significant devaluation without the population knowing precisely when, silver was a sure bet. Evaluated by weight and not on how it was worked, it became a guarantee of security (although relative) for the middle and upper classes of the population; it provided a possible answer to the insecurity caused by the rumours that spread from one citizen to another in Québec. This at least is the interpretation suggested by the price curve for silver (Graph 13, Chapter 6).

While the price of silver had remained around 30 *livres* per mark (245 g) since the beginning of the War of the League of Augsburg, starting in 1708-09, it began to rise slowly but surely. The devaluation announced by the Navy Treasurer in 1714 marked the beginning of the inflationary spiral. In one year the price of precious metals increased 67%. Two years later it reached unequalled heights: 180 *livres* per mark or an increase of 386% in three years. Then prices began to fall. During the 1720s silver showed significant fluctuations. Even though efforts were made to stabilize its price, this was only achieved again around 1730. But the "inflationary upheaval" left its mark: while silver stabilized at 48 *livres* per mark, this represented an increase of 60% with relation to the end of the 17th century.

In short, whether it was a regional or imported good, each commodity reacted differently depending upon whether it was a harvested or manufactured
product and was transported over a long haul or a short distance. Climatic,
demographic, political, and economic factors all affected, each in their own
fashion, the products sold to consumers in Québec in the 18th century.

Nonetheless, several crucial periods should be emphasized, during
which two or more of these factors combined to produce price increases
or decreases. First, the period covering the War of the League of
Augsburg and the beginning of the War of the Spanish Succession; that
is, 1690 to 1706, stands out. While the first years in this period were
marked by numerous price jumps, prices fell during the last few years.
The poor harvests and problems with importing caused by the war can
explain the upward fluctuations at the beginning of the period. Starting
in 1697 there were problems with the fur trade, which led to the failure
of the Compagnie de la Colonie in 1705. On the demographic level, the
smallpox epidemic in 1702-03 caused a mortality crisis; and all these
factors had a definite effect on the levels of consumer prices, which
mostly fell considerably between 1702 and 1706.

Starting in 1707-08, the prices of several products were on the rise.
This upswing was maintained by the Navy Treasurer's decision to re-
deem Canadian currency at only 50% of its 1714 value. The consequence of this was to fuel the inflationary spiral, which evened out only
at the beginning of 1720, when the term "Canadian currency" "disappeared." Subsequently, prices took several years to stabilize; until about
1725. This long interval was broken up into two distinct phases; 1707-
08 to 1713-14, and from this date until 1725-26.

From 1707 to 1714, the war stimulated the urban and regional economies.
The government invested massively in public works and, like harbour captain
and merchant Louis Prat, individuals invested in shipbuilding. However, it
was more difficult for imports to arrive in the capital. The Treaty of Utrecht,
which ended the war, may have been good news on the political level. On the
economic level, however, the war effort had left the coffers bare and an enormous public debt in both the kingdom and the colony.

This situation partly justified the Navy Treasurer's decision to devalu-
ate; this decision, in turn, led to uncertainty among the residents of Québec respecting their currency rates. Consequently, in order to protect
themselves against any erosion of their purchasing power, everyone in-

GRAPH 15

COST OF LIVING BASED ON 9 PRODUCTS
QUÉBEC, 1690-1749

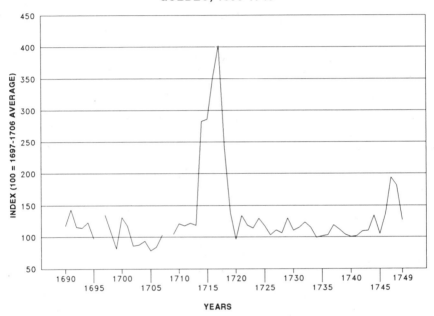

creased their prices. The uncertainty lasted three full years so that when
the devaluation was finally announced, merchants and producers had to
adjust their prices to take the new reality into account.

From 1726-27 until the end of the 1730s, prices remained relatively
stable despite the commercial and economic effervescence that characterized activities in the capital during this period. The only dark spot
was the smallpox epidemic, which led to a new mortality crisis.

Poor harvests from 1737 to 1744 affected the price structure only
slightly, except for the price of wheat. Later, the war and the massive
investments it provoked on the part of the government, together with the
inevitable difficulties concerning supplies, caused a new inflationary
outburst between 1745 and 1749, the last year included in this study.

Compiling a Price Index

Having identified these products, as well as their price movements, we can construct an index that depends upon the movement of all of these different prices. There are several ways to proceed; statisticians and economists manage by multiplying the statistical operations on a single product or a series of products as weighted by their importance in terms of their use by the average household. While this method is valid in the case of modern-day needs, it becomes difficult to apply to historical data, if only in terms of identifying a weight factor that takes into account the use or annual production of that product. Furthermore, would this weighting operation considerably modify the data? Paquet and Wallot answer this question in the negative.[25]

Since this is the case, we must use the formula of the relative price; that is, the price of a product for the year under consideration, divided by the base price for the same product.[26] While the first element does not present any problems, the second becomes more difficult to identify. The debate gravitates around the price during the base year: should we use a single year or several years? Choosing a decade allows us to eliminate any sudden movements in the situation and level the playing field. But which decade should we choose? Taking our data into account, the period from 1697 to 1706 seems to be the most appropriate on the basis of several criteria.

The first criterion, the economic and political circumstances, must be chosen so that we do not let the war affect price movements too much, and they remain relatively stable. The period chosen is divided equally between times of peace and times of war. Second, it is important to respect the existing data: thus, for the base price, we must have an annual price seven out of ten times for each product. Only two decades come close to meeting these criteria: the period retained and 1730-39; during the first (1697-1706) the criterion applies for all the products, except pepper.[27] Thus it corresponds more closely to the criteria set. The average price of each of the products during this decade thus became the base price.

Once we have done this, it is possible to obtain a relative price index. We have only to add the quotient resulting from the division of the annual price by the base price of each of the products; then, to divide it by the number of observations; and finally to multiply the result by a factor of 100.[28] Graph 15 shows the compiled relative index for the nine prod-

GRAPH 16

COST OF LIVING BASED ON 17 PRODUCTS
QUÉBEC, 1690-1749

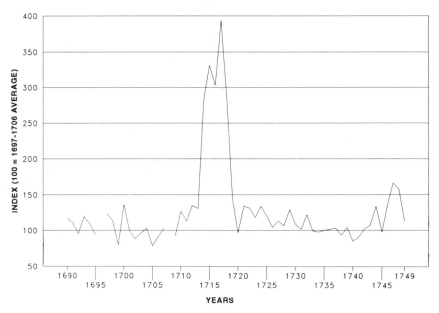

ucts mentioned for the period between 1690 and 1749. Several observations can be made. Apart from the strong inflationary thrust during 1714-18, which has already been well established, this phenomenon reappeared only at the end of the War of the Austrian Succession.[29] Furthermore, the base decade was the only one during which, in some years, the cost of living was below the 100 index; in short, these were years when it cost less to live in Québec.[30] It was during these same years that the price of wheat (Hamelin) was at its lowest.

This parallel between the general price index and the price of wheat sold by the Seminary was not limited to this decade alone. The curves show remarkable homogeneity; besides, the upsurge from 1714 to 1719 showed that similar phenomena were taking place at the same times. All this would lead one to believe that the clerks used wheat as an evaluation scale, or even better, that they had shops themselves, which in

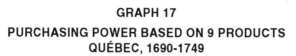

GRAPH 17

PURCHASING POWER BASED ON 9 PRODUCTS
QUÉBEC, 1690-1749

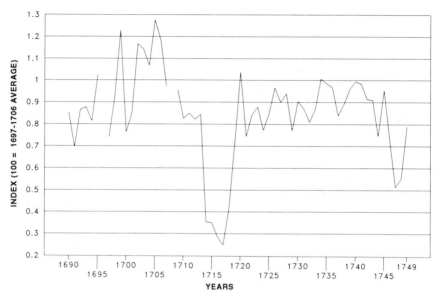

some cases was actually true. In short, this curve of the cost of living indices confirms the curve for the price of wheat compiled by Hamelin.

It is also important to point out that if the wider range of 17 products had been chosen it would not have upset the index curves too much;[31] although there would have been a few annual adjustments. However, the base period would still be the one during which the cost of living was lowest; the years of high inflation remained the same (from 1714 to 1719 and 1746 to 1748). On the other hand, the cost of living stabilized during the 1730s, after the previous decade had so to speak played the role of filter for the inflationary residues. But this period of calm was fleeting; the War of the Austrian Succession inevitably brought about effects on prices (Graph 16).

Graph 15, which illustrates the cost of living from 1690 to 1706, shows that on the whole prices tended to fall, except for 1691 and 1701-02. This period overall corresponds to a movement of deflation; while from 1707 to 1713, the residents of Québec felt the effects of inflation as they did in 1745-49. The period from 1726 to 1736 appears to have been one of "relative stability" just like the period from 1737 to 1744. According to the graph though, the years from 1714 to 1726 appear to be highly inflationary. What was the reason for this situation?

The buying power of Québec citizens seems to have been rapidly eroded between 1714 and 1720.[32] The 1717 *livre* was only worth one quarter of its value or 5 *sols*. This was the true value of the monetary unit; the difference (15 *sols* or 300%) would correspond to a value added to face the increase in costs (Table 70 and Graph 17). Along the same lines, the 1690 *livre* was only worth 17 *sols*; and the 1748 *livre* was only worth 11. Still we cannot measure inflation for a given period using this criteria; for the period between 1714 and 1720, the rate of inflation for the goods under consideration, without taking into account the 62.5% devaluation of currency, was 1.77% or 0.25% per year.[33] For the whole period between 1714 and 1725, the annual rate of inflation was 7.7%, taking the devaluation into account. When considered separately, this rate of inflation drops to 2.31%. According to Table 70, the rate of inflation for the period from 1690 to 1706 changed into one of deflation since consumer prices dropped at a rate of 2.24% annually. For the subsequent period (1707-13), there was an increase in the cost of living of about 7% per year. Between 1726 and 1744, residents of Québec experienced annual decreases of 0.64% in prices; while between 1737 and 1744, they climbed by 3.7% per year. Between 1745 and 1749, prices rose at a rate of 5.9% per year and this trend continued afterwards.

These figures are surprising since they challenge the traditional interpretation which sees the rebirth of maritime trade as ensuring a certain prosperity for Québec. It is undeniable that there was some prosperity, but we must qualify and limit this statement. First, we should emphasize the deflationary and inflationary swings, which translated into socio-economic movements: "Inflation is supposed to reduce unemployment, deflation to cause it to go up," writes John Garraty.[34] Inflation means increased demand and deflation means the opposite. While economic development is created by deflation, deflation implies unemployment or at least under-employment. Shipbuilding and intercolonial trade were born or rather reborn once inflation was controlled; thus, returns were not eaten up by inflation. Prosperity also implies a certain magnetism: newcomers flock in; competition keeps salaries low, and productivity increases, but on the other hand incomes decrease.

This consideration of the work force represents the reflections of numerous thinkers in the 17th and 18th centuries: there could not be too many workers because prosperity derived from work. But the corollary, as Arthur Young wrote: "Everyone but an idiot knows that the lower classes must be kept poor or they will never be industrious."[35] In 1710 when Raudot defended the idea of competition,[36] he was reflecting a new type of thinking on political economy. Thirty years later, one of his successors, Hocquart, expressed serious reservations about extreme competition.[37] As early as 1732, thus in the middle of a boom period, the same Hocquart wrote to Maurepas that the colony was on the road to ruin unless it was rescued by public funds.[38] Under-employment was being felt sharply. All in all, the boom of 1727-30 created a lot of hope, but few expectations were actually fulfilled.

This economic movement was accompanied by a movement of men as is confirmed by the rates of population growth.[39] The only exception to this rule was the period from 1727 to 1736 when the capital posted its greatest growth. Here again, the formula reads as follows: many are called, few are chosen and some remember after a while that they still have links that call them back to their original parishes. Already, during 1714 and 1720, the strong inflationist surge had pushed more than one citizen outside the city limits.

A final phenomenon arises from our analysis of inflation in Québec in the 18th century. And Hocquart's statement already points in this direction: the importance of government intervention to stimulate the economy. The only two periods during which the economy in Québec showed signs of full employment, 1707-13 and 1745-49, correspond to years when public expenditures were growing quickly. Between 1706 and 1713, the government spent at least 250 000 *livres* on the construction of defensive works, and this sum amounted to over 750 000 *livres* between 1745 and 1749.[40] In short, the government was the force behind and the best stimulus for growth of the urban economy. This aspect of Hocquart's reasoning on political economy, in which he gives us to understand that the government must favour the rise of an independent Canadian business-class nevertheless marks a return to the debate of the

TABLE 70
ANNUAL PRICE INDEX, QUÉBEC, 1690-1749
(in *livres*)

Year	Silver quot. 1 30.09	Lard quot. 2 0.187	Flour quot. 3 2.614	Wood quot. 4 3.186	Wheat quot. 5 2.505	Butter quot. 6 0.2621	Salt quot. 7 2.159	Pepper quot. 8 1.5564	Candles quot. 9 0.424	Average	Composite Index	Annual Inflation Rate	Purchasing Power	Average Inflation Rate
1690	0.930				1.197					1.173	117.26		0.853	
1691	0.996		1.147	0.999	2.395	1.4114				1.434	143.41	22.31	0.697	
1692	0.996			1.176	1.347		1.389		1.061	1.156	115.61	-19.39	0.865	
1693	1.096		1.434	0.999	0.797		1.042		0.919	1.140	114.00	-1.40	0.877	
1694	0.971	1.600	0.715		0.598	1.2779	1.042	1.2014	2.216	1.228	122.79	7.72	0.814	
1695	0.884			1.117		0.9918	1.213		1.061	0.978	97.79	-20.36	1.023	
1696														
1697	0.934	1.173	1.721	0.941	1.796	1.1444	1.301		1.509	1.346	134.62		0.743	
1698	0.996			1.088					0.872	1.081	108.07	-19.72	0.925	
1699	1.121		0.788	0.586	0.746				0.825	0.814	81.37	-24.71	1.229	-2.24 (1691-1706)
1700	0.897		1.721	1.176	1.796	1.5640	0.694			1.308	130.84	60.80	0.764	
1701	1.028	1.173	1.692	1.117	1.683	1.3542	0.694	0.9380	0.872	1.173	117.27	-10.37	0.853	
1702	0.996	1.093		1.088	0.674	0.7120	0.738	0.7196	1.061	0.857	85.67	-26.95	1.167	
1703	0.995	1.050	0.573	1.059	0.583	0.8710	0.791	0.9393	0.985	0.875	87.55	2.19	1.142	
1704	1.035	0.800	0.573	0.941	0.648	0.7820	1.389	1.2014		0.936	93.63	6.95	1.068	
1705	0.996	0.907	0.501		0.573					0.784	78.40	-16.27	1.275	
1706	0.996	0.800	0.428			0.5722	1.389	1.2014	0.872	0.845	84.49	7.76	1.184	
1707	0.996			1.057	0.497					1.027	102.73	21.59	0.973	
1708														
1709	1.121	0.693	0.680	1.029		0.8583	1.505	1.4456		1.048	104.78		0.954	
1710	1.146	1.049	0.860	1.176	0.947	0.9346	1.910	1.8054	1.061	1.210	121.03	15.51	0.826	7.009 (1707-1713)
1711	1.186	1.093	0.932	1.000	0.747	1.1444	1.563	1.7251	1.191	1.176	117.59	-2.84	0.850	
1712	1.370	1.227	0.679	1.294	0.784	1.4114	1.736			1.215	121.50	3.32	0.823	
1713	1.229			0.999	1.096	1.4114				1.184	118.42	-2.53	0.844	
1714	2.056	2.401	1.792	1.412		2.3651	6.946	4.1763	2.429	2.829	282.89	138.88	0.353	
1715	1.909	1.974	2.582	2.353	2.544	3.3315	4.445	4.8188	2.641	2.861	286.08	1.13	0.350	
1716	5.981		2.725	1.647	2.245	2.8610	5.210	3.8550	2.641	3.516	351.64	22.92	0.284	
1717	3.356				2.993	5.7220	5.557			4.021	402.10	14.35	0.249	
1718	2.423	3.859	2.008	1.686	2.993	1.9327		1.9275		2.405	240.46	-40.20	0.416	
1719	1.711	1.974	0.988	0.941	1.197	1.4305		1.4456	1.415	1.388	138.80	-42.28	0.720	

TABLE 70 (Con't)
ANNUAL PRICE INDEX, QUÉBEC, 1690-1749
(in *livres*)

Year	Silver quot. 1 30.09	Lard quot. 2 0.187	Flour quot. 3 2.614	Wood quot. 4 3.186	Wheat quot. 5 2.505	Butter quot. 6 0.2621	Salt quot. 7 2.159	Pepper quot. 8 1.5564	Candles quot. 9 0.424	Average	Composite Index	Annual Inflation Rate	Purchasing Power	Average Inflation Rate
1720	1.329		0.765		0.798					0.964	96.42	-30.53	1.037	7.713 (1714-1725)
1721	1.617	1.156	0.765	0.784		1.9073	0.926	2.2487		1.344	134.36	39.35	0.744	includes 62.5%
1722	1.993	1.067	0.765	0.941	0.798	1.1444	1.157	1.6062	1.179	1.184	118.37	-11.90	0.845	devaluation
1723	2.126		0.765	0.941	0.898			0.9637		1.139	113.90	-3.78	0.878	
1724	1.865	1.600	0.956	1.237	1.097	1.0172	1.412	1.0440	1.415	1.294	129.40	13.61	0.773	
1725	1.433	1.067	0.956	1.098	1.197	1.5258	1.273	0.9637	1.179	1.178	117.77	-8.99	0.849	
1726	1.358	1.067	0.669	1.333	0.598	0.9536	0.926	0.8834	1.179	1.035	103.53	-12.09	0.966	
1727	1.329	0.978				1.1444			1.179	1.111	111.15	7.36	0.900	
1728	1.329	0.800								1.065	106.48	-4.20	0.939	
1729	1.437	1.654								1.297	129.65	21.77	0.771	
1730	1.566	1.067	0.765	1.255	0.798	1.5258	0.694	0.9637	1.179	1.107	110.65	-14.65	0.904	-0.64 (1726-1736)
1731	1.628	1.067		0.941		1.1444				1.149	114.90	3.84	0.870	
1732	1.578	1.067	0.860	1.255	0.898	1.0490	0.897	1.1243	2.358	1.232	123.21	7.23	0.812	
1733	1.609	1.547		0.941		1.0490	1.157	1.1779	0.589	1.153	115.32	-6.40	0.867	
1734	1.565	1.333	0.717	0.836	0.698	1.1444	0.810	0.8513	0.982	0.994	99.35	-13.85	1.007	
1735	1.571	1.156	0.573	0.941	0.798	1.1444	0.926	0.9637	1.061	1.015	101.52	2.18	0.985	
1736	1.590	0.818	0.573	1.255	0.578		1.234		1.179	1.033	103.29	1.75	0.968	
1737	1.652	1.067		0.941	0.898		1.389			1.190	118.96	15.17	0.841	
1738	1.528									1.122	112.17	-5.71	0.892	
1739	1.566	0.800	0.573	1.157		0.7629	1.389	0.9637	0.872	1.042	104.17	-7.13	0.960	
1740	1.611	0.800				0.9536	0.926	0.8352	0.825	1.005	100.53	-3.50	0.995	
1741	1.608	0.746				1.2079	0.879			1.018	101.77	1.23	0.983	3.760 (1737-1743)
1742	1.580		0.956	1.098	0.598	0.9536	0.694	0.9637		1.094	109.37	7.47	0.914	
1743	1.617	1.333		1.098		0.5722			1.415	1.099	109.93	0.51	0.910	
1744	1.570	1.467	1.147	0.941	1.397	1.5258	0.780	0.8031		1.342	134.16	22.04	0.745	
1745	1.595	1.200	1.004		0.997	0.9536	2.045	1.6062	0.766	1.048	104.78	-21.90	0.954	
1746	1.606	1.814	0.765	1.412	0.698	1.6212	2.489	3.8550		1.371	137.06	30.81	0.730	
1747	1.638	1.920	1.083	1.464	1.197	1.9073		1.2850		1.945	194.46	41.88	0.514	5.979 (1744-1749)
1748	1.506	3.334		1.952	0.997					1.815	181.52	-6.65	0.551	
1749	1.595	1.520		2.105	0.698	1.3351	0.810	0.6425	1.415	1.265	126.53	-30.30	0.790	

previous century on the subject of the government's role in the economy.[41]

*****

This analysis of inflation in Québec in the first half of the 18th century has made it possible to identify six different phases in the capital's economic cycle. From 1690 to 1706 consumer prices fell. They increased from 1707 to 1713. The increase in the cost of living slowed down after 1713, although prices continued to rise. From 1727 to 1736, prices fell slightly and began to increase again after 1737, modestly until 1744, and then more rapidly. These price movements coincided with the movement of men looking for employment.

The period of deflation experienced by Québec in the middle of an era of "prosperity" does not mean, however, that this prosperity did not occur, on the contrary; but the movement turned out to be very limited. It lasted from 1727 to 1731 as shown by the movement in building[42] and in land grants.[43] Subsequently the economic cycle was only stimulated sparingly. This was the background for Hocquart's distress signal in 1732.

While Québec experienced a drop in consumer prices between 1727 and 1736, this phenomenon did not arise spontaneously. It began at the end of the war in 1713, as soon as the government ceased investing massively in public construction; and the monetary crisis only served to accentuate the recession (should we say depression?) As a result, this emphasizes the importance of the welfare state in stimulating the economy.

APPENDIX C
DISTRIBUTION OF HEADS OF HOUSEHOLDS BY DISTRICTS AND STREETS, AND BY PROFESSION, 1716 AND 1744

Street	Total		Services		Business		Artisan		Unskilled	
	1716	1744	1716	1744	1716	1744	1716	1744	1716	1744
Upper Town										
Depuis le fort		12		4		3		4		1
Grison		10		1		4		2		3
Carrières	2	10	0	0	1	1	1	7	0	2
Saint-Louis	45	37	13	12	4	10	19	12	9	3
Jardins	5	11	3	3	0	3	2	4	0	1
Buade	8	28	4	10	3	10	1	7	0	1
Sainte-Anne	13	20	4	4	2	7	7	5	0	4
Trésor	2	0	0	0	1	0	1	0	0	0
Fabrique	11	12	4	6	2	4	4	2	1	0
Saint-Jean	7	73	1	3	3	20	2	35	1	15
Pauvres		21		4		9		7		1
Rempart		8		1		3		3		1
Saint-Joseph		23		3		6		12		2
Couillard	17	27	5	3	1	4	5	12	6	8
Nouvelle		15		3		4		8		0
Saint-Flavien		9		0		0		5		4
Saint-François		16		2		5		4		5
Sainte-Famille	7	19	2	5	0	2	3	9	2	3
Voisine Sainte-Famille		1		0		0		0		1
Rempart		8		1		2		3		2
Lavallée		7		1		0		3		3
	117	367	36	66	17	97	45	144	19	60

DISTRIBUTION OF HEADS OF HOUSEHOLDS
BY DISTRICTS AND STREETS, AND BY PROFESSION, 1716 AND 1744

Street	Total		Services		Business		Artisan		Unskilled	
	1716	1744	1716	1744	1716	1744	1716	1744	1716	1744
Palace										
Saint-Nicolas	14	22	3	8	2	5	7	7	2	2
Saint-Roch		11		2		2		6		1
Saint-Vallier		26		2		7		11		6
Saint-Charles		56		5		9		36		6
Canoterie	1	0	1	0	0	0	0	0	0	0
subtotal	15	115	4	17	2	23	7	60	2	15
Lower Town										
Sault-au-Matelot	39	68	8	6	13	26	12	29	6	7
Champlain		55		6		16		20		13
De Meulle	40	42	4	4	16	17	19	20	1	1
Escalier		10		0		1		9		0
Cul-de-sac	20	25	2	1	12	19	6	3	0	2
Sous-le-fort	37	26	8	1	21	16	6	8	2	1
Saint-Pierre		33		7		23		3		0
Notre-Dame	20	19	6	4	12	15	2	0	0	0
Place Royale		11		1		10		0		0
Côte de la Montagne	26	43	5	9	3	10	16	22	2	2
subtotal	182	332	33	39	77	153	61	114	11	26
Total (city)	314	814	73	122	96	273	113	318	32	101

APPENDIX D
1716 CENSUS

Street	Households		Population			Adults					Children				Servants		Live-ins	
	No.	%	Pers.	%	Pers./Hou.	Men No.	Men Age	Women No.	Women Age	Adult/Hou.	Boys	Girls	Chi./Hou.	Age?	No.	Ser./Hou.	No.	Ser./Hou.
Upper Town																		
Carrières	3	0.65	24	1.05	8.000	2	46.000	3	34.330	1.67	12	5	5.67	2	0	0	0	0
Saint-Louis	47	10.22	244*	10.72	5.190	45	42.840	47	34.520	1.96	65	72	2.91	5	8	0.170	0	0
Jardins	10	2.17	45	1.98	4.500	9	39.875	11	37.200	2.00	14	11	2.50	0	0	0	0	0
Sainte-Anne	14	3.04	74	3.25	5.290	14	42.770	14	37.540	2.00	19	24	3.07	0	3	0.210	0	0
Buade	9	1.96	52*	2.28	5.770	9	54.875	11	42.250	2.00	14	12	2.89	0	5	0.550	0	0
Trésor	3	0.65	14	0.61	4.670	3	38.330	3	29.660	2.00	5	3	2.67	0	0	0	0	0
Fabrique	16	3.48	70*	3.07	4.375	9	45.500	13	40.850	1.375	21	18	2.44	3	5	0.310	0	0
Saint-Jean	8	1.74	32*	1.41	4.000	7	36.860	9	39.875	2.00	5	7	1.50	0	3	0.375	0	0
Sainte-Famille	7	1.52	44	1.93	6.290	7	47.290	7	41.710	2.00	18	12	4.29	0	0	0	0	0
Couillard	19	4.13	108	4.74	5.680	19	47.190	21	40.050	2.00	33	35	3.58	0	0	0	0	0
	136	29.56	707	31.06	5.200	124	44.090	139	37.570	1.88	206	199	3.02	10	24	0.18	0	0
PalaceQuarter																		
Saint-Nicolas	21	4.56	129	5.67	6.140	22	41.450	24	34.680	2.20	35	45	3.20	1	2	0.09	0	0
Canoterie	2	0.43	17	0.75	8.500	2	45.000	1	40.000	1.50	7	4	5.50	0	3	1.50	0	0
	23	5.00	146	6.41	6.350	24	41.750	25	34.910	2.13	42	49	3.96	1	5	0.22	0	0
Lower Town																		
Sault-au-Matelot	79	17.17	384*	16.87	4.860	76	39.400	74	34.860	1.90	104	104	2.63	5	20	0.25	0	0
Côte de la Montagne	27	5.87	163*	7.16	6.040	28	39.000	30	32.590	2.00	46	45	3.52	1	11	0.40	1	0.04
Notre-Dame	28	6.09	149	6.55	5.320	24	41.000	30	33.500	1.86	34	35	2.54	0	25	0.90	1	0.04
De Meulle and Champlain	81	17.61	334	14.67	4.120	70	39.400	75	34.450	1.79	89	92	2.23	6	2	0.02	0	0
Cul-de-sac	31	6.74	159	6.98	5.130	31	41.430	30	38.700	1.97	39	47	2.77	0	12	0.38	0	0
Sous-le-fort	49	10.65	190	8.35	3.880	43	37.560	47	34.560	1.84	41	39	1.63	1	19	0.39	0	0
	295	64.13	1379	60.59	4.670	272	39.430	286	34.730	1.87	353	362	2.42	13	89	0.30	2	0.01
Petite Rivière	6	1.30	44*	1.93	7.330	4	31.500	5	29.600	1.50	15	14	4.83	2	2	0.33	1	0.16
Total	460		2276		4.950	424	41.920	455	36.330	1.91	616	624	2.68	26	120	0.26	3	0.01

*The total includes those absent.

APPENDIX E
1744 CENSUS

Street	Households No.	Households %	Population Pers.	Population %	Population Pers./Hou.	Men No.	Men Age	Women No.	Women Age	Adult/Hou.	Children Boys	Children Girls	Chil./Hou.	Age ?	Servants No.	Servants Ser./Hou.	Live-ins No.	Live-ins Ser./Hou.
Upper Town																		
Depuis le Fort	13	1.23	52	1.04	4.00	14	38.00	12	34.16	1.92	14	12	2.08	0	0	0	0	0
Grison	14	1.33	74	1.48	5.29	15	39.66	14	35.86	2.00	23	21	3.21	1	0	0	0	0
Carrières	13	1.23	59	1.18	4.54	10	41.10	11	37.60	1.61	19	19	2.92	0	0	0	0	0
Saint-Louis	74	7.02	416	8.31	5.62	73	44.13	75	42.67	1.99	117	120	3.20	2	24	0.32	6	0.08
Jardins	18	1.71	72	1.44	4.00	13	38.50	19	41.59	1.72	16	17	1.89	2	4	0.22	1	0.05
Buade	25	2.37	119	2.38	4.76	20	43.17	20	36.42	1.60	27	23	2.00	0	27	1.08	2	0.08
Sainte-Anne	16	1.52	81	1.62	5.06	16	43.88	15	39.29	1.94	21	27	3.00	1	0	0	1	0.06
Fabrique	13	1.23	82	1.64	6.31	11	38.55	17	36.08	1.85	16	20	3.08	0	10	0.77	8	0.61
Saint-Jean	82	7.78	371	7.41	4.52	79	41.88	81	38.50	1.95	93	98	2.33	1	13	0.16	6	0.07
Pauvres	21	1.99	97	1.94	4.62	17	38.00	20	32.59	1.76	20	26	2.19	2	14	0.67	1	0.05
Rempart	9	0.85	36	0.72	4.00	9	41.33	9	34.33	2.00	9	5	1.55	2	2	0.22	0	0
Saint-Joseph	23	2.18	115	2.30	5.00	21	45.74	23	40.45	1.91	33	31	2.78	1	0	0	6	0.26
Couillard	36	3.41	154	3.08	4.28	33	44.29	30	40.89	1.75	27	51	2.17	1	6	0.17	6	0.17
Nouvelle	17	1.61	101	2.02	5.94	17	42.94	17	37.18	2.00	29	27	3.29	0	9	0.53	2	0.12
Saint-Flavien	9	0.85	46	0.92	5.11	9	34.75	10	33.11	2.00	13	9	2.67	0	2	0.22	3	0.33
Saint-François	20	1.90	95	1.90	4.75	18	42.28	18	39.80	1.90	31	22	2.80	1	0	0	0	0
Sainte-Famille	24	2.28	117	2.34	4.87	24	50.14	25	43.91	2.00	28	23	2.17	0	11	0.46	6	0.25
Voisine Sainte-Famille	7	0.66	32	0.64	4.57	7	36.71	7	32.86	2.26	6	10	2.29	0	1	0.14	1	0.14
Rempart	12	1.14	67	1.34	5.58	13	40.25	12	34.83	2.14	17	25	3.58	0	0	0	0	0
Lavallée	12	1.14	53	1.06	4.42	11	35.27	12	33.25	1.92	15	14	2.42	0	0	0	1	0.08
Total	458	43.45	2242	44.80	4.89	430	41.03	451	37.27	1.90	574	600	2.60	14	123	0.27	50	0.11
Palace Quarter																		
Saint-Nicolas	19	1.80	85	1.70	4.47	22	42.82	21	37.44	2.26	16	21	2.21	1	3	0.16	1	0.05
Saint-Charles	70	6.64	302	6.03	4.31	63	37.07	70	35.94	1.90	76	75	2.16	2	11	0.16	5	0.07
Total	89	8.44	387	7.73	4.35	85	39.94	91	38.69	1.98	92	96	2.11	3	14	0.15	6	0.07

APPENDIX E (Cont'd)
1744 CENSUS

Street	Households		Population			Adults					Children				Servants		Live-ins	
						Men		Women		Adult/	Boys	Girls	Chil.	Age		Ser./		Ser./
	No.	%	Pers.	%	Pers./Hou.	No.	Age	No.	Age	Hou.			Hou.	?	No.	Hou.	No.	Hou.
Saint-Roch																		
Suburb																		
Saint-Roch	21	1.90	109	2.18	5.19	23	38.20	22	40.05	2.14	28	20	2.43	1	13	0.62	2	0.09
Saint-Vallier	31	2.94	163	3.26	5.26	31	42.83	29	38.72	1.93	46	40	2.77	1	8	0.26	7	0.23
	52	4.93	272	5.43	5.23	54	40.51	51	39.38	2.02	74	60	2.58	2	21	0.40	9	0.17
Lower Town																		
Sault-au-Matelot	111	10.53	517	10.33	4.66	101	41.28	111	37.19	1.91	140	128	2.41	1	21	0.19	16	0.14
Champlain	69	6.55	289	5.77	4.19	65	43.43	72	39.09	1.94	77	66	2.12	0	4	0.06	6	0.09
De Meulle	44	4.17	188	3.76	4.27	38	44.45	46	41.10	1.86	31	52	1.93	1	13	0.29	6	0.14
Escalier	9	0.85	29	0.58	3.22	9	33.33	8	29.62	1.89	3	3	0.67	0	4	0.44	2	0.22
Cul-de-sac	30	2.85	124	2.48	4.13	25	43.22	31	40.37	1.83	28	30	1.97	0	7	0.23	3	0.10
Sous-le-fort	29	2.75	103	2.06	3.55	28	40.85	30	37.15	1.96	13	13	0.93	0	11	0.38	8	0.28
Saint-Pierre	41	3.89	199	3.98	4.85	36	40.29	36	37.36	1.76	59	44	2.51	0	15	0.37	8	0.19
Notre-Dame	20	1.90	94	1.88	4.70	19	43.94	19	38.94	1.90	20	23	2.15	0	14	0.70	0	0
Place Royale	8	0.76	40	0.80	5.00	10	43.38	6	44.33	1.75	7	8	2.12	0	10	1.25	0	0
Côte de la Montagne	48	4.55	248	4.96	5.17	43	42.05	46	37.98	1.85	55	69	2.58	1	24	0.50	11	0.23
	409	38.80	1831	36.59	4.48	374	41.72	405	38.31	1.88	433	436	2.15	3	123	0.30	60	0.15
Suburb																		
Séminaire	18	1.77	115	2.30	6.39	19	42.87	18	41.80	2.00	33	36	3.89	0	6	0.33	3	0.17
Côte Saint-Jean	8	0.76	42	0.84	5.25	8	45.71	10	40.75	2.00	13	9	3.00	0	2	0.25	0	0
Saint-Charles River	20	1.90	115	2.30	5.75	21	42.53	22	38.83	2.00	39	30	3.60	0	3	0.15	0	0
	46	4.36	272	5.44	5.91	48	43.70	50	40.46	2.00	85	75	3.61	0	11	0.24	3	0.06
Total	1054		5004		4.75	992	41.35	1049	37.89	1.94	1259	1267	2.40	22	292	0.28	128	0.12

ABBREVIATIONS AND ACRONYMS

ALQ	Assemblée législative du Québec
AN	Archives nationales (France)
ANQQ	Archives nationales du Québec, Québec
ASQ	Archives du séminaire de Québec
CHAAR	*Canadian Historical Association Annual Report*
CHR	*Canadian Historical Review*
CLF	Cercle du livre de France
DCB	*Dictionary of Canadian Biography*
DFC	Dépôt des fortifications des colonies
IHAF	Institut d'histoire de l'Amérique française
IQRC	Institut québécois de recherche sur la culture
NA	National Archives of Canada
PRDH	Programme de recherches en démographie historique, Université de Montréal
PUF	Presses universitaires de France
PUL	Presses de l'université Laval
PUM	Presses de l'université de Montréal
RAPQ	*Rapport de l'archiviste de la province de Québec*
RHAF	Revue d'histoire de l'Amérique française
UTP	University of Toronto Press

NOTES

Introduction

1 Nevertheless this scenario is based on real examples.

2 Y. Desloges, The Study of the Urban Past and its Many Approaches: A Historiographic Review," *Research Bulletin*, No. 197 (June 1983), Ottawa.

3 J.C. Perrot, *Genèse d'une ville moderne, Caen au XVIIIe siècle* (Paris and La Haye: Mouton, 1975), Vol. 1, pp. 12-13, and 51.

Chapter 1
Demographic Characteristics, 1688-1755

1 R. Chénier, "L'urbanisation de la ville de Québec, 1660-1690," Manuscript on file, Québec, Canadian Parks Service, 1979, pp. 178-201. The situation is also valid for Montréal in the 17th century: L. Dechêne, *Habitants et marchands de Montréal au XVIIe siècle* (Paris and Montréal: Plon, 1974), pp. 98-100.

2 AN, Colonies, G1, 460-61. The general censuses cover the following years: 1692, 1695, 1698, 1706-07, 1712-14, 1716, 1718-24, 1726-27, 1730, 1732, 1736-37 and 1739.

3 Canada, Statistics of Canada, *Census of Canada, 1665 to 1871* (Ottawa: I.B. Taylor, 1876), Vol. 4, pp. 2-61. It is important to emphasize that this publication deals only with nine censuses (1692, 1695, 1698, 1706, 1719, 1720, 1721, 1734 and 1739). Moreover, this publication does not contain all the data in the original manuscripts.

4 H. Charbonneau and J. Légaré, *Répertoire des actes de baptêmes, mariages, sépultures et des recensements du Québec ancien* (Montréal: PUM, 1980-), Vol. 8, pp. 557-76, and Vol. 18, pp. 757-800. L. Beaudet, *Recensement de la ville de Québec, 1716* (Québec: A. Côté, 1887); *RAPQ, 1919-1940*, "Le recensement de Québec en 1744" (Québec, Rédempti Paradis, King's Printer, 1940), pp. 1-154. Canada, *Statistics [...]*, p. 27. The abundance of sources and the almost total lack of data on the subject of their treatment leaves many questions unanswered. It is important to emphasize certain incongruities in the statistical censuses. For example, apart from the disparities that may exist between a copy and the original, we should point out that the 1712 census does not indicate the number of men present in Québec, so that the figure for the total population is not complete. Furthermore we should remember that the figures published in the collections of Canadian statistics are generally over-

evaluated. In 1692, the original shows a total population of 1439 people while the published version shows 1570 for a difference of 131 individuals or 9.1%. In fact 131 children including 61 boys and 70 girls were added to the total without any explanation. The same is true of the censuses of 1695 and 1698. In the first case there was an over-evaluation of 9.8%. If there was an over-evaluation for Québec, it is quite likely that the evaluation of the population of the colony was also higher than it was in fact. In summary, it is better to refer to the original documents rather than to the published censuses because, until now, there has been no careful analysis of the way the census data were recorded.

5   Until now the terms "family" and "household" were used interchangeably. In order to avoid confusion, it would be preferable to use the term "family" when speaking of statistical censuses. On the other hand, according to demographers the term "household" corresponds to a physical unit; in other words, it is used to designate all the people living under the same roof. G. Olivier-Lacamp and J. Légaré, "Quelques caractéristiques des ménages de la ville de Québec entre 1666 et 1716," *Histoire sociale/Social History*, Vol. 12, No. 23 (May 1979), p. 67. However, as will be shown in Part 2, this definition should be revised.

6   Even though our colleague, R. Chénier, gives an annual increase of 10%, it is important to add a detail concerning the calculation of the rate of growth. The figure advanced by Chénier is the intercensal rate of growth rather than the annual rate of growth as understood by demographers. The 10% was calculated using the following formula: $\dfrac{P^t - P^o}{P^o}/t$ where P^t represents the population at the end of the period under consideration, P^o that at the beginning, and t the time elapsed. In order to calculate the annual rate of growth, we should use the following formula: $\dfrac{100\,(P^t - P^o)}{0.5\,(P^t + P^o)}/t$

At least this is what suggests demographer Michel P. Paillé, "Accroissement et structure de la population à Québec au début du XIXe siècle," *Histoire sociale/Social History*, Vol. 9, No. 17 (May 1976), pp. 188-90. R. Chénier, *op. cit.*, pp. 184 and 408.

7   That is, an intercensal rate of 7.1%. R. Chénier, *op. cit.*, pp. 184 and 408.

8   *Ibid.*, p. 409.

9   *Ibid.*, pp. 187, 412-13.

10   L. Dechêne, *Habitants[...]*, pp. 98 and 493-95.

11   *Ibid.*, p. 98.

12   R. Chénier, *op. cit.*, p. 188.

13   *Ibid.*, pp. 189-92.

14   *Ibid.*, pp. 193-95.

15   According to L. Dechêne (*Habitants[...]*, p. 99), there are curious anomalies in the distribution of the sexes in people under 15; enough to make us doubt the accuracy of the censuses.

16   AN, Colonies, G1, Vol. 460-61, General Censuses; L. Dechêne, (*Habitants[...]*, p. 493). Moreover, we should emphasize that the white population of the colony of

Massachusetts, even though more numerous, increased at a slower pace during the course of this period. In 1690, there were 49 500 inhabitants; in 1720, 91 000; and in 1750, 188 000; for a rate of growth of 1.97% between 1690 and 1720, and 2.32% between 1720 and 1750. D.L. Jones, *Village and Seaport; Migration and Society in Eighteenth Century Massachusetts* (Hanover and London: University Press of New England, 1971), p. 23.

17 L. Dechêne, "La croissance de Montréal au XVIIIe siècle," *RHAF*, Vol. 27, No. 2 (September 1973), p. 164. These figures are different from those contained in *Habitants et marchands de Montréal*. It is important to remember that the figures for Montréal do not include the suburbs.

18 The figures in Table I were obtained from four sources: L. Dechêne, *Habitants[...]*, p. 493; L. Dechêne, "La croissance[...]," p. 164; R. Chénier, *op. cit.*, pp. 406-09, and AN, Colonies, G1, 460-61, General Censuses. The rates of growth were obtained from figures obtained in the statistical census of 1716. The use of the figures obtained by the priest for Québec will slightly lower the rate of growth.

19 The data on Portsmouth were derived from K.E. Andersen, "The Layered Society; Material Life in Portsmouth N.H., 1680-1740," PhD thesis, University of New Hampshire, 1982, p. 60. Those for Newport and Providence were derived from R.V. Wells, *The Population of the British Colonies in America before 1776. A Survey of Census Data* (Princeton N.J.: Princeton University Press, 1975), p. 98; the others from C. Bridenbaugh, *Cities in the Wilderness; The First Century of Urban Life in America, 1625-1742* (New York: Oxford University Press, 1971), p. 6; C. Bridenbaugh, *Cities in Revolt; Urban Life in America, 1743-1776* (New York: Oxford University Press, 1973), p. 5.

20 That is, 419 in Québec and 40 in Petite-Rivière. According to the statistical census the town also included the suburbs.

21 J. Hamelin, *Économie et société en Nouvelle-France* (Québec: PUL, [1960]), pp. 16 and 58-65; L. Dechêne, *Habitants[...]*, pp. 131 and 162-63.

22 J. Mathieu, *Le commerce entre la Nouvelle-France et les Antilles au XVIIIe siècle* (Montréal: Fides, 1981), pp. 29 and 153.

23 J. Hamelin, *op. cit.*, p. 64.

24 A. Charbonneau, Y. Desloges and M. Lafrance, *Québec, ville fortifiée du XVIIe au XIXe siècle* (Québec: Pelican and Parks Canada, 1982), pp. 300-301; J. Mathieu, *Le commerce[...]*, p. 29. This table could never have been compiled without the help of my colleague Marc Lafrance, who had the idea of redefining the areas covered in the statistical censuses, especially those carried out toward the end of the 17th and the beginning of the 18th century. We should also point out that the figures in Table 3 apply only to civilians. The 1755 figure was obtained from a note written by James Murray at the bottom of the summary table for the 1761 census. Finally indices for the cost of living, as defined in Appendix B, correspond to this chronological distribution. This does not include the many other indices that will be developed in subsequent chapters.

25 A. Charbonneau, Y. Desloges and M. Lafrance, *op. cit.*, pp. 301-04, 375-76, and 418-20. Certainly beggars invaded the towns during the crisis years of 1742-43; but how

many were there and where did they come from? Could not they have originated in the city?

26 R. Chénier, *op. cit.*, pp. 187-89.

27 L. Dechêne, *Habitants[...]*, pp. 98-99.

28 R. Chénier, *op. cit.*, p. 187.

29 It is important to remember that the proportion of male representation plunged during the censuses of 1706, 1707, 1713, 1718, 1719, 1730, 1736 and 1739. In terms of the first three, they overlap the war periods while in 1718 and 1719, the difficult times encouraged the more enterprising members of the population to move elsewhere in order to ensure their subsistence. As far as the last three are concerned, we do not know the possible cause of this regression in male representation, but we should point out that there was a steady decrease in the number of men since 1720.

30 J. Henripin, *La population canadienne au début du XVIIIe siècle: nuptialité, fécondité, mortalité infantile* (Paris: PUF, 1954), pp. 18-20.

31 During the course of 1690-1749, the parish priests celebrated 2256 marriages, baptized 11 267 children and buried 7114 people. The figures of the Hôpital-Général and the Hôtel-Dieu Hospital are included in these data. These births, marriages and deaths registers were collected by PRDH researchers. H. Charbonneau and J. Légaré, *op. cit.*, Vols. 1, 8 and 18.

32 Adding the percentages or absolute numbers provides incomplete results because marriages between people who came from other countries or whose geographic origins are unknown were not included. The survey only asked about urban dwellers.

33 There were 213 marriages involving one spouse from outside the parochial area between 1690 and 1749. Of this number, 23 came from Europe (20%), 777 (64%) from France, 105 (8.5%) from other areas in the colony and 308 (25%) from the government of Québec.

34 Since the censuses show only the number of men older than 50, we have calculated that the number of women in this age category was equal to that of men, which probably represents an underevaluation of the phenomenon as we will see later. In the case of the 1739 census, the 50 men marked absent were added to the 15-49 year-old group.

35 L. Dechêne, *Habitants[...]*, pp. 100-101, note 7.

36 G. Olivier-Lacamp and J. Légaré, *op. cit.*, p. 70.

37 This average seems a little high because the 1737 census shows only 5.7 people per family. Jacrau's figures in 1744 which were initially underestimated show only 4.7 people per "household"; this situation may be explained by the slow-down in growth experienced by the capital between 1737 and 1744.

38 P. Goubert, *Cent mille provinciaux au XVIIe siècle; Beauvais et la Beauvaisis de 1600 à 1730* (Paris: Flammarion, 1968), p. 53.

39 J. Henripin, *op. cit.*, p. 95. As far as the situation in Montréal is concerned, it corresponds closely to the results obtained by the demographer. L. Dechêne, *Habitants[...]*, pp. 104-05.

40 At least in Beauvaisis, according to P. Goubert, *op. cit.*, p. 59. It is important to point out that although women were more numerous in the nominal rolls of 1716 and 1744, these two dates fall in periods of economic slow down.

41 This figure was derived from the analysis of succession inventories of the population of Québec. It was obtained by subtracting the date of death from that of marriage for 276 marriages.

42 The figure is also close to the Canadian and Montréal averages. J. Henripin, *op. cit.*, p. 95; L. Dechêne, *Habitants[...]*, p. 107, note 24.

43 Henripin observed the inverse situation for the colony as a whole, where 18.5% of the men and 14.1% of the women married.

44 The figures in Table 8 are read as follows: the absolute numbers divided by the number of days in the month give the number of days, whose added total gives the denominator of the monthly index. The quotient obtained must be multiplied by 12. H. Charbonneau and M.L. Marcilio, *Démographie historique* (Paris: PUF, 1979), p. 64.

45 H. Charbonneau, *Vie et mort de nos ancêtres; étude démographique* (Montréal: PUM, 1975), pp. 180-82; L. Dechêne, *Habitants[...]*, pp. 109-10.

46 According to Goubert, 1% of the births in Beauvaisis were illegitimate, while in Montréal they totalled 1.87%. The average for Canada as a whole varied between 0.2% and 1.2%. P. Goubert, *op. cit.*, p. 54; L. Dechêne, *Habitants[...]*, p. 114.

47 According to Goubert, by taking into account the last births, the period of fertility was only 16 to 20 years. P. Goubert, *op. cit.*, p. 56.

48 L. Dechêne, *Habitants[...]*, p. 111.

49 Total births were only 10 984, and not 11 267; that is a difference of 283 which can be explained by the fact that 83 births of children of unknown sex and 200 births of native children, foreigners (outside the urban area) and even newly converted anglophones were not included.

50 The calculations were carried out in the same way as those for Table 7. See note 44.

51 L. Dechêne, *Habitants[...]*, p. 113.

52 Infants of unknown sex were not included.

53 Demographers Henripin and Charbonneau have warned researchers about the difficulties they could meet if they decide to count deaths. On the whole, they say that the births, marriages and deaths registers underevaluate the number of deaths. The same would be true in Beauvaisis. This seems to hold for both France and Canada. L. Dechêne, *Habitants[...]*, p. 116; P. Goubert, *op. cit.*, pp. 62-63.

54 P. Goubert, *op. cit.*, p. 63; L. Dechêne, *Habitants[...]*, pp. 116-17.

55 H. Charbonneau, "À propos de démographie urbaine en Nouvelle-France; réflexions en marge d'*Habitants et marchands de Montréal* de Louise Dechêne," *RHAF*, Vol. 30, No. 2 (September 1976), p. 263.

56 That is, a mortality rate of 211 per 1000. The figures in the table include acts that do not indicate the age; that is, 653 or about 11% of the dead civil population, since soldiers and seamen were considered to be a floating population and are not included.

57 This proportion is much higher than that obtained by the demographer Charbonneau who estimated that in 1713, 52.5% of the number of dead children were under 15. H. Charbonneau, "À propos[..]," p. 267.

58 According to a study on domestic servants, female children between 4 and 13 provided a recruitment base for domestic service. F. Barry, "Familles et domesticité féminine au milieu du 18e siècle," in N. Fahmy-Eid and M. Dumont, eds., *Maîtresses de maison, maîtresses d'école; femmes, famille et éducation dans l'histoire du Québec* (Montréal: Boréal Express, 1983), p. 231.

59 P.-G. Roy, *La ville de Québec sous le régime français* (Québec: King's Printer, 1930), Vol. 2, p. 18. This figure seems questionable because the births, marriages and deaths registers show 322 burials for these two years. As Roy has pointed out, these deaths could not have all been the result of smallpox. In the absence of a systematic analysis of these deaths it may be better to retain this number.

60 AN, Colonies, C^{11}A, Vol. 21, fol. 41-43, Callières and Beauharnois to the Minister, 27 April 1703. These figures are nevertheless deceiving because we must subtract from them that infant mortality that would have occurred in any case.

61 According to Jacques Dupaquier, there are six different intensities in mortality crises to which he attributes the following indices: minor crisis (between 1 and 2); moderate crisis (between 2 and 4); major crisis (between 4 and 8); massive crisis (between 8 and 16); mammoth crisis (between 16 and 32); catastrophe (over 32). In order to calculate these indices we must add the deaths in the 10 years preceding the event, obtain the average, and then calculate the average deviation in accordance with the following equation: $I = \dfrac{D_x - M_x}{\sigma_x}$

The index is equal to the number of deaths in year X, from which we subtract the average of the 10 previous years; the difference is divided by the standard deviation of the 10 reference years. H. Charbonneau and A. Larose, eds., *Les grandes mortalités: étude méthodologique des crises démographiques du passé* (Liège: Ordina, 1979), pp. 85-93.

62 L. Dechêne, *Habitants[...]*, p. 119.

63 F. Rousseau, *L'oeuvre de chère en Nouvelle-France; le régime des malades à l'Hôtel-Dieu de Québec* (Québec: PUL, 1983), p. 37.

64 H. Charbonneau and A. Larose, *op. cit.*, p. 89.

65 J. Hamelin, *op. cit.*, p. 60. We will come back to this in Appendix B when we discuss the curve of the price of wheat.

66 Hamelin notes that, during the course of 1727-33, the shortage of wheat was the result, not of poor harvests, but rather of large wheat exports to the West Indies. J. Hamelin, *op. cit.*, p. 60.

67 Furthermore, the Swedish traveller Kalm says that the large and beautiful farms in the neighbourhood of Québec belonged to its citizens. P. Kalm, *Voyage de Pehr Kalm au Canada en 1749; traduction annotée du Journal de route*, translation J. Rousseau, G. Béthune and P. Morisset (Montréal: CLF, 1977), p. 312.

68 J. Mathieu, *et al.*, "Les alliances matrimoniales exogames dans le gouvernement de Québec, 1700-1760," *RHAF*, Vol. 35, No. 1 (June 1981), p. 14.

Chapter 2
Of Men, Neighbourhoods and Trades

1   These considerations will be analyzed in the two subsequent parts of this work.

2   The question here is not to analyze the social structures, but rather those of the socio-professional character of the neighbourhood or the particular street.

3   A. Charbonneau, Y. Desloges and M. Lafrance, *op. cit.*, p. 353.

4   *Ibid.*, p. 357. It should be noted that this number represents an increase of 2.6% for 1745.

5   A few explanations are in order concerning the figures contained in Table 14. First, it should be pointed out that the figures on Upper Town include the residents of the future suburbs of Saint-Louis and Saint-Jean. In the present state of research, it is impossible to decide which is which. The construction of the wall in 1745 made the task of dividing up the residents easier; however, this demarcation did not exist when Father Jacrau did his compilation. The Palace Quarter, which was to be called by several different names over the years, was limited to Saint-Nicolas and Saint-Charles streets. Residents of Saint-Vallier and Saint-Roch streets were considered residents of the Saint-Roch suburb. Finally, the 1716 suburb appears to have been highly underestimated since it had had over 200 inhabitants from the end of the 17th century. Father Thibault limited himself to the immediate inner suburb, ignoring the Côte Sainte-Geneviève and the Côte Saint-Jean. This latter consideration derives from observations made by my colleague Marc Lafrance.

6   Did the physical obstacles represented by the cliff and the river lead to the over-pricing of lots and houses in this sector to the point that only merchants and the well-to-do had access to it? This hypothesis will be analyzed in the second part of this work.

7   The number of garrisoned servicemen was not very large during this period; there were about 100 including officers.

8   According to figures obtained by demographers of the Université de Montréal, there were 2281 people distributed among 462 households. We eliminated the household formed by the governor and his family plus another household which was a duplicate.

9   Here again the governor and the duplicate households were eliminated. The printed version of the PRDH shows 1056 households including the governor's family.

10 These figures differ from those in the previous chapter. It is not our intention to substitute them for the figures in statistical censuses. To the contrary they allowed us to define two phenomena: on one hand, the priest's under-evaluation in 1716 and on the other, the mobility of the population according to the enumeration of 1744. If the number of people per family was 6.7 in 1739, it is highly possible that this figure had dropped to the level reported by the priest, since the five years separating the two censuses were difficult ones due to poor harvests. Some people migrated. In short,

we have juxtaposed the censuses instead of comparing them, and the size of the families in the statistical censuses is explained by the considerable number of migrants from bordering parishes (that is, people whose demographic behaviour differs from those of people from urban neighbourhoods).

11   As the analysis of the growth rates in the previous chapter showed.

12   Among researchers there is no general agreement on this question of contraception; however, women have much fewer children than their biological potential would allow. M. Laget, *Naissances: l'accouchement avant l'âge de la clinique*, (Paris: Seuil, 1982), pp. 64-66. It should also be pointed out that 72.3% of all children in 1716 were under the age of 15, and that this proportion reached 75.3% in 1744.

13   G. Olivier-Lacamp and J. Légaré, *op. cit.*, p. 70.

14   P. Goubert mentions that in theory women can have children up to the age of 45 or 50; in reality, it has been established that women had their last child at 41, so that a 43-year-old woman "is often an old woman." P. Goubert, *op. cit.* pp. 55-56.

15   G. Olivier-Lacamp and J. Légaré, *op. cit.*, p. 70.

16   J.-P. Gutton, *Domestiques et serviteurs dans la France de l'Ancien Régime* (Paris: Aubier-Montaigne, 1981), pp. 8 and 73.

17   L. Dechêne, "Quelques aspects de la ville de Québec au XVIIIe siècle d'après les dénombrements paroissiaux," *Cahiers de géographie du Québec*, Vol. 28, No. 75 (December 1984), pp. 489-90.

18   L. Dechêne, *Habitants[...]*, p. 375. It seems that this concept is more flexible, despite the ambiguity in the classification of certain professions such as that of servant which, in our opinion, should be put in the fourth sector rather than in the first. Nevertheless, since these are figures for the professions of the heads of households, this situation does not arise very frequently. It should be noted that in this text the "services" sector excludes clergymen.

19   L. Dechêne, "Quelques aspects[...]," p. 498.

20   It should be noted that only 20 trades appear in Table 16; this selection (based on the trade being mentioned three times or more) allowed for a more adequate comparison between the censuses. Still this means that this selection contains 78% of the heads of households whose trade was identified in 1716, and 77% of those in 1744. Ship carpenters and wig-makers were excluded in the absence of comparative data.

21   The term "domestic" includes not only the people identified as such, but also footmen, housemaids, manservants, governesses, domestics, slaves, apprentices and labourers. These two latter categories may seem surprising. But they are justified by a *de facto* situation: the contracts of apprenticeship often stipulated that the young apprentice would have to carry out domestic tasks. Although this does not mean that the apprentice was a journeyman, it should be noted that this custom was widespread in France. J.-P. Hardy and D.T. Ruddell, *Les apprentis artisans à Québec, 1660-1815* (Montréal: PUQ, 1977), p. 54; J.-P. Gutton, *op. cit.*, pp. 14 and 69-70.

22   A. Charbonneau, *et al.*, "Le Parc de l'Artillerie et les fortifications de Québec," Historical studies presented to the Learned Societies Conference in Québec, Parks Canada, 1976, p. 71.

23 For specific data on each of the streets, see Appendixes C, D and E.

24 J.-P. Gutton, *op. cit.*, p. 7-8; D. Roche, *Le peuple de Paris,* (Paris: Aubier-Montaigne, 1981), pp. 26-30.

25 F. Barry, "Famelles et domesticité fémenine au milieu du 18ᵉ siècle," in N. Fahmy-Eid and M. Dumont, eds., *op. cit.*, pp. 232-33.

Chapter 3
The Urban Landscape

1 L. A. de Lom d'Arce, baron de Lahontan, *Nouveaux voyages en Amérique septentrionale* (Montréal: Hexagone/Minerve, 1983), letter 3, pp. 72-73.

2 J.-P. Bardet, *Rouen aux XVIIᵉ et XVIIIᵉ siècles; les mutations d'un espace social* (Paris: Société d'édition d'enseignement supérieur, 1983), Vol. 1, p. 25; L. Teisseyre-Sallmann, "Urbanisme et société; l'exemple de Nîmes aux XVIIᵉ et XVIIIᵉ siècles," *Annales, E.S.C.,* Vol. 35, No. 4 (July-August 1980), p. 967; M. Trudel, *Initiation à la Nouvelle-France* (Montréal: Holt, Rinehart and Winston, 1968), p. 142.

3 P. Kalm, *op. cit.*, p. 317 (fol. 772).

4 *Ibid.*

5 *Ibid.*, p. 324 (fol. 777).

6 *Ibid.*, pp. 320-21 (fol. 775).

7 These dimensions were obtained using the surface area of Lower Town shown on Chaussegros de Léry's 1742 plan. [One *toise* equals 6.5 (English) feet]. NA, National Collection of Maps and Plans, PH/430, Québec, 1742.

8 These place names are from R. Brisson, *La charpenterie navale à Québec sous le régime français* (Québec: IQRC, 1983), p. 57.

9 R. Chénier, *op. cit.,* p. 107-08.

10 A. Charbonneau, Y. Desloges and M. Lafrance, *op. cit.,* p. 342.

11 It is important to point out that at present these width standards have remained about the same for Sault-au-Matelot and Saint-Pierre streets or for Petit Champlain Street, which is 18.4 (French) feet or 6 metres. This information was obtained from the Highway Department of the City of Québec.

12 R. Chénier, *op. cit.,* pp. 107-108; ANQQ, NF-7, declarations and enumerations, fief of Sault-au-Matelot, fol. 598, 20 August 1737.

13 A. Charbonneau, Y. Desloges and M. Lafrance, *op. cit.,* p. 339.

14 It is very difficult to measure the space taken up by the docks and military installations. This is why they are not discussed. It must be pointed out that these are maximum figures.

15 It should be added that the habitable area increased slightly over the same period.

16 Saint-Nicholas Street was 42 (French) feet wide, Saint-Charles was 22, and de la Digue and Lacroix lanes were respectively 18 and 15 feet wide. ANQQ, NF-7, declarations and enumerations, Hospitalières of the Hôtel-Dieu land, 3 July 1739. NA, National Collection of Maps and Plans, PH/350, Québec 1739, Plan of the Colonial Administrator's Palace by Chaussegros de Léry.

17 P. Kalm, *op. cit.*, p. 324 (fol. 777).

18 C. Lacelle, "Military Property in Quebec City, 1760-1871," *History and Archaeology*, No. 57 (1978), p. 180.

19 The Paupers of the Hôtel-Dieu Property covered 2.27 hectares including the cemetery; the Hôtel-Dieu land accounted for 3.42 hectares; the Jesuits occupied 2.05 hectares; the Ursulines, 2.74 hectares; the Seminary, 2.71 hectares; North-Dame Parish, 3.33 hectares; the Bishopric, 1.56 hectares; and the Recollects, 1.48 hectares. This was space occupied by properties of institutions in Upper Town as described in the testimony and enumeration or measured on Chaussegros de Léry's 1742 plan. It does not include landholdings belonging to the religious communities in the city.

20 Including the following streets and lanes, Saint-Louis, Saint-Jean, Saint-Stanislas, Sainte-Ursule, des Jardins, des Pauvres (Côte du Palais) streets, du Grison, Saint-Denis, du Mont-Carmel, Sainte-Hélène (MacMahon), Laporte, Sainte-Geneviève, Dauphine, des Carrières, Sainte-Anne, Major or du Chateau (du Fort), Frontenac, Buade, de l'Evêché, du Trésor, Côte de la Fabrique, Saint-Joseph (Garneau), de la Sainte-Famille, Saint-Vallier (Hébert), sur les Remparts, du Séminaire, Saint-Joachim, Saint-François, Saint-Flavien, Nouvelle (Christie) and Couillard. Around 1737, there were two Saint-Vallier Streets, the second one (which still exists) was in the Saint-Roch suburb.

21 It should be pointed out that when he built his ramparts farther to the west in 1745, Chaussegros de Léry pushed back the physical limits of Upper Town and thus increased the habitable area of the district by almost 45% (around 16 hectares). This figure was calculated on the basis of Chaussegros de Léry's 1752 plan (NA, National Collection of Maps and Plans, PH/340, Québec, 1752).

22 Actually, this figure of 35 hectares turns out to be inflated, since again we have to subtract the area covered by religious buildings (19.6 hectares) and part of the road network (about 3.4 hectares), not to mention some public buildings. Only 12 hectares remain for house construction.

23 The territorial boundaries of the cities and their suburbs generally follow those of the ecclesiastical jurisdiction. See J.C. Perrot, *op. cit.*, Vol. 1, pp. 12-13, 51.

24 RAPQ, 1921-1922, "Procès-verbaux sur la commodité et incommodité dans chacune des paroisses de la Nouvelle-France par Mathieu-Benoît Collet, procureur général du roi au Conseil Supérieur de Québec" (Québec: L.-A. Proulx, 1922), p. 362.

25 A. Charbonneau, Y. Desloges and M. Lafrance, *op. cit.*, p. 424.

26 ANQQ, records of C. Barolet, inventory taken after the death of J.-B. Couillard de Lespinay, 16 March 1735.

27 For example, the fief of Sault-au-Matelot owned by the Seminary covered about 7% of the city's total area.

28   The surface areas shown refer only to the lots meant for building houses and not prairie and pastureland lots which would considerably distort the estimate. As for Joachim Girard, he received his lot from the Paupers of the Hôtel-Dieu so that he should not be considered to be a landowner. However, for purposes of comparison, it was preferable to identify him in a special way in order to bring out the land-speculation operation looming behind his action.

29   Explanations should not be limited to reasons exclusively related to the physical characteristics of the land, since the small size of the lots ceded by the Seminary can also be explained by that institution's financial difficulties. The same would be true of the Hôtel-Dieu, which does not seem to have had available large amounts of money to care for the needy. N. Baillargeon, *Le Séminaire de Québec de 1685 à 1760* (Québec: PUL, 1977), pp. 270-78; F. Rousseau, *op. cit.*, pp. 79-108.

30   It is difficult not to see a land-speculation operation in Joachim Girard's land subdivision: the area ceded by the shoemaker was 22.5% smaller than that ceded almost on the same spot by the Paupers of the Hôtel-Dieu, in spite of the topography in this section of the city. Moreover, the payments required from and by Girard unquestionably confirm this hypothesis: even though the shoemaker had to pay 5 *livres* per *arpent* per year to the Paupers of the Hôtel-Dieu; in return, he received from these lots an annual payment of 325 *livres* per *arpent* (although they could be bought back). ANQQ, NF-7, declarations and enumerations, Paupers of the Hôtel-Dieu property, 12 December 1739.

31   A factor that may explain the difference in area is the fact that docks were added along the river to the lots on Saint-Pierre Street.

32   ANQQ, NF-7, declarations and enumerations, Paupers of the Hôtel-Dieu property, 12 December 1739.

33   We estimated that the sector of the land located to the west of des Pauvres Street, of which three-quarters were required for the construction of Chevalier de Beaucour's fortifications, measured 2500 square *toises*. ANQQ, NF-7, declarations and enumerations, Hospitalières of the Hôtel-Dieu, 3 July 1739.

34   *Ibid.*, Jesuits property, 20 February 1733.

35   P. Kalm, *op. cit.*, p. 329 and 319 (fol. 717 and 773).

36   *Ibid.*, p. 319 (fol. 774).

37   ANQQ, NF-7, declarations and enumerations, fief of Sault-au-Matelot, 20 August 1737.

38   *Ibid.*, declarations and enumerations, Cap-aux-Diamants property, 17 March 1740; Notre-Dame land, 20 May 1740.

39   P. Kalm, *op. cit.*, p. 318 (fol. 773).

40   Measurements from Chaussegros de Léry's 1742 plan.

41   *Ibid.*

42   R. Etlin, "L'air dans l'urbanisme des Lumières," *Dix-huitième siècle* (1977), pp. 123-29.

43 Although there were quite a few vacant lots around 1744, this was due to a combination of circumstances involving either fires, recent concessions or administrative delays (for example, the officer in charge of public roads was slow in defining the statutory building lines). It does not seem to have been the accepted thing in the 18th century to wait very long before building. There had been no regulations setting a deadline for the King's new rent payers to enclose their lots or building on them, since that put in place by Colonial Administrator Raudot in March 1707. Moreover, most of the vacant lots were in Upper Town. ANQQ, NF-2, Vol. 1, fol. 28, order by J. Raudot, 19 March 1707.

44 This percentage was obtained by adding the block surface of houses to that of secondary structures in relation to the entire ceded area. ANQQ, NF-7, declarations and enumerations, 1723-58, *passim.*

45 ANQQ, NF-7, declarations and enumerations, Paupers of the Hôtel-Dieu property, 12 December 1739, fol. 715.

46 D. Roche, *op. cit.*, p. 100.

47 G.-P. Léonidoff, "L'habitat de bois en Nouvelle-France; son importance et ses techniques de construction," *Bulletin d'histoire de la culture matérielle* (Spring 1982), p. 24.

48 R. Chénier, *op. cit.*, pp. 161-67.

49 ALQ, *Édits, ordonnances royaux, déclarations et arrêts du Conseil d'État concernant le Canada* (Québec: E.R. Fréchette, 1854-1856), Vol. 2, pp. 314-21, 7 June 1727.

50 For example, section 187 of the *Coutume de Paris* specifies that the owner of the land may build as high as he wishes so that Intendant Dupuy could not have been unaware of it. C. de Ferrière, *Commentaire sur la Coutume de la Prévôté et Vicomté de Paris* (Paris: Libraires associés, 1788), Vol. 1, pp. 433-34.

51 A. Charbonneau, Y. Desloges and M. Lafrance, *op. cit.*, pp. 252-53. In Chapter 6 we will touch upon the economic situation again.

52 ALQ, *Jugements et délibérations du Conseil souverain de la Nouvelle-France* (Québec: A. Côté, 1888), Vol. 3, p. 327, 18 April 1689.

53 *Ibid.*, Vol 2, p. 946, 10 April 1684.

54 ANQQ, NF-20, insinuations de la Prévôté de Québec (M65/3), Vol 11, p. 238, order dated 5 September 1748.

55 ALQ, *Jugements[...] du Conseil souverain [...]*, Vol. 6, p. 39, 24 March 1710; AN, Colonies, F3, Vol. 10, fol 313, 22 October 1726.

56 A battering ram was described as follows: "a piece of round wood 12 to 14 feet long and 5 inches in diameter on the large end, in which a hole is pierced in order to introduce three pegs two feet long and from one-half to two inches in diameter each, the first of which is set at a distance of half a foot from the small end and the two others are at three feet from the large end." AN, Colonies, F3, Vol. 13, fol., 241-241v, order dated 11 August 1746. This apparatus recalled the old war machines used to knock

down fortified walls. From this, we can assume that four to six persons were necessary to handle it, and that the tool had to be kept close to the house or adjacent to it.

57   ALQ, *Jugements[...] du Conseil souverain[...]* Vol. 5, p. 446, ruling dated 22 November 1706.

58   AN, Colonies, F3. Vol 3, fol. 399, order dated 7 July 1670.

59   ANQQ, NF-2, (M5/2), fol. 31v-32, order of J. Raudot, 30 May 1711.

60   AN, Colonies, F3, Vol. 12, fol. 375, order dated 20 September 1740. Six years later, a new order made the fines heavier; henceforward, offenders would be liable to a fine of 50 *livres* and even three months in prison, and to twice that in case of a repeat offence. P.-G. Roy, *Inventaire des ordonnances des intendants de la Nouvelle-France conservées aux Archives provinciales de Québec* (Beauceville: L'Éclaireur, 1919), Vol. 3, pp. 86-87, order dated 26 September 1746.

61   ALQ, *Édits, ordonnances royaux [...]*, Vol. 2, p. 302, ruling dated 5 October 1740.

62   ALQ, *Jugements[...] du Conseil souverain[...]*, Vol. 6, pp. 39-40, order dated 24 March 1710.

63   ANQQ, NF-20, insinuations de la Prévôté de Québec (M65/1), Vol. 4, p. 185, order dated 23 May 1721.

64   ALQ, *Édits, ordonnances royaux [...]*, Vol. 2, pp. 368-69, order dated July 12, 1734.

65   ALQ, *Jugements[...] du Conseil souverain[...]*, Vol. 3, p. 327, police regulations dated 18 April 1689.

66   *Ibid.*, Vol. 5, p. 281, order dated 22 March 1706; *ibid.*, Vol 5, p. 472, order dated 13 December 1706.

67   *Ibid.*, Vol. 5, p. 446, order dated 22 November 1706.

68   *Ibid.*

69   P.-G. Roy, *Inventaire des ordonnances [...]*, Vol. 2, p. 208, order dated 1 August 1736.

70   After December 1691, the Sovereign Council allowed the inhabitants of Lower Town to equip themselves at their own cost with a "Holland pump used to spray water on burning houses," ALQ, *Jugements[...] du Conseil souverain[...]*, Vol. 3, p. 591, police regulation dated 4 December 1691.

71   AN, Outremer, DFC, No. 365, memoirs of Levasseur de Neré, [1700]. Even though Levasseur listed only one well at the end of the French régime, there was certainly a second one, on Place d'Armes, as shown in an engraving by Richard Short (see Figure 5).

72   *Ibid.*, No. 374, note dealing with water, 8 November 1708.

73   On this subject, note that the Jesuit College, where the British army was stationed at the end of the 18th century, allowed the public to use its fountain. Beside, the commander of the troops, Sir Isaac Brock, ran into trouble with the population when he withdrew this established right from them.

74   C. de Ferrière, *op. cit.*, Vol. 1, section 193, p. 439.

75   ALQ, *Jugements[...]du Conseil souverain[...]*, Vol. 5, p. 233, police regulation dated 1 February 1706.

76   *Ibid.*, Vol. 5, p. 336 and 353, 28 June and 2 August 1706.

77   *Ibid.*, Vol. 3, p. 327, police regulations dated 18 April 1689.

78   *Ibid.*, Vol. 4, p. 159, police regulations dated 22 February 1698.

79   P.-G. Roy, *Inventaire des ordonnances[...]*, Vol. 2, pp. 13-14, order dated 18 June 1727.

80.   *Ibid.*, Vol. 3, pp. 160-61, order dated 17 July 1751. On this subject, we should mention the practice of Pierre Guy of Montréal, who promised to collect manure and take it to his land. It was a way of solving the problem of lack of fertilizer.

81   ANQQ, NF-19, registres de la Prévôté de Québec (M27/5), No. 1446, order dated 5 April 1745.

82   ALQ, *Édits, ordonnances royaux[...]*, Vol. 2, p. 38, order dated 8 April 1743.

83   P.-G. Roy, *Inventaire des ordonnances[...]*, Vol. 3, p. 38, order dated 8 April 1743.

84   ALQ, *Jugements[...]du Conseil souverain[...]*, Vol. 5, p. 233, police regulations dated 1 February 1706.

85   A. Charbonneau, Y. Desloges and M. Lafrance, *op. cit.*, p. 262. We will return to this question in Chapter 5.

86   ALQ, *Jugements[...] du Conseil souverain[...]*, Vol. 5, p. 233, police regulations dated 1 February 1706.

87   *Ibid.*, Vol. 4, p. 159, police regulations dated 22 February 1698.

88   P.-G.Roy, *Inventaire des ordonnances[...]*, Vol. 1, p. 64, order by Raudot, 22 August 1708; AN, Colonies, F3, Vol. 9, fol. 123, order dated 22 August 1708. It should be noted that the market for vegetables and fruits was on Fridays and the meat market on Saturdays. This situation arises from the fact that Fridays and Saturdays were days when meat was not eaten. It was due to the lack of facilities for keeping meat (see Chapter 5) that the meat market had to be held off until Saturday.

89   *Ibid.*, Vol. 1, pp. 59 and 66, orders by Raudot, 8 June 1708 and 23 October 1708. AN, Colonies, F3, Vol. 9, fol. 129, 23 September 1708. This situation had lasted since 1694!

90   ALQ, *Jugements,[...] du Conseil souverain[...]*, Vol. 3, p. 870, police regulations dated 2 April 1694.

91   ANQQ, NF-2, Book 4, order dated 16 April 1710.

92   AN, Colonies, F3, Vol. 9, fol. 184, order dated 18 September 1710. At least in a precisely defined zone.

93   AN, Colonies, F3, Vol. 12, fol. 47, order by Hocquart, 16 May 1732.

94   P.-G. Roy, *Inventaire des ordonnances[...]*, Vol. 2, p. 165, order by Hocquart, 8 May 1734.

95 Fines increased from three *livres* in 1734 to six *livres* in 1739. *Ibid.*, Vol. 2, p. 269, order by Hocquart, 26 April 1739.

96 ALQ, *Édits, ordonnances royaux[...]*, Vol. 3, p. 403, order by Bigot, 17 May 1750.

97 P.-G. Roy, *Inventaire des ordonnances[...]*, Vol. 1, p. 262, 25 June 1742; AN, Colonies, F3, Vol. 11, fol. 66, order dated 10 March 1727; *ibid.*, fol. 67, 21 May 1727.

98 P.-G. Roy, *Inventaire des ordonnances[...]*, Vol. 1, p. 219, order dated 22 April 1722.

99 ALQ, *Édits, ordonnances royaux[...]*, Vol. 3, p. 420, order dated 4 August 1707; P.-G. Roy, *Inventaire des ordonnances*, Vol. 2, p. 147, order dated 23 June 1733.

100 AN, Colonies, F3, Vol. 11, fol 96, order dated 8 August 1727; ALQ, *Édits, ordonnances royaux[...]*, Vol. 3, p. 427, order dated 20 August 1709.

Chapter 4
A Tenant's Town

1 M. Garden, "Quelques remarques sur l'habitat urbain. L'exemple de Lyon au XVIIIe siècle," *Annales de démographie historique* (1975), p. 32; J.-P. Bardet, "L'habitat: une interrogation," *Annales de démographie historique* (1975), p. 19.

2 AN, Colonies, G1, 1688 and 1739 Censuses; M. Lafrance, "Etude sur l'evolution physique de la ville de Québec, 1608-1763," manuscript on file (Ottawa: Canadian Inventory of Historic Building, Canadian Parks Service, 1972), p. 101. The author identifies 660 buildings; we find it reasonable to deduct 10%, in order to take into account sheds and other non-residential buildings, since he obtained this figure from an examination of plans from the period. This number must, however, be compared to the number of houses visited by John Franks in August 1778; that is, 628 houses. Taking into account the devastating effects of the war on real estate and the population of the city, we may assume that this evaluation basically corresponds to the number advanced for the end of the French régime. NA, RG4, A1, Vol. 23, p. 7690, Visite des maisons et cheminées de cette ville, 11 September 1778. I wish to thank Christine Chartré for having graciously provided me with this reference.

3 That is about two-thirds of the houses on the 1740 plan.

4 We will henceforth use this rate.

5 L. Dechêne, "La croissance[...]," p. 169.

6 J. P. Bardet, *Rouen[...]*, p. 179.

7 The small number of labourers listed as landlords seems stunning; this may stem from the source used, that of the leases. One of the most probable explanatory factors is the small size of the houses owned by workers, making them unsuitable for subdivision for purposes of renting. For example, François Cliche, a worker living in the Saint-Roch suburb, owned a one-floor house made of half timbers that measured 15 by 20 feet. We cannot say that non-skilled workers never owned land; the example of François Cliche prevents us from doing so. However, as we will see below, given the

land and house purchasing costs, the number of journeymen who were landlords could not have been very high. We must add that Cliche purchased his land from Hiché in June 1753, during an economic boom when public investment and the shipping trade flourished. ANQQ, notary S. Sanguinet, No. 860, succession inventory of François Cliche, 3 January 1757.

8   The figures on Table 21 were derived from an analysis of rental leases. It is a cumulative total for the entire period, and not for a given time. What do these leases mean in terms of the capital's rental market? This is a question that is impossible to answer since this assumes a knowledge of the rental stock and a recreation of the rental history of each building for the period under consideration, as a function of the various owners and rentals involved. For example, we found 23 rental leases for 1695. The same year the census shows 213 houses and cabins. This could mean that 10.8% of the houses were rented; however, this was not the case, since not all owners may have wanted to rent their buildings, in whole or in part. This figure cannot meet the requirements of an evaluation of rental stock, which would be much too high, given the unknown number of owners who did not rent their buildings.

9   ANQQ, notary C. Rageot, No. 002, 29 January 1696. ANQQ, notary J. Pinguet, No. 2628, 8 March 1741.

10   Widows made up 18% of all parties contracting marriage in Québec. See Chapter 1.

11   We should specify here that regardless of the number of leases or the number of individuals, the proportions vary only in the order of 1%. This is also true of Table 21.

12   While widows pose a problem in terms of identifying their trade, we can say that, with a few exceptions such as the widow Fornel, they did not have a specialized trade. However, there is reason to believe that these proportions come close to reality since, according to the two 18th-century nominal rolls, the four sectors involved represent 19%, 32%, 37% and 11% of the labour force respectively. The proportions in the leases are 19%, 30%, 35% and 15%, not counting the widows.

13   Nevertheless, some landlords were afraid to rent to publicans; they prohibited the sale of alcohol or subletting to publicans. About 15 leases dated between 1690 and 1759 contain such clauses. A few examples are: ANQQ, notary C. Barolet, 20 March 1753 and 7 April 1752; notary F. Lacetière, 5 December 1713, 6 May 1716 and 19 April 1722. We will return to these later.

14   This activity goes hand in hand with the movement of the population (Chapter 1) and prices (Appendix B).

15   ANQQ, NF-25, file 264, lease of 16 July 1696. I would like to thank my colleague G. Proulx for providing me with this reference.

16   Compared with Father Jacrau's enumeration, the 1744 plan showing the properties expropriated for the shipyard's needs, illustrates the presence of large numbers of tenants quite well.

17   The issue of transportation will be analyzed in the next chapter.

18   J.-P. Bardet, *Rouen[...]*, p. 175.

19   These data are from succession inventories for the period 1690-1749.

20 D. Roche, *op. cit.*, pp. 113-14.

21 Please note that this applies to renting houses. As most rentals were of this type, it seems worthwhile to stay with only this aspect of the rental market.

22 Note that this refers to the renewal of leases and not previous rental periods which are rarely identified. We should also point out that the 21 streets described are those where rental activity was most widespread; they include 84% of all registered leases.

23 ANQQ, notary C. Barolet, 7 November 1734, lease of M. Cureux *dit* St-Germain; notary L. Chambalon, 27 April 1708, 5 May 1713 and 29 May 1715, leases of Hélène Meschin, Guillaume Fabas and Angélique Hédouin; notary C.H. Dulaurent, 8 August 1754, lease of Florent Michaud; notary P.A.F. Lanoullier des Granges, 15 March 1750, lease of Geneviève Janson-Lapalme; notary P. Rivet, 21 May 1713, lease of Simon Soupiran.

24 Amazingly only 3% of the tenants came from outside the city. This situation raises several questions: is this due to a problem of under-recording? Or does it indicate a process whereby new immigrants came mainly looking for work and, having found it, decided to settle down? Nothing in the present state of research offers a definite answer to this question.

25 Landlords could also ask to be paid annually, monthly, quarterly, bimonthly or in advance. The *Coutume de Paris* law set the standard at quarterly payments (every three months).

26 How many houses were equipped with bread ovens? This is a difficult question to answer. However, taking into account the figures put forward in the last chapter, we could say that this would be about one-third of the houses also.

27 This was the case of Paul Guillot, who received the full amount for the rent for an apartment located on des Pauvres Street from Jacques Gagnon. ANQQ, notary J.E. Dubreuil, lease of 10 May 1733.

28 Subletting means not only renting to a third party a whole house that has already been rented, but also renting part of that same house to a third party.

29 This was particularly the case of a lease by the Gaillard estate to Barthelemy Coton, who was in fact acting for Charles Gaillard. ANQQ, notary H. Hiché, 7 September, 1730. The same situation arose when a former resident of New England, Barthelemy Collins, rented Claude Morillonet-Berry's house on Saint-Louis Street. ANQQ, notary C.H. Dulaurent, lease of 25 September 1747.

30 This is a security pledge, as described by C. de Ferrière, *op. cit.*, Vol. 1, art. 161-63, pp. 377-83.

31 The following examples are from ANQQ, NF-20, Pièces détachées de la Prévôté de Québec. From another point of view, the historian J.A. Dickinson specifies that, between 1685 and 1753, the cases heard by the Québec provost involved property disputes in an proportion that increased from 8% to 20% of the cases. However, we should point out that the term property is used here in its wider sense, and that the cases involved both Québec and the whole region. J.A. Dickinson, *Justice et justiciables; la procédure civile à la prévôté de Québec, 1667-1759* (Québec: PUL, 1982), pp. 121-25.

32   ANQQ, NF-20, No. 876, 12 July 1732, and No. 1004, 18 September 1734.

33   ANQQ, notary C. Barolet, leases of 20 April 1752 and 20 March 1753; notary L. Chambalon, 31 October, 1692.

34   ANQQ, notary N.-G. Boucault de Godefus, lease of 24 July 1751; notary J. Pinguet-Vaucour, 15 March 1734.

35   ANQQ, F. Genaple, lease of 29 December, 1691; notary F. Lacetière, 19 April 1722.

36   The ban on subletting to tavern-keepers or running a tavern seems to have been rare (barely 1% of the leases). Thus, the hypothesis of a wish to protect the market as opposed to the building seems to have some merit. However, only a reconstruction of the network of public houses would allow a final answer to this question.

37   ANQQ, notary F. Lacetière, lease of 5 December, 1703.

38   ANQQ, notary N.-G. Boucault de Godefus, leases of 4 July 1737 and 17 August 1745.

39   ANQQ, notary M. Laferté-Lepailleur, lease of 17 July 1702; notary P. Rivet, lease of 20 January 1712. This despite the fact that ordinances made it mandatory for people to keep pigs and cattle in their basements if they did not have auxiliary buildings, such as barns and stables, as discussed in Chapter 3.

40   ANQQ, notary F. Lacetière, 26 April 1703; notary C.H. Dulaurent, 30 April 1747.

41   ANQQ, notary F. Lacetière, (M41), lease of 23 October 1711.

42   ANQQ, notary F. Lacetière, (M41), lease of 28 March 1716; notary J.-C. Panet, leases of 1 March 1745 and 15 April 1757.

43   ANQQ, notary C. Barolet, leases of 22 May 1732 and 7 September 1732.

44   ANQQ, notary J.-C. Panet, lease of 4 March 1752.

45   Without taking too great a step, it is important first to stop to consider the cost of purchasing land. Without a rigorous reconstruction of land records that could show us not only the location of the land, but also the time frame when the act took place, it becomes difficult to specify an average cost for the purchase of land.

46   L. Dechêne, "La rente du faubourg Saint-Roch à Québec, 1750-1850," *Revue d'histoire de l'Amerique française*, Vol. 34, No. 4 (March 1981), p. 579.

47   ANQQ, NF-7, declarations and enumerations, Paupers of the Hôtel-Dieu property, 12 December 1739. We must emphasize that Joachim Girard, who rented lots outside the wall at 3 *sols* per square foot, sold his subdivided lots for between 1*s*.3*d*. and 8*s*. per square foot, for a profit of over 400%, which confirms the shoemaker/tavern-keeper's speculative manoeuvres.

48   *Ibid*, declarations and enumerations, Hospitalières of the Hôtel-Dieu land, 3 July 1739.

49   *Ibid*, declarations and enumerations, property of the Jesuits, 20 February 1733.

50   *Ibid*, declarations and enumerations, property of the Ursulines, 27 May 1737.

51   *Ibid*, declarations and enumerations, fief of Sault-au-Matelot, 20 August 1737.

52　*Ibid*, declarations and enumerations, Cap-aux-Diamants and Notre-Dame lands, 17 March 1740 and 20 May 1740.

53　L. Dechêne, "La rente[...]", pp. 579-80; see also ASQ, Seigneury funds, 6, No. 23, sale 17 June 1726.

54　ASQ, Seigneury funds, 6, Nos. 54 and 54B, sale 1 July 1696; transfer 17 October 1705.

55　L. Dechêne, "La rente [...]", p. 580.

56　A. Charbonneau, Y. Desloges and M. Lafrance, *op. cit.*, pp. 251-52.

57　ANQQ, notary G. Rageot, No. 4032, sale of 28 May 1690.

58　ANQQ, notary F. Lacetière, No. 1528, 29 January 1726.

59　ANQQ, notary F. Lacetière, (M41), No. 2044, 8 November, 1719.
All the prices shown are in French currency.

60　*Ibid.*, No. 2208, 20 March 1724.

61　A review of the taxation (lods et ventes) involving building transactions in Québec in 1758 confirm these figures in terms of sale prices, despite the galloping inflation experienced by the capital during this period. AN, Colonies, $C^{11}A$, Vol. 103, fol. 528ss, Lods et ventes, Québec, 1758. I would like to thank my colleague M. Lafrance for providing me with this reference.

62　ANQQ, notary H. Hiché, No. 508, 29 October 1735.

63　J.-P. Bardet, *Rouen[...]*, pp. 178-79.

Part Three
Introduction

1　D. Roche, *op. cit.*, p. 69.

Chapter 5
The Domestic Environment

1　While the source mainly provides information on landlords (as shown in Appendix A), there is reason to believe that tenancy did not stop people from buying goods, especially when these are easily portable items. However, we should point out that, with two exceptions (construction workers and labourers), landlords owned more furnishings than tenants. Thus, we can expect to find the same objects among both groups, but in higher numbers among landlords.

2　L. Dechêne, *Habitants [...]*, p. 319.

3　ANQQ, notary L. Chambalon, 10 January 1701, succession inventory of Jean Lepicart. It becomes difficult to evaluate the evolution of the prices of consumer goods as descriptions of these objects are rarely complete. In the case of horses their breed, age and obviously use must be considered.

4   ANQQ, notary J.-C. Panet, 12 December 1749, succession inventory of Marie Dupéré.

5   P. Kalm, *op. cit.*, p. 300.

6   P.-G. Roy, *Inventaire des ordonnances[...]*, Vol. 3, p. 117, ordinance of 28 December 1748; ALQ, *Édits, ordonnances royaux[...]*, Vol. 3, p. 415-16, ordinance of 10 November 1706.

7   ANQQ, NF-2, file 36 (M5/8), fol. 70-77, ordinance of 21 April 1749. This ordinance arose from a specific context: while any newcomer from the surrounding countryside could become a carter during the 18th century, because he owned a horse, the economic boom of the years 1744-45 stirred the blood of too many horse owners. This regulation, limiting the number of carters and forcing a public trustee, Martial Vallet, a clerk of the Superior Council, on them, arose from this situation. He set up a list, and watched to ensure that carters identified their horses with a number. When making trips longer than three days outside the city, carters had to inform the Lieutenant-General. On the other hand, anyone leaving the job had to give at least two months notice, and only residents of the city were eligible to apply for the position created.

8   ANQQ, notary J.E. Dubreuil, 11 March 1715, succession inventory of Anne Guay. There are many other examples.

9   In Table 30, poultry owners were actually slightly more numerous, because we have not included those who owned turkeys or owners of pigeons or geese, but the proportions do not vary significantly.

10 F. Rousseau, *op. cit.*, p. 155.

11 ANQQ, notary F. Lacetière, leases of 26 April 1703 and 23 October 1711; notary C.H. Dulaurent, lease of 30 April 1747; notary P. Rivet, lease of 20 March 1717.

12 Since F. Rousseau has already conducted a tasty analysis of foods, we did not feel it was worthwhile doing so again; we will only analyze new or different elements.

13 Store and personal inventories were combined in this compilation of listed products. Obviously, since fresh products only last from a few hours to a few days, the succession inventories are most useful for learning about what products could be stored most easily during the season when the death occurred, especially since half of the inventories were conducted in the winter. This explains why beans, cabbages, onions and peas are the most frequently mentioned vegetables.

14 F. Rousseau, *op. cit.*, pp. 167-68.

15 ANQQ, notary C.H. Dulaurent, lease of 25 September 1747.

16 ANQQ, notary C. Barolet, 21 November 1747, succession inventory of François Chasle.

17 ANQQ, notary N. Boisseau, 13 January 1734, succession inventory of Jean Crespin.

18   ANQQ, notary J.C. Louet Senior, 13 August 1722, succession inventory of Jean-François Martin Delino.

19   Public ovens existed in the Palace Quarter. Does this mean that they were also found in other neighbourhoods? It is impossible to answer that question at this time. These ovens would have served the employees of the naval shipyards.

20   It seems difficult to believe that the city's bakers would have the opportunity to stockpile cereals, due to the situation of under-production.

21   ALQ, *Jugements[...] du Conseil souverain[...]*, Vol. 6, pp. 794-96, decree of 16 July 1714.

22   *Ibid.*, Vol. 5, p. 1011, decree of 5 August 1709.

23   *Ibid.*, Vol. 6, pp. 53 and 113, decrees of 5 May and 5 September 1710.

24   *Ibid.*, Vol. 5, p. 514, 7 February 1707.

25   These were crisis prices, which is to say that prices were usually lower. On the other hand, while these prices are inflated, they nevertheless reveal the importance of the "crisis." All prices are in *deniers*. See A.J.E. Lunn, "Economic Development in New France, 1713-1760," PhD thesis, McGill University, 1942, p. 407, for more on increases in wheat production.

26   The figures on Table 31 are from various regulations and ordinances. They are not exhaustive, but are indicative. ALQ, *Jugement[...] du Conseil souverain[...]*, Vol. 3, p. 591, police regulations, 4 December 1691; *ibid.*, Vol. 4 p. 394, 15 February 1700; *ibid.*, Vol. 5, p. 505, bakers' appeal, 31 January 1707; *ibid.*, Vol. 6 p. 53, decree of 5 May 1710; P.-G. Roy, *Inventaire des ordonnances[...]*, Vol. 2, p. 90, ordinance of 23 January 1731; P.-G. Roy, *Inventaire des jugements et délibérations du conseil supérieur de la Nouvelle-France de 1717 à 1760* (Beauceville: L'Éclaireur, 1935), Vol. 3, p. 162, 23 January 1737; *ibid.*, Vol. 4, p. 99, decree of 25 October 1742. Note that in 1737 the price of bread rose by two and a half times after the first regulation, and the price shown on the table is the average price set by these two decrees.

27   F. Rousseau, *op. cit.*, p. 149.

28   ANQQ, notary J. Barbel, 7 December 1719, inventory of François Chasles. They are found regularly in later inventories.

29   "In the 18th century, cod was a favoured and sought after food in France, and its consumption seems to have been particularly high among well-off citizens." L. Turgeon, "Consommation de morue et sensibilité alimentaire en France au XVIIIe siècle," *Historical Papers/Communications historiques* (1984), pp. 21-41. Québec was no exception since 76% of the people who had cod were merchants. The others were Councillors or administrators except for one shipowner.

30   Oyster shells were used in lime production and to dye fabrics and furs. On this subject, see H. Deslauriers and C. Rioux, "Les conditions de vie dans la Dauphine de 1760 à 1800," manuscript on file (Québec: Canadian Parks Service, 1982), pp. 141-47.

31   P. Kalm, *op. cit.*, p. 314.

32   H.N. Nicol, "The Domestic Economy of Two Québec City Houses (1740-1830)," manuscript on file (Ottawa: Canadian Parks Service, 1982), p. 95. We admit that this study, based on a zootechnic analysis of bones found in archaeological digs at a site on des Carrières street, is incomplete; nevertheless, it opens several avenues of research.

33   F. Rousseau, *op. cit.*, pp. 162-63.

34   Salt was not as rare and expensive as some people expected. See Appendix B on this subject.

35   ANQQ, notary F. Genaple, 8 January 1704, inventory of the possessions of Claude de Xainte.

36   P. Kalm, *op. cit.*, p. 225.

37   ANQQ, notary F. Genaple, 31 August 1703, inventory of the possessions of Marie-Anne Milot.

38   ANQQ, notary J.C. Panet, 21 November 1746, inventory of Marie-Hélène Lemieux.

39   ANQQ, notary J. Pinguet, 28 March 1742, inventory of Jourdain Lajus.

40   F. Rousseau, *op. cit.*, p. 217. Note that today this product is made as much of vegetables as of herbs, particularly leeks, carrots, celery and onions.

41   *Ibid.*, p. 191.

42   ANQQ, notary C.H. Dulaurent, 28 November 1749, inventory of Paul Lambert *dit* Saint-Paul.

43   F Rousseau, *op cit.*, p. 183.

44   Was this product made from sugar beets as opposed to other types of sugars?

45   ANQQ, notary J. Pinguet, 28 March 1742, inventory of Jourdain Lajus.

46   ANQQ, notary H. Hiché, 9 November 1733, inventory of Françoise Foucault.

47   ANQQ, notary J. Pinguet, 2 November 1739, inventory of Étienne Marchand; notary E. Barolet, 12 November 1747, inventory of Françoise Chasle.

48   ANQQ, notary J. Barbel, 17 December 1732, inventory of Louise-Elizabeth Duguay. According to Barbara Ketcham Wheaton, *L'office et la bouche; histoire des moeurs de la table en France, 1300-1789* (Paris: Calmann-Lévy, 1984), pp. 34 and 228-29, almond powder "enriched" with fish concentrate had been used to replace meat bouillons since the Middle Ages. This was part of the art of imitation in the kitchen during the days of abstinence. In the 18th century, cooking had evolved considerably, and powdered almond was mainly used in confectionery and added to candied fruit.

49   ANQQ, notary C.H. Dulaurent, 28 November 1749, inventory of Paul Lambert *dit* Saint-Paul.

50   ANQQ, notary L. Chambalon, leases of 11 March 1712 and 7 April 1712; notary J.E. Dubreuil, lease of 11 May 1725; notary C.H. Dulaurent, lease of 25 September 1747. Kalm's numerous references to this subject should not be forgotten.

51 Only 10% of the deceased had alcohol in their homes between 1690 and 1759. Personal communication from my colleague G. Proulx, who is preparing a study on tavern-keepers and publicans in Québec under the French régime.

52 ANQQ, notary F. Genaple, 26 April 1694, inventory of Marie-Anne Pinguet.

53 This was not derived from mentions of snuff, but rather from the number of snuff tins of all types found in inventories.

54 P. Kalm, *op. cit.*, p. 224 and 240.

55 ALQ, *Jugements[...] du Conseil souverain[...]*, Vol. 3, p. 621.

56 The Superior Council required butchers to have a licence, costing 50 *livres* annually. *Ibid.*, Vol. 5, p. 256, 1 March 1706.

57 These two prices did not vary significantly over the course of the 18th century except during periods of high inflation.

58 The lard prices are from Table 69 in Appendix B. The prices of the other meats are from the ALQ *Jugements[...] du Conseil souverain[...]*, Vol. 3, p. 621, regulation of 24 March 1692; *ibid.*, Vol. 3, p. 872, regulation of 4 April 1694; *ibid.*, Vol. 5, p. 256, order of 1 March 1706; *ibid.*, Vol. 6, p. 44, regulation of 7 April 1710; P.-G. Roy, *Inventaire des jugements[...] du Conseil supérieur[...]*, Vol. 1, p. 44, 25 April 1718; *ibid.*, Vol. 1, p. 62-63, 6 March 1719; *ibid.*, Vol. 2, p. 99, decree of 24 March 1730; *ibid.*, Vol. 4, p. 224, decree of 18 January 1745; *ibid.*, Vol. 4, p. 227, regulation of 25 January 1745; P.-G. Roy, *Inventaire des ordonnances[...]*, Vol. 3, p. 101, ordinance of 3 February 1748; *ibid.*, Vol. 3, p. 113, ordinance of 25 November 1748; *ibid.*, Vol. 3, p. 123, ordinance of 31 March 1749; *ibid.*, Vol. 3, p. 129, ordinance of 1 June 1749; *ibid.*, Vol. 3, p. 137, ordinance of 20 December 1749. Comparisons of fresh and salted meat pose problems. How should we evaluate the retail price of the amount of brine required to salt a pound of meat? Certainly not at the six *deniers* per pound that had to be paid between 1731 and 1744. On the other hand, according to J.-L. Flandrin, fat was always worth more than lean in both beef and pork in France in the 17th and 18th centuries. This situation arises solely because of the difference between supply (low) and demand (high). In short fat was rarer. Was this true in the colony? It seems that it was. J.-L. Flandrin, "Le goût et la nécessité: sur l'usage des graisses dans les cuisines d'Europe occidentale (XIVᵉ-XVIIIᵉ siècles)," *Annales E.S.C.*, Vol. 38, No. 2 (March-April 1983), pp. 369-401.

59 P.-G. Roy, *Inventaire des jugements[...] du Conseil supérieur[...]*, Vol. 1, pp. 20-21, 14 May 1717.

60 *Ibid.*, Vol. 1, p. 44, 25 April 1718; *ibid.*, Vol. 1, p. 67, 2 May 1719.

61 ANQQ, NF-20, insinuations de la Prévôté de Québec (M27/5), No. 1417, 4-5 February 1745.

62 ASQ, fonds Séminaire, No. 7, folder 72A, Journal de Récher, November 1757 to March 1758.

63 ANQQ, NF-20, (M27/5), No. 1454, 3 May 1745.

64 This proportion arises from the actual usable amount of butcher's beef. Today, a young steer weighs an average of 1200 pounds. According to Kalm, Canadian ani-

mals were small; this is why we assumed a lower weight. We would like to thank Bernard Godbout of the National Meat Institute for his help on this subject.

65 F. Rousseau, *op. cit.*, p. 272.

66 ALQ, *Jugements[...] du Conseil souverain[...]*, Vol. 3, p. 872, regulation of 4 April 1694.

67 *Ibid.*, Vol. 5, p. 256, 1 March 1706.

68 P.-G. Roy, *Inventaire des ordonnances[...]*, Vol. 3, pp. 113, 123 and 129, 25 November 1748, 31 March 1749, and 1 June 1749.

69 ALQ, *Jugements[...] du Conseil souverain[...]*, Vol. 3, p. 621, regulation of 24 March 1692.

70 F. Rousseau, *op. cit.*, p. 157.

71 ALQ, *Jugements[...] du Conseil souverain[...]*, Vol. 6, p. 44, 7 April 1710.

72 ANQQ, notary F. Lacetière, 15 February 1703, inventory of Nicolas Vollant.

73 ANQQ, notary P. Rivet, 20 March 1717, lease of Michelle Mars to Gabriel Greysac.

75 There were on average 20.5% fewer guns than militiamen in Québec between 1714 and 1739, and the percentage increased throughout the 18th century. Y. Desloges, "La corvée militaire à Québec au XVIIIe siècle," *Histoire sociale/Social History*, Vol. 15, No. 30 (Nov. 1982), p. 354, note 120.

76 AN, Colonies, C^{11}A, Vol. 79, fol. 251v, Hocquart to Bigot and Duquesnel, 1743.

77 H.N. Nichol, *op. cit.*, p. 93-97. We should point out that in the bones analyzed, second place belonged to mutton/goat. This can be explained by the fact that the bones came from a stratum covering the period 1740-80. During a period of both political and economic difficulty, the 1710 comment on the subject of mutton was again relevant. The proportions of meats were as follows: beef, 58%; mutton, 21%; pork, 15%; dog, 3%.

78 This also confirms P. Kalm (*op. cit.*, p. 298).

79 D. Roche, *op. cit.*, pp. 140 and 154.

80 ANQQ, notary J. Barbel, 16 February 1724, succession inventory of Françoise Lemaître-Lamorille. This appearance of various dyed fabrics corresponds to the extension of commerce from the Levant to England. France did not wish to remain behind England, therefore the proclamation by Maurepas, the minister responsible for the colonies, who was worried about the British textile industry. R. Lamontagne, *Textiles et documents Maurepas* (Montréal: Leméac, 1970), p. 37ss. Also see A. Lespagnol, "Cargaisons et profits du commerce indien au début du XVIIIe siècle; les opérations commerciales des compagnies malouines — 1707-1720," *Annales de Bretagne et des pays de l'ouest* (1982), pp. 313-50.

81 The number of inventories was reduced to 677 after grouping by trades. Since we decided to use only the trades specified in the inventories, "habitants," priests, foreign merchants, and some others were excluded, which is why there are 21 fewer than on the previous table.

82 Clocks included hourglasses. This proportion of objects indicating the time becomes much larger if watches, such as pocket watches that became more and more popular during the 18th century, are added. Quebeckers were of their era (the wealthier ones at least) as one of the main obsessions of the 18th century was time. On this subject, see D.J. Boorstin, *The Discoverers* (New York: Random House, 1983), pp. 26-78. This preoccupation should be compared with the phenomenon of public clocks (Chapter 3).

83 D. Roche, *op. cit.*, p. 155.

84 If we had included religious jewellery such as rosaries or crucifixes, the phenomenon would have been identical, or even smaller; most of the time, according to the marriage contracts, women's jewellery belonged to them. This may explain the low proportion of religious jewellery (3%) in the inventories. Furthermore, what could be more significant than the following quotation found on gifts made by donors who "wished to rid themselves of worldly goods, and only concentrate on their salvation." The donors were usually aged 50 or more.

85 These figures are for simple, undecorated mirrors smaller than 100 square inches, not the large, ornate, gilded mirrors. We should also emphasize that, among the small ones, trade mirrors quickly spread through the population. ANQQ, notary L. Chambalon, 10 January 1701, succession inventory of Jean Lepicard; notary C. Barolet, 20 September 1745, succession inventory of Marguerite Prevost.

86 The analysis of the age at death was made possible by comparisons with births, marriages and deaths registers. See Appendix A for more on this subject.

87 Whale fishing itself had a less enviable fate, becoming "casual" during the 1730s and 1740s. A. Laberge, "État, entrepreneurs, habitants et monopole: le 'privilège' de la pêche au marsouin dans le bas Saint-Laurent, 1700-1730," *RHAF*, Vol. 37, No. 4 (March 1984), p. 553.

88 This considering that we found a quote on the price of candles more than twice as often as that of oil, not counting tallow. See Table 65 in Appendix B for more on this subject. Also see E.I. Woodhead, C. Sullivan, and G. Gusset, *Lighting Devices in the National Reference Collection, Parks Canada* (Ottawa: Parks Canada, 1984), p. 29.

89 L. Décarie-Audet, N. Genêt and L. Vermette, *Les objets familiers de nos ancêtres* (Montréal: Éditions de l'Homme, 1974), pp. 119 and 148-49. Tin or copper chandeliers, lamps, candleholders and sconces were for interior lighting, compared to lamps and lanterns. All interior light sources except lamps used candles as a light source. The differences are in their forms; as a result, the choice of one or another becomes not only a question of taste but also of practical use; a flat candleholder can be hung easily, for example.

90 P. Kalm, *op. cit.*, p. 297

91 While Table 42 shows the brick stove and the stove plate separately (in order to respect the inventory nomenclature), we believe that these two categories should be combined. Thus we find 230 brick stoves compared to 252 iron ones. We should add that among the 187 inventories where no heat source was mentioned, the notaries did include fireplace implements (andirons, coal scoops, etc.) in one-third of the cases. Finally, these are mentions of the types of devices but not of their numbers.

92 ANQQ, NF-25, fol. 1090, complaint of Pierre Léger, 10 December 1735. I would like to thank my colleague G. Proulx for providing me with this reference.

93 ANQQ, notary L. Chambalon, 13 June 1702, succession inventory of François Provost; *ibid.*, 29 March 1703, succession inventory of François Allaire.

94 P. Kalm, *op. cit.*, p. 292.

95 Note that for the purposes of Table 43, the types of devices shown on Table 42 have been grouped.

96 It becomes very difficult to establish an average cost since we have no idea of the size of the device or its decoration; the prices we have given should be those of small stoves, if they are compared to prices of the era. ANQQ, notary F. Genaple, 5 March 1691, succession inventory of Hughes Cochran *dit* Floridor.

97 ANQQ, notary C.H. Dulaurent, 11 September 1748, succession inventory of Marie Renée Roussel.

98 The plate itself is 25% to 33.3% cheaper. ANQQ, notary L. Chambalon, 10 December 1698, succession inventory of François Poisset; notary C. Rageout, succession inventory of Guillaume Guillot *dit* Larose, 3 March 1701; notary C.H. Dulaurent, 18 August 1749, inventory of Anne Bernier; notary J. Pinguet, 9 February 1745, inventory of François Paris; notary C. Barolet, 20 June 1748, inventory of Marie Ann Lemieux; notary G. Boucault de Godefus, 8 January 1743, inventory of Marie-Anne Labadie.

99 NA, MG1, C^{11}A, Vol. 112-2, fol. 171, cited by M. Mousette in *Le chauffage domestique au Canada, des origines à l'industrialisation* (Québec: PUL, 1983), p. 85.

100 The penetration of stoves from the Saint-Maurice Forges into the urban market in Québec may seem too low to some; this was, however, the first decade of production.

Chapter 6
Insecurity in the Midst of Prosperity

1 See Appendix A for a critical analysis of succession inventories as sources.

2 A. Shortt, *Documents relatifs à la monnaie, au change et aux finances du Canada sans le régime français* (Ottawa: King's Printer, 1925), 2 vols.

3 J. Hamelin, *op. cit.*, pp. 60-66.

4 L. Dechêne, *Habitants [...]*, pp. 131-40.

5 *Ibid.*, p. 138; A. Charbonneau, Y. Desloges and M. Lafrance, *op. cit.*, pp. 47-49.

6 On this subject see Appendix B.

7 ANQQ, notary F. Lacetière, No. 1145, succession inventory of Pierre Metayer *dit* Saint-Onge, 8 June 1716.

8 A. Shortt, *op. cit.*, Vol. 1, pp. 398-402 and 410 ss.

9 ANQQ, notary F. Lacetière (M41), No. 1897 fol. 208, lease by P. Lefebvre to Marie-Madeleine and Thérèse Robitaille, 30 August 1717. Note that the financial clauses read as follows: "1000 *livres* a year taking into account the legal tender where 500 *livres* hard cash is the equivalent of 375 French *livres*." This is the only mention found identifying a different exchange rate for cash. The Royal Edict of 5 July 1717 implied that the 50% reduction refers to cash and the additional 12.5% to the playing cards.

10 ANQQ, notary F. Lacetière, succession inventories of Jacques Bernier and of Pierre Dasilva, No. 1207 and No. 1209, 17 and 22 January 1718.

11 ANQQ, notary J.E. Dubreuil, No. 979, lease by L. Normand Labrière to Jean Baptiste Halle, 14 March 1718.

12 ANQQ, notary F. Lacetière, No. 1219, inventory of Marie Maillou, 16 April 1718; *ibid,* (M41) No. 1970, 22 April 1718, lease by Elisabeth Marchand to Pierre Frontigny.

13 A. Vachon, "Lacetière, Florent de," *DCB*, Vol. 2, p. 325.

14 It has been suggested that the cut-off date tends to obscure the overall picture since the source, that is the succession inventory, contains the outcome of the accumulation of the preceding years, with the result that those that overlap the time of death and even go some years beyond it describe what would have happened during the previous period. This choice was made taking into account the indications respecting the demographic and economic movements. Yet, it must be pointed out that, if this date had been moved by several years, the results would have remained the same since the movement had started during the previous decade.

15 From 1691 to 1726, the cost of living rose at a rate of 2.6% annually (including the 62.5% devaluation in money); from 1727 to 1749, it rose 2.1% annually. When considering assets, wealth or balance sheets, the situation remained almost the same in relation to the effects of inflation. On this subject see Appendix B.

16 While the proportion of those with less than 1000 *livres* drops between Tables 45 and 47, the difference can be explained by the fact that, between 1690 and 1749, 22% were landowners; most of those checked between 1727 and 1749 (70%) had a fortune of 750 *livres* or less. Composed mainly of widows, artisans or workmen engaged in the maritime trade, these owners were concentrated in Lower Town on Escalier, Champlain, or de Meulle streets or in the Palace Quarter on Saint Nicolas Street. There they occupied mostly small wooden houses as was pointed out in Chapter 3.

17 Meaning dowry or previous right in the case of "debts," but then none of the sums mentioned included the bed or the furnished room.

18 The dowry belonged to the children, and the wife had only a life interest in it; for this she had to render an accounting. The children had to choose between their share of the inheritance or the dowry, depending on the best option, with the result that in most cases the dowry was not applicable. C. de Ferrière, *op. cit.*, Vol. 2, title XI, sec. 249 and 253, pp. 120-25.

19 In the case of life annuities, we considered that the capital corresponded to one-twentieth of the annual revenue. On the other hand, annuities, especially favoured by merchants and officers, only represented 7% of the dowries. It must also be pointed out

that this proportion was obtained from the total value of the joint estate's fortune; since half of the goods fell to one of the two parties, it must then be supposed that the spouse had control over the other half. If we agree that half of this fortune was personal, then two out of five spouses could not pay their debts, this proportion being 27% for those who died before 1727 and almost 52% for those deceased after that date.

20 ANQQ, notary C. Barolet, succession inventory of Jean Boucher *dit* Belleville, 3 May 1745. By way of comparison, it should be noted that Jean Maillou, who died in 1753, had loans valued at almost 29 000 *livres*. ANQQ, notary C. Barolet, succession inventory of Jean Maillou, 21 September 1753.

21 ANQQ, notary C. Barolet, No. 372 and No. 654, succession inventories of François Foucault and Pierre Denis *dit* Legris, 22 July 1734 and 22 May 1737.

22 *Ibid.*, No. 654, succession inventory of Pierre Denis *dit* Legris, 22 May 1737.

23 ANQQ, notary L. Chambalon, No. 1290, inventory of Raymond Dubosc, 29 March 1697.

24 For this, we have to establish the retail sales price and subtract all related expenses.

25 ANQQ, notary J. Pinguet, No. 2505, succession inventory of Louis Beaudouin, 27 July 1740.

26 ANQQ, notary F. Lacetière, No. 1171, succession inventory of Robert Drouard, 4 March 1717.

27 This figure, based on data from 11 inventories, confirmed Miquelon's statement on the subject of margins of profit, but our data indicates beyond a doubt that this margin was not even, either among the merchants, or within the inventoried stocks. D. Miquelon, *Dugard of Rouen: French Trade to Canada and the West Indies, 1729-1770* (Montréal: McGill-Queen's University Press, 1978), pp. 74-76. The succession inventories consulted were the following: ANQQ, notary J. Barbel, No. 648, 24 March 1722, Ambroise Renoyer; No. 735, 11 January 1724, Jacques Richard; No. 745, 16 February 1724, Françoise Lemaître-Lamorille; No. 763, 30 May 1724, Nicolas Pinault; No. 811, 17 April 1725, Jean Petit; No. 1185, 17 December 1732, Charlotte Elisabeth Duguay; notary H. Hiché, 12 August 1733, Jean-Baptiste Demeule; notary J. Barbel, No. 1243, 16 June 1734, Jacques Guion-Fresnay; notary C. Barolet, No. 331, 22 July 1734, François Foucault; No. 654, 22 May 1737, Pierre Denis Legris; notary J. Pinguet, No. 2505, 22 July 1740, Louis Beaudouin.

28 L. Dechêne, *Habitants [...]*, p. 215.

29 This table was drawn from references to the geographic origins of the debtors; each time that the origins were not mentioned, we assumed that citizens or suburban dwellers were involved; they were not included in the table. The category "unknown" includes references to obscure areas such as Cap à l'Arbre, while "Québec" includes the villages located within a radius of 50 kilometres, from Cap-Santé to Saint-Joachim on the North Shore, and from Sainte-Croix to Saint-Pierre de Montmagny on the South Shore. The villages downstream became "the lower river"; Lotbinière, upstream, was included in the administration of Trois-Rivières (this only happened in about a dozen cases). Likewise, Montréal took in the western outposts (here again,

there were exceptions). The categories "France" and "West Indies" most often include suppliers that had a balance due.

30 ANQQ, notary J.-C. Louet, Sr., No. 58, 27 January 1721, succession inventory of Marie-Catherine Lepicard. It must be noted that Véron de Grandmesnil lived in Montréal between 1713 and 1715. Roland-J. Auger, "Véron de Grandmesnil, Étienne," *DCB*, Vol. 3, p. 642.

31 ANQQ, notary J. Barbel, No. 745, 16 February 1724, succession inventory of Françoise Lemaître-Lamorille. We should also determine whether Guillemin eventually drew on part of his credits. It must also be noted that Guillemin lived in Montréal from time to time, according to his biographer D. J. Horton, "Guillemin, Charles," *DCB*, Vol. 2, pp. 268-69.

32 This trend is contrary to that described by J. Dickinson, *op. cit.*, p. 154. True, the capital turned toward the sea with the rise of the maritime industries; but this was nothing new, merely an acceleration, because Québec from its very beginnings had depended on the sea.

33 Certainly the socio-professional classification of these people lends itself to criticism. On this subject see Appendix A.

34 This list of French suppliers is evidently very incomplete; it was the result of the only references contained in the succession inventories. However, it is consistent with the picture painted by J. Pritchard, "Ships, Men and Commerce: a Study of Maritime Activity in New France," PhD thesis, University of Toronto, 1971, pp. 304-43.

35 See Appendix B on this subject.

36 It would have cost too much to have an inventory drawn up, so the labourer or his wife would have preferred to avoid this expense. On the other hand, servants were young and few died, which would explain why they had no succession inventories. On this subject, see J.-P. Hardy and T. Ruddell, *op. cit.*, pp. 56-58; F. Barry, "Familles et domesticité féminine au milieu du 18e siècle," in N. Fahmy-Eid and M. Dumont, eds., *op. cit.*, p. 231.

37 D. Roche, *op. cit.*, pp. 78-79 and 84.

38 J.A. Garraty, *Unemployment in History; Economic Thought and Public Policy* (New York: Harper and Row, 1978). p. 55.

39 D. Miquelon, *op. cit.*, pp. 70-71 and 233, note 9. As well, only the shop inventories needed to be considered to verify the phenomenon of competition; all merchants sold fabrics to their clientele, some making this a specialty.

40 AN, Colonies C^{11}A, Vol. 75, fol. 9v, Mémoire de Desauniers à Beauharnois, 1741.

41 D. Miquelon, *op. cit.*, p. 79, Table 9. In 1754, Colonial Administrator Bigot said that the 14 Protestant business houses in Québec controlled three-quarters of the retail business. J.F. Bosher, "French Protestant Families in Canadian Trade, 1740-1760," *Histoire sociale/Social History*, Vol. 7, No. 14 (November 1974), pp. 179-201.

42 D.J. Horton, "Guillemin, Charles," *DCB*, Vol. 2, pp. 268-69.

43 ANQQ, NF-2, book 4 (M5/1), fol. 55v-56, ordinance by J. Raudot, 6 May 1710. The preamble read thus: For the good of everyone there must be in a town more than one

person in the same profession, as much for the impetus this would give to contractors and workers to improve their wares in order to have a market for them, as because both parties in the future would charge a more reasonable price, which never happens when a profession is controlled by one person[...]." [Translation].

44   A. Charbonneau, Y. Desloges and M. Lafrance, *op. cit.*, p. 50.

45   *Ibid.*, pp. 246-53.

46   As has been shown by the analysis of the geographic origins of the spouses as well as the analysis of the rate of growth.

47   Concerning butchers and bakers, see the preceding chapter and Appendix B.

48   M. Thivierge, "Les artisans du cuir au temps de la Nouvelle-France, Québec, 1660-1760," in J.-C. Dupont and J. Mathieu, eds., *Les métiers du cuir* (Québec: PUL, 1981), p. 34.

49   R. Brisson, *op. cit.*, p. 62.

50   J. Mathieu, *La construction navale royale à Québec, 1739-1759* (Québec: Société historique de Québec, 1971), pp. 76-77.

51   P.N. Moogk, "Lajus, Jourdain," *DCB*, Vol. 3, pp. 344-45.

52   A. Charbonneau, Y. Desloges and M. Lafrance, *op. cit.*, p. 247.

53   ANQQ, notary F. Lacetière, engagement of Jean Marie Dasilva *dit* Portugais to Jean Maillou, 7 May 1724.

54   This means the presence of a shop recorded by the notary; the number read 42 out of 117 before 1727, and 25 out of 83 after that date.

55   J.A. Garraty, *op. cit.*, p. 5.

56   P.N. Moogk, "In the Darkness of a Basement: Craftsmen's Associations in Early French Canada," *CHR*, Vol. 57, No. 4 (December 1976), pp. 418-19.

57.   *Ibid.*, pp. 436-37 and 422.

58   *Ibid.*, p. 435. A limited partnership meant an association in which one of the partners furnished the capital and the others money and work, or only work. *Ibid.*, p. 425.

59   A. Charbonneau, Y. Desloges and M.Lafrance, *op. cit.*, pp. 255-62.

60   Y. Desloges, "L'habitat militaire à Québec au XVIIIe siècle," Manuscript Report Series No. 431 (1980), Parks Canada, Ottawa, pp. 135-61.

Appendix A
The Value of Succession Inventories

1   Since the now celebrated article by G. Paquet and J. P. Wallot, "Les inventaires après décès à Montréal au tournant du XIXe siècle: préliminaires à une analyse," *RHAF*, Vol. 30, No. 2 (September 1976), pp. 163-221, articles on and discussions of this source alone have become more and more numerous. For example, the article by

Y. Morin, "La représentativité de l'inventaire après décès; l'étude d'un cas, Québec au début du XIXe siècle," *RHAF*, Vol. 34, No. 4 (March 1981), pp. 515-33; or, again the workshop held during the IHAF's Annual Meeting held in Compton, Québec, in 1983. On the French side, we must not forget the excellent study by D. Roche entitled, *Le peuple de Paris*.

2   This marvellous team which had to work under difficult conditions has earned congratulations for their diligent and especially hard work: Louise Déry, Adrienne Labbé, Johanne Lacasse, Rénald Lessard and Gérald Sirois as well as Janis Richmond who left due to illness. My colleague G. Proulx completed the team. I must thank them warmly; without their contributions, this study would not have been possible.

3   My colleague G. Proulx, who was working at the same time on the same sources, but on different subjects, chose to isolate the period between 1690 and 1759. This permitted the identification of nearly 1000 inventories, with nearly 300 more for the last decade alone.

4   Lacking an analysis of the trades of deceased persons; such information is left out of births, marriages and deaths registries most of the time.

5   In the case of an inventory for an artisan who owned a shop, the bailiff entrusted the evaluation to another person in the same line of work. The same was true for merchants.

6   ANQQ, notary N. Boisseau, No. 93, succession inventory of Jean Crespin, 13 January 1734.

7   ANQQ, notary F. Lacetière, No. 1118, inventory Étienne Landron, 29 October 1715.

8   *Ibid.*, No. 1145, Inventory of Pierre Métayer *dit* Saint-Onge, 8 June 1716.

9   *Ibid.*, No. 1219, inventory of Marie Maillou, 16 April 1718.

10   *Ibid.*, No. 1364, inventory of Marie Jacquette Damour, 16 January 1722.

11   M. Guyot, *Répertoire universel et raisonné de jurisprudence civile, criminelle, canonique et bénéficiale* (Paris: Pankouke, 1775-1784), Vol. 16, pp. 493-94. Regarding appreciation, the example of Louise Roussel, widow of watch-maker and jeweller Jacques Pagé may clear up this obscure legal question. Pagé died without issue; besides his wife he left nephews and nieces "who claimed to be entitled to inherit." A lawsuit between the widow and the nephews rested upon the evaluation and appreciation. Pagé and Roussel were married in 1715, a period of inflation; they had set a prior right before distribution of 800 *livres* as well as a clause of mutual donation. When the time came for the inventory to be drawn up in 1742, the widow was opposed to doing this on the basis of "the true value of things, without appreciation." She claimed that the mutual donation must not prejudice her prior right. In fact, she wanted to maximize the amount guaranteed in her marriage contract. Following a legal battle, a compromise was reached: the widow agreed to have the household furniture and the household goods appraised and estimated at their true value without appreciation; on the other hand, the watchmaking and jewellery tools were to be "listed below their true value," it being understood, at the same time, that the tools "shall be sold at auction in the usual manner, to the highest bidder." ANQQ, notary J. Pinguet, 19 July 1742, succession inventory of Jacques Pagé.

12   This was notably the case of the record of the sale of the goods of notary Jacques
     Pinguet de Vaucour when there was a gain of 60%. Another similar example, the es-
     tate of labourer Jean Bessière brought in 111% more when sold. These were not the
     only examples. All the records would have to be analyzed, in order to determine
     what the surplus represented before we could decide if inflation was a compensating
     factor; even better, we would have to check the articles one by one in order to decide
     if all the inventoried objects had been included in the public auction. Our team
     checked nearly 160 of these documents, which represents about 75% of the records,
     taking into account that 30% of the 703 inventories had been subject to inflation.
     This is a long and arduous task for those who wish to undertake it.... ANQQ, notary
     G. Boucault de Godefus, No. 762, 5 May 1749; *ibid.*, No. 856, 4 December 1749.

13   M. Guyot, op. cit., Vol. 16, pp. 490 and 493. Certain commodities such as coinage,
     precious metals (gold and silver), and consumer products were not subject to appreciation.

14   L. Lavallée, "Les archives notariales et l'histoire social de la Nouvelle-France,"
     RHAF, Vol. 28, No. 3 (December 1974), p. 389. The marriage contract was signed
     before a notary in almost 80% of the cases.

15   H. Charbonneau, *Vie et mort [...]*, p. 153.

16   The average age of death and the length of the marriage represent only two of the
     variables likely to affect the comparisons between joint estates. Yet, as the following
     data emphasize, it is difficult to establish absolute criteria. For example, inventories
     of officers were essentially for remarried widowers and widows, as shown by the
     average ages, compared with the length of the marriage. In this regard, they represent
     exceptions to the rule, as do the inventories of the male workers in the iron trades.
     This situation partly explains why there were so many inventories of senior public
     servants and officers, but this is valid only for this socio-professional group.

Group	Average Age				Average length of marriage			
	Men	No.	Wom.	No.	Men	No.	Wom.	No.
Services								
Officers	58.5	36	48.9	25	6.75	38	6.7	22
Public Servants	57.9	13	42.9	17	19.05	17	15.16	16
Business								
Merchants	48.5	32	42.5	16	17.37	36	15.71	13
Food	43.3	7	39.3	9	17.33	10	12.56	8
Transportation	47.75	8	35.5	6	15.16	11	10.53	7
Artisan								
Construction	55.43	14	37.15	26	23.23	12	11.65	20
Iron	44.3	13	39.36	14	8.36	14	18.62	12
Leather	51.4	5	63.5	2	18.29	6	23.5	2
Clothing	48.8	5	37.8	8	12.05	6	10.62	6
Wood	57.8	5	30.0	11	20.75	4	14.95	9
Labourers	41.5	2	38	3	28.64	1	27.94	1

17 C. de Ferrière, *op. cit.*, Vol.2, art. 241, pp. 98-101.

18 G. Paquet and J.-P. Wallot, "Les inventaires[...]," pp. 176-77.

19 C. de Ferrière, *op. cit.*, Vol. 2, art. 240, pp. 83-98.

20 This question of renunciation proved very theoretical though. If the joint estate had contracted a loan or an obligation, more often than not the notarized document specified that the husband had "authorized" his wife to assume joint responsibility. Once this obligation was accepted, the wife could no longer avoid her legal commitments. This explains why the deeds contain very few renunciations of joint estates.

21 C. de Ferrière, *op. cit.*, Vol. 2, art. 168, pp. 390-91.

22 It is important to remember that the age retained was 15 or the age of bearing arms for a boy, and not 25, which is the legal age of majority. Moreover, all the demographic studies show an average age of 20 for the marriage of women; but since they ran the risk of death in childbirth, the age of 15, although slightly below reality, is nevertheless compatible with this and contributes only slightly to lowering the quotient of relative value. The figures are from H. Charbonneau and J. Legaré, *Répertoire[...]*. Monks and nuns, soldiers and sailors were not included in the compilation of both deaths and inventories.

23 Y. Morin, *op. cit.*, p. 518.

24 See Chapter 1.

25 This practice was not peculiar to the 18th century as pointed out in an article by Y. Morin, *op. cit.*, p. 521.

26 We chose rather to separate deaths for children into groups of under one year and under 15; and for adults, into those under 50 and over 50.

27 In Table 60, the centiles in the "Charbonneau" column are from the work of H. Charbonneau, *Vie et mort[...]*, p. 233; they resulted from the "Ensemble" total, after subtracting those under 15.

28 It was very rare to find an inventory drawn up at the request of a creditor, although he might have brought pressure to bear on the survivors to hire a notary.

29 This classification is the work of Louise Dechêne, *Habitants [...]*, p. 375. Although various criticisms could be levelled against it, this grouping by large sectors of activity makes it possible to obtain quickly an overall view of the component elements of a society. The groups representing each of the sectors were discussed in Chapter 2.

30 This analysis of marriage contracts, done jointly with Marc Lafrance, was the subject of a paper presented at the meeting of the French Colonial Historical Society, held at Laval University in May 1985. It was later published in the form of an article: Y. Deslosges and M. Lafrance, "Dynamique de croissance et société urbaine, Québec au XVIIIe siècle," *Histoire sociale/Social History*, Vol. 21, No. 42 (Nov. 1988), pp. 251-67.

31 On this subject, see Chapter 4. Perhaps it would have been better to divide the unknowns between owners and tenants, but in what proportions? At least this was suggested by the analysis of the worldly goods of various socio-professional groups, especially businessmen, minor public servants and transporters, while the value of

the personal estates of some unknowns closely approached that of owners. It must be noted that this proportion of owners stayed the same decade after decade.

32 Furthermore, the proportion of owners obtained from the inventories closely resembled the one that emerged from the rental leases (Chapter 4). J.-P. Bardet, *Rouen[...]*, pp. 178-79.

33 L. Déry and R. Lessard, "Esquisse de la situation socio-materiélle des forgerons, menuisiers et charpentiers de Québec, 1792-1835," manuscript on file (Ottawa: National Museum of Man, History Division, 1984), pp. 20-21. G. Paquet and J.-P. Wallot, "Les inventaires[...]," pp. 216 and 219. Among the ironworkers, owners accounted for 91% of the deceased; among the carpenters, for 73%; and among framers, for 65%.

34 For example, we should add that the value of real estate during the last decade of the French régime represented 35.8% of the assets of the owners. In short, the proportion differed very little and remained constant. I must thank my colleagues G. Proulx and M. Lafrance for bringing this to my attention.

35 Our team, however, found nearly 200 references to partitions for the period between 1690 and 1759.

36 Some partitions only took place about twenty years later, as for example, in the case of the successions of Marie Gignard or Louise Guillot (26 years) or even those of Blaise Lepage or Pierre Vallière (21 years).

37 ANQQ, notary G. Boucault de Godefus, No. 339, 3 February 1745, succession inventory of Yves Arguin.

38 ANQQ, notary G. Boucault de Godefus, No. 488, 23 September 1746, record of the succession of the late Arguin, Sr.

39 ANQQ, notary C.H. Dulaurent, No. 466, 13 April 1743, record of the succession of the late Levasseur Marguerite, wife of the late Duroy Pierre. A copy was also found in AN, Colonies, Series E, folio 209.

40 ANQQ, notary C. Louet Jr., No. 8, 15 December 1739, succession inventory of Marguerite Levasseur.

41 On this subject, see Chapter 3.

42 The evaluation of an inheritance showed one characteristic; it contained a third item identified as "recovery," which meant the total of the amounts entered as assets and as real estate, and from which the heirs had not yet fully profited at the time the document was prepared. In short, the document deals mainly with the amount to be divided, with the result that Arguin's heirs only shared 15 521 *livres*, and Duroy's heirs, 14 798 *livres*.

Appendix B
Price Index Fluctuations

1 J. Hamelin, *op. cit.*, pp. 61-62.

2 Our research on the cost of stone for construction has shown this same phenomenon. On this subject, see A. Charbonneau, Y. Desloges and M. Lafrance, *op. cit.*, pp. 307-09; F. Rousseau, *op. cit.*, pp. 72 and 74.

3 It would take too long to name all the documents produced by Paquet and Wallot. We will mention only the following two articles: "Aperçu sur le commerce international et les prix domestiques dans le Bas-Canada, 1793-1812," *RHAF*, Vol. 21, No. 3 (December 1967), pp. 447-73; "Crise agricole et tensions socio-ethniques dans le Bas-Canada, 1802-1812: éléments pour une ré-interprétation," *RHAF*, Vol. 26, No. 2 (September 1972), pp. 185-237.

4 F. Ouellet, J. Hamelin and R. Chabot, "Les prix agricoles dans les villes et les campagnes du Québec d'avant 1850: aperçus quantitatifs," *Histoire sociale/ Social History,* Vol. 15, No. 29 (May 1982), pp. 83-127.

5 L. Dechêne, *Habitants[...],* p. 521; J. Hamelin, *op. cit.,* p. 61.

6 J. Hamelin, *op. cit.,* p. 59.

7 As F. Rousseau has shown, *op. cit.,* pp. 70-74.

8 In fact, we have only found a few references for the end of the 17th century. As an example, ALQ, *Jugements[...] du Conseil souverain[...],* Vol. 3, p. 379, 9 January 1690.

9 G. Paquet and J.-P. Wallot, "Les inventaires[...]," pp. 181-82.

10 *Ibid.*, pp. 202-08.

11 The boundaries of the urban area of Québec in the 18th century were described in Chapters 1 and 3.

12 Obviously any mention of flour described as being "rat-infested" or in bad or unhealthy condition was not retained.

13 M. Guyot, *op. cit.*, Vol. 16, p. 493.

14 It is impossible to decipher the prices using Hamelin's graph and only the table on page 59 allows us to make a comparison. J. Hamelin, *op. cit.*, pp. 59-61.

15 Note that the price of wheat taken from the Hôtel-Dieu's account books follows this same trend. F. Rousseau, *op. cit.*, p. 72.

16 In decreasing order of annual entries, these products included silver (57), firewood (45), wheat and butter (43), lard (42), salt (39), flour (38), pepper and candles (33), tallow and tobacco (27), peas (24), white sugar (23), nutmeg (22), olive oil and cloves (21), vinegar (20), raw sugar (18), eels, oats, and bran (17), cinnamon (16), rice and lamp oil (14), maple sugar and coffee (11), plums (9), molasses and chocolate (7), salted beef (6) and eggs (4). The compilation of the annual price always refers to an average.

17 Imported tobaccos from Brazil, Saint Vincent or elsewhere were more expensive and were left out. We should not be surprised to observe the absence of wine, brandy and other alcoholic beverages. They were not often mentioned in inventories (scarcely 16%, according to G. Proulx who studied innkeepers); also, we usually have the price by the cask. All our other products had unit prices. The problem raised by the men-

tion of a price per cask has to do with measurement. Depending upon the port of origin, the contents of the cask may have varied considerably. AN, Colonies, B Series, 76:7, Minister of the Navy to Hocquart, 2 March 1743.

18   The years of poor harvests are confirmed by judgements and deliberations of the Superior Council; see ALQ, *Jugements[...] du Conseil souverain[...]*.

19   Was this wheat flour, rye flour or some other flour that can be used to make bread? The indications gathered from the inventories lead us to believe that it was wheat, which corroborates the statement by J. Hamelin (*op. cit.*, p. 66), that "the basis of the diet was a single food: wheat." See Chapter 5 on this subject.

20   A statistical analysis produced a close correlation between the prices of the two products. The coefficient of our relation was 0.87 for the whole period.

21   The information on harvests between 1714 and 1750 is from A.J.E. Lunn, *op. cit.*, pp. 95-104 and 447.

22   This expression is Jean Hamelin's: *op. cit.*, p. 62. During this time, the products did not reach a peak at the same time. For example, salt cost almost seven times its 1714 base price and stabilized at five before going down again, while the cost of pepper was highest in 1716.

23   There is little probability that an excess of exports caused this rise in prices, especially since part of the pork consumed came from French imports. However, it seemed these imports were used to feed the troops and not the population. AN, Colonies, $C^{11}A$, 75:301, shipments from the port of Rochefort destined for the King's stores in Québec, 4 September 1741.

24   In case of emergency, authorities sent ships to Labrador where fishermen from France stored large quantities of salt for their fish preserving needs.

25   G. Paquet and J.-P. Wallot, "Aperçu sur le commerce[...], p. 469, note 21. It would be appropriate to point out here the contribution of Solange Dion, mathematician employed by the Socio-Economic Research Section, who guided us in working out the statistical validations of the various prices.

26   This leads to the formula P1/Po. It solves the problem that the various products have variable unit prices, taking into account the unit of measure.

27   The price of pepper only appears for five years.

28   The formula should read: $I = \Sigma\,(P^n/P^o)\,x\,\,100/N$

29   At least during the period under consideration. According to an anonymous report drawn up during the Seven Years' War, the inflationary spiral reached new heights between 1751 and 1759. APC, MG5, B1, 11:72v-73v, Exhibition of the Prices of Goods in Canada.

30   It should be noted that the price of a *toise* of masonry for house construction was also at its lowest during these years. (*Toise* is an old French unit of length equal to 1.949 metres.) A. Charbonneau, Y. Desloges and M. Lafrance, *op. cit.*, p. 307.

31   Some sceptics will have quickly challenged the value of silver or pepper as goods likely to supply indications on the cost of living in Québec. It should be sufficient to specify here that the indices, whether based on 9 or 17 products, were also compiled

without silver. The price fluctuation is subject only to a small change after silver was eliminated. All in all, silver represents a weight in the calculation of the cost of living index because its price changes slowly.

32 In order to measure buying power, it is sufficient to divide the base index of 100 by the annual index. The quotient becomes the coefficient to be applied to the given values for a year in order to eliminate the inflation in the cost of a product.

33 The combined increase in the index is 177 points and the subsequent drop, 113 points. These numbers are obtained by establishing the increase or decrease of the annual quotient from the preceeding annual report. For example, the difference between the 1711 report from the 1710 one and so on; then one adds up the quotients and divides by the number of years used.

34 J.A. Garraty, *op. cit.*, p. 1.

35 *Ibid.*, p. 42.

36 ANQQ, NF-2, (M5/1), book 4, fol. 55v-56, edict dated 6 May 1710.

37 AN, Colonies, C^{11}A, 75:9v, Desauniers' Report to Beauharnois, 1741.

38 A. Charbonneau, Y. Desloges and M. Lafrance, *op. cit.*, p. 50-51.

39 See Chapter 1 on this subject.

40 A. Charbonneau, Y. Desloges and M. Lafrance, *op. cit.*, p. 303. These figures only refer to construction of fortifications and barracks and not all military expenses, such as supplies, etc.

41 J.A. Garraty, *op. cit.*, p. 37.

42 See Chapters 3 and 6 as well as A. Charbonneau, Y. Desloges and M. Lafrance, *op. cit.*, pp. 246-53.

43 See Chapter 3.

SOURCES OF TABLES

1

AN, Colonies, G1, Vol. 460-61; L. Dechêne, *Habitants et marchands de Montréal au XVIIe siècle* (Paris and Montréal: Plon, 1974), p. 493; *ibid.*, "La croissance de Montréal au XVIIIe siècle," *RHAF*, Vol. 27, No. 2 (September 1973), p. 164; R. Chénier, "L'urbanisation de la ville de Québec, 1660-1690," manuscript on file (Québec: Canadian Parks Service, 1979), pp. 406-09.

2

C. Bridenbaugh, *Cities in the Wilderness: The First Century of Urban Life in America, 1625-1742* (New York: Oxford University Press, 1971), p. 6; *ibid., Cities in Revolt; Urban Life in America, 1743-1776* (New York: Oxford University Press, 1973), p. 5; K.E. Anderson, "The Layered Society: Material Life in Portsmouth, N.H., 1680-1740," PhD thesis, University of New Hampshire, 1982, p. 60; R.V. Wells, *The Population of the British Colonies in America before 1776. A Survey of Census Data* (Princeton N.J.: Princeton University Press, 1975), p. 98.

3

AN, Colonies, G1, Vol. 460-61; *RAPQ, 1939-1940*, "Le recensement de Québec en 1744" ([Québec], Rédempti Paradis, King's Printer, 1940).

4 and 6

AN, Colonies, G1, Vol. 460-61.

5, 7-13

H. Charbonneau and J. Légaré, *Répertoire des actes de baptêmes, mariages, sépultures et des recensements du Québec ancien* (Montréal: P.U.M., 1980-).

14-19

H. Charbonneau and J. Légaré, *Répertoire des actes de baptêmes, mariages, sépultures et des recensements du Québec ancien* (Montréal: P.U.M., 1980-); L. Beaudet, *Recensement de la ville de Québec, 1716* (Québec: A. Côté, 1887); *RAPQ, 1939-1940*, "Le recensement de Québec en 1744" ([Québec], Rédempti Paradis, King's Printer, 1940).

20

ANQQ, NF-7, Declarations and enumerations, 1723-58.

21-24, 26-28

ANQQ, Records of the Notaries of Québec, 1690-1759, rental leases.

25, 29-30, 33-57, 63-64, 66, 69-70

ANQQ, Records of the Notaries of Québec, 1690-1749, succession inventories.

31

ALQ, *Jugements et délibérations du conseil souverain de la Nouvelle-France* (Québec: A. Côté, 1885-91), 6 vols.; P.-G. Roy, *Inventaire des ordonnances des intendants conservées aux Archives provinciales de Québec* (Beauceville: L'Éclaireur, 1919), 3 vols.; *ibid., Inventaire des jugements et délibérations du conseil supérieur de la Nouvelle-France de 1717 à 1760* (Beauceville: L'Éclaireur, 1935), 7 vols.

32

ANQQ, Records of the Notaries of Québec, 1690-1749, succession inventories; ALQ, *Jugements et délibérations du Conseil souverain de la Nouvelle-France* (Québec: A. Côté, 1885-91), 6 vols.; P.-G. Roy, *Inventaire des jugements et déliberations du conseil supérieur de la Nouvelle-France de 1717 à 1760* (Beauceville: L'Éclaireur, 1935), 7 vols.; *ibid., Inventaire des ordonnances des intendants conservées aux Archives provinciales de Québec* (Beauceville: L'Eclaireur, 1919), 3 vols.

58, 60-62, 65

ANQQ, Records of the Notaries of Québec, 1690-1749, succession inventories; H. Charbonneau and J. Légaré, *Répertoire des actes de baptêmes, mariages, sépultures et des rencensements du Québec ancien* (Montréal: P.U.M., 1980-).

67

ANQQ, Notary G. Boucault de Godefus, No. 339, 3 February 1745; No. 488, 23 September 1746.

68

ANQQ, Records of the Notaries of Québec, 1690-1749, succession inventories; J. Hamelin, *Économie et société en Nouvelle-France* (Québec: P.U.L., [1960]), pp. 59-61.

BIBLIOGRAPHY

Manuscript Sources

Canada. National Archives
Manuscripts Division
> MG5, B1, ministère des Affaires étrangères — Paris, reports and documents, America, 1592-1785.
> RG4, A1, correspondence of the offices of civil and provincial secretaries

National Map and Plans Collection
> PH/350, Québec, 1739
> PH/430, Québec, 1742
> PH/340, Québec, 1752

France. National Archives
Fonds des Colonies
> Series $C^{11}A$, general correspondence, Canada. Letters and other documents sent from the colony to the Minister of the Navy, 1604-1760.
> Series E, Personal files, 1626-1760
> Series F3, Moreau de Saint-Méry collection. Various documents on the colonies, 1604-1760
> Series G1, births, marriages and deaths registers, censuses and other documents

Overseas Section
> Fortifications of the colonies. North America. Documents on engineering works, 1660-1760.

Québec (province). Archives nationales à Québec. Public archives.
Records of the Notaries from the 17th and 18th centuries, passim.
Nouvelle-France (NF-2), Intendants' ordinances, 1666-1760
Nouvelle-France (NF-7), declarations and enumerations, 1723-1758.
Nouvelle-France (NF-19), registres de la Prévôté de Québec, 1666-1759.
Nouvelle-France (NF-20), insinuations de la Prévôté de Québec, 1668-1759.
Nouvelle-France (NF-25), collection de pièces judiciaires et notariales, 1638-1759.

Québec (seminary). Archives
Fonds Séminaire, 1660-1760, 5, 6, and 8.
Fonds Seigneuries, 6 and 7.

Printed Sources

Beaudet, Abbé Louis
Recensement de la ville de Québec, 1716. A. Côté, Québec, 1887.

Canada. Statistics of Canada/Statistiques du Canada
Census of Canada, 1665 to 1871 / Recensements du Canada, 1665 à 1871. I.B. Taylor, Ottawa, 1876, Vol. 4.

Charbonneau, Hubert, and Jacques Légaré
Répertoire des actes de baptêmes, mariages, sépultures et des recensements du Québec ancien. PUM, Montréal, 1980- , 26 vols.

Québec. Assemblée législative
Édits, ordonnances royaux, déclarations et arrêts du Conseil d'État concernant le Canada. E.R. Fréchette, Québec, 1854-56, 3 vols.
———. *Jugements et délibérations du Conseil souverain de la Nouvelle-France.* A. Coté / J. Dussault, Québec, 1885-91, 6 vols.

Rapport de l'archiviste de la province de Québec, 1921-1922
"Les notaires au Canada sous le régime français," L.A. Proulx, King's Printer, Québec, 1922, pp. 1-58.
———. "Procès-verbaux sur la commodité et incommodité dans chacune des paroisses de la Nouvelle-France par Mathieu-Benoît Collet, procureur général du roi au Conseil Supérieur de Québec," L.A. Proulx, King's Printer, Québec, 1922, pp. 262-362.

Rapport de l'archiviste de la province de Québec, 1939-1940
"Le recensement de Québec en 1744," Rédempti Paradis, King's Printer, Québec, 1940, pp. 1-154.

Shortt, Adam
Documents relatifs à la monnaie, au change et aux finances du Canada sans le régime français. King's Printer, Ottawa, 1925, 2 vols.

Inventories

Roy, Pierre-Georges
Inventaire des ordonnances des intendants de la Nouvelle-France conservées aux Archives provinciales du Québec. L'Éclaireur, Beauceville, 1919, 3 vols.
———. *Inventaires des jugements et délibérations du conseil supérieur de la Nouvelle-France de 1717 à 1760.* L'Éclaireur, Beauceville, 1932-35, 7 vols.

Legal Dissertations

Ferrière, Claude de
Commentaire sur la Coutume de la Prévôté et Vicomté de Paris. New edition, Librairies associés, Paris, 1788, 2 vols.

Guyot, M.
Répertoire universel et raisonné de jurisprudence civile, criminelle, canonique et bénéficiale. Pankouke, Paris, 1775-84, 64 vols.

Dictionaries

Dictionary of Canadian Biography. UTP, Toronto, 1966-, Vol. 1: 1000-1700; Vol. 2: 1701-1740; Vol. 3: 1741-1770.

Furetière, Antoine
Dictionnaire universel contenant généralement tous les mots français tant vieux que modernes et les Termes des Sciences et des Arts. 2nd ed., Arnoud et Reinier, Rotterdam, 1701.

Studies

Andersen, Karen E.
"The Layered Society: Material Life in Portsmouth, N.H., 1680-1740," PhD thesis, University of New Hampshire, 1982.

Baillargeon, Noël
Le Séminaire de Québec de 1685 à 1760. PUL, Québec, 1977.

Bardet, Jean-Pierre
Rouen aux XVIIe et XVIIIe siècles; les mutations d'un espace social. Société d'édition d'enseignement supérieur, Paris, 1983, 2 vols.

Bouchard, Gérard
Le village immobile; Sennely-en-Sologne au XVIIIe siècle. Plon, Paris, 1972.

Boorstin, D.J.
The Discoverers. Random House, New York, 1983.

Bridenbaugh, Carl
Cities in the Wilderness; The First Century of Urban Life in America, 1625-1742. Oxford University Press, New York, 1971.
———. *Cities in Revolt; Urban Life in America, 1743-1776.* Oxford University Press, New York, 1973.

Brisson, Réal
La charpenterie navale à Québec sous le régime français, IQRC, Québec, 1983.

Charbonneau, A., *et al.*
"Le Parc de l'Artillerie et les fortifications de Québec," Historical Study presented to the Learned Societies Conference, Parks Canada, Québec, 1976.

Charbonneau, A., Y. Desloges, and M. Lafrance
Québec, the fortified city: from the 17th to the 19th century. Parks Canada, Ottawa, 1982.

Charbonneau, Hubert
Vie et mort de nos ancêtres; étude démographique. PUM, Montréal, 1975.

Charbonneau, Hubert, and André Larose, editors
Les grandes mortalities: étude méthodologique des crises démographiques du passé. Ordina, Liège, 1979.

Charbonneau, Hubert, and Maria Luisa Marcilio
Démographie historique. PUF, Paris, 1979.

Chénier, Rémi
"L'urbanisation de la ville de Québec, 1660-1690," manuscript on file, Canadian Parks Service, Québec, 1979, (published as *Québec: A French Colonial Town in America, 1660 to 1690*). Canadian Parks Service, Ottawa, 1991.

Décarie-Audet, L., N. Genêt, and L. Vermette
Les objets familiers de nos ancêtres. Éditions de l'Homme, Montréal, 1974.

Dechêne, Louise
Habitants et marchands de Montréal au XVIIe siècle. Plon, Paris and Montréal, 1974.

Déry, Louise, and Rénald Lessard
"Esquisse de la situation socio-matérielle des forgerons, menuisiers et charpentiers de Québec, 1792-1835," manuscript on file, National Museum of Man, History Division, Ottawa, 1984.

Deslauriers, Hélène, and Christian Rioux
"Les conditions de vie dans la Dauphine de 1760 à 1800," manuscript on file, Canadian Parks Service, Québec, 1982.

Desloges Yvon
"L'habitat militaire à Québec au XVIIIe siècle," Manuscript Report Series No. 431 (1980), Parks Canada, Ottawa.

Dickinson, John Alexander
Justice et justiciables; la procédure civile à la prevoté de Québec, 1667-1759. PUL, Québec, 1982.

Dupont, Jean-Claude, and Jacques Mathieu, editors
Les métiers du cuir. PUL, Québec, 1981.

Fahmy-Eid, Nadia, and Micheline Dumont, editors
Maîtresses de maison, maîtresses d'école, femmes, famille et éducation dans l'histoire du Québec. Boréal Express, Montréal, 1983.

Garraty, John A.
Unemployment in History; Economic Thought and Public Policy. Harper and Row, New York, 1978.

Goubert, Pierre
Cent mille provinciaux au XVIIe siècle; Beauvais et le Beauvaisis de 1600 à 1730. Flammarion, Paris, 1968.

Gutton, Jean-Pierre
Domestiques et serviteurs dans la France de l'ancien régime. Aubier-Montaigne, Paris, 1981.

Hamelin, Jean
Économie et société en Nouvelle-France. PUL, Québec, 1960.

Hardy, Jean, and Thierry Ruddell
Les apprentis artisans à Québec, 1660-1815. PUQ, Montréal, 1977.

Henripin, Jacques
La population canadienne au début du XVIIIe siècle: nuptialité, fécondité, mortalité infantile. PUF, Paris, 1954.

Jones, D.L.
Village and Seaport; Migration and Society in Eighteenth Century Massachussetts. University Press of New England, Hanover and London, 1981.

Kalm, Pehr
Voyage de Pehr Kalm au Canada en 1749; traduction annotée du Journal de route. J. Rousseau, G. Bethune and P. Morisset, transl. CLF, Montréal, 1977.

Lacelle, Claudette
"Military property in Québec City, 1760-1871," *History and Archeology No. 57* (1982), Parks Canada, Ottawa.

Lafrance, Marc
"Étude sur l'évolution physique de la ville de Québec, 1608-1763," manuscript on file, Canadian Inventory of Historic Building, Canadian Parks Service, Ottawa, 1972.

Laget, Mireille
Naissances; l'accouchement avant l'âge de la clinique. Seuil, Paris, 1982.

Lahontan, Louis Armand de Lom d'Arce, baron de
Nouveaux voyages Amérique septentrionale. Hexagone/Minerve, Montréal, 1983.

Lamontagne, Roland
Textiles et documents Maurepas. Leméac, Montréal, 1970.

Lunn, Alice J.E.
"Economic Development in New France, 1731-1760," PhD thesis, McGill University, 1942.

Mathieu, Jacques
La construction navale royale à Québec, 1739-1759. Société historique de Québec, Québec, 1971.
———. *Le commerce entre la Nouvelle-France et les Antilles au XVIIIe siècle.* Fides, Montréal, 1981.

Miquelon, Dale
Dugard of Rouen; French Trade to Canada and the West Indies, 1729-1770. McGill-Queen's University Press, Montréal, 1978.

Moogk, Peter N.
Building a House in New France; An Account of the Perplexities of Client and Craftsmen in Early Canada. McClelland and Stewart, Toronto, 1977.

Moussette, Marcel
Le chauffage domestique au Canada, des origines à l'industrialisation. PUL, Québec, 1983.

Nicol, H.N.
"The Domestic Economy of Two Québec City Houses (1740-1830)," manuscript on file, Canadian Parks Service, Ottawa, 1982.

Perrot, Jean-Claude
Genèse d'une ville moderne, Caen au XVIIIe siècle. Mouton, 1975, Paris and The Hague, 2 vols.

Pritchard, James
"Ships, Men and Commerce: A Study of Maritime Activity in New France," PhD thesis, University of Toronto, 1971.

Queneday, Raymond
L'habitation rouennaise; étude d'histoire, de géographie et d'archéologie urbaines. 2nd ed., G. Montfort, Brionne, 1977.

Roche, Daniel
Le peuple de Paris. Aubier-Montaigne, Paris, 1981.

Ross, Lester A.
"Archeological metrology: English, French, American and Canadian systems of weights and measures for North American historical archaeology," *History and Archeology,* No. 68 (1983), Parks Canada, Ottawa.

Rousseau, François
L'oeuvre de chère en Nouvelle-France; le régime des malades à l'Hôtel-Dieu de Québec. PUL, Québec, 1983.

Roy, Pierre-Georges
La ville de Québec sous le régime français. King's Printer, Québec, 1930, 2 vols.

Trudel, Marcel
Initiation à la Nouvelle-France. Holt, Rhinehart and Winston, Montréal, 1968.

Wells, Robert V.
The Population of the British Colonies in America before 1776. A Survey of Census Data. Princeton, N.J., Princeton University Press, 1975.

Wheaton, Barbara Ketcham
L'office et la bouche; histoire des moeurs de la table en France, 1300-1789. Calmann-Lévy, Paris, 1984.

Woodhead, E.I., C. Sullivan, and G. Gusset
Lighting Devices in the National Reference Collection, Parks Canada. Studies in Archeology, Architecture, and History, Parks Canada, Ottawa, 1984.

Articles

Bardet, Jean-Pierre
"L'habitat: une interrogation," *Annales de démographie historique* (1975), pp. 19-29. Paris.

Bosher, J.F.
"French Protestant Families in Canadian Trade, 1740-1760," *Histoire sociale/Social History,* Vol. 7, No. 14 (Nov. 1974), pp. 179-201. Ottawa.

Charbonneau, Hubert
"A propos de démographie urbaine en Nouvelle-France; réflexions en marge d'*Habitants et marchands de Montréal* de Louise Dechêne," *Revue d'histoire de l'Amérique française,* Vol. 30, No. 2 (Sept. 1976), pp. 263-69. Montréal.

Dechêne, Louise
"La croissance de Montréal au XVIIIe siècle," *Revue d'histoire de l'Amérique française,* Vol. 27, No. 2 (Sept. 1973), pp. 163-80. Montréal.
———. "La rente du faubourg Saint-Roch à Québec, 1750-1850," *Revue d'histoire de l'Amérique française,* Vol. 34, No. 4 (March 1981), pp. 569-96. Montréal.
———. "Quelques aspects de la ville de Québec au XVIIIe siècle d'après les dénombrements paroissiaux," *Cahiers de géographie du Québec,* Vol. 28, No. 5 (Dec. 1984), pp. 485-505. Québec.

Desloges, Yvon
"La corvée militaire à Québec au XVIIIe siècle," *Histoire sociale/Social History,* Vol. 15, No. 30 (Nov. 1982), pp. 333-56. Ottawa.
———. "The Study of the Urban Past and its Many Approaches: A Historiographic Review," *Research Bulletin,* No. 197 (1983), Parks Canada, pp. 1-15. Ottawa.

Desloges, Yvon, and Marc Lafrance
"Dynamique de croissances et société urbaine, Québec au XVIIIe siècle," *Histoire sociale/Social History,* Vol. 21, No. 42 (Nov. 1988), pp. 251-67.

Etlin, R.
"L'air dans l'urbanisme des Lumières," *Dix-huitième siècle* (1977), pp. 123-34. Paris.

Flandrin, J.-L.
"Le goût et la nécessité: sur l'usage des graisses dans les cuisines d'Europe occidentale (XIVe-XVIIIe siècles)," *Annales E.S.C.*, Vol. 38, No. 2, (March-April 1983), pp. 369-401. Paris.

Garden, Maurice
"Quelques remarques sur l'habitat urbain. L'exemple de Lyon au XVIIIe siècle," *Annales de démographie historique* (1975), pp. 29-35. Paris.

Laberge, Alain
"État, entrepreneurs, habitants et monopole: le 'privilège' de la pêche au marsouin dans le bas Saint-Laurent, 1700-1730," *Revue d'histoire de l'Amérique française*, Vol. 37, No. 4 (March 1984), pp. 543-56. Montréal.

Lavallée, Louis
"Les archives notariales et l'histoire sociale de la Nouvelle-France," *Revue d'histoire de l'Amérique française*, Vol. 28, No. 3 (Dec. 1974), pp. 385-404. Montréal.

Léonidoff, Georges-Pierre
"L'habitat de bois en Nouvelle-France; son importance et ses techniques de construction," *Material History Bulletin/Bulletin d'histoire de la culture matérielle* (Spring 1982), pp. 19-35. Ottawa.

Lespagnol, A.
"Cargaisons et profits du commerce indien au début du XVIIIe siècle; les opérations commerciales des compagnies malouines — 1707-1720," *Annales de Bretagne et des pays de l'ouest* (1982), pp. 313-50. Rennes.

Mathieu, J., *et al.*
"Les alliances matrimoniales exogames dans le gouvernement de Québec, 1700-1760," *Revue d'histoire de l'Amérique française*, Vol. 35, No. 1 (June 1981), pp. 3-32. Montréal.

Moogk, Peter N.
"In the Darkness of a Basement: Craftmen's Associations in Early French Canada," *Canadian Historical Review*, Vol. 57, No. 4 (Dec. 1976), pp. 399-439. Toronto.

Morin, Yvan
"La représentativité de l'inventaire après décès; l'étude d'un cas, Québec au début du XIXe siècle," *Revue d'histoire de l'Amérique française*, Vol. 34, No. 4 (March 1981), pp. 515-33. Montréal.

Olivier-Lacamp, Gael, and Jacques Légaré
"Quelques caractéristiques des ménages de la ville de Québec entre 1666 et 1716," *Histoire sociale/Social History*, Vol. 12, No. 23 (May 1979), pp. 66-78. Ottawa.

Ouellet, F., J. Hamelin, and R. Chabot

"Les prix agricoles dans les villes et les campagnes du Québec d'avant 1850: aperçus quantitatifs," *Histoire sociale/Social History*, Vol. 15, No. 29 (May 1982), pp. 83-127. Ottawa.

Paillé, Michel P.

"Accroissement et structure de la population à Québec au début du XIXe siècle," *Histoire sociale/Social History*, Vol. 9, No. 17 (May 1976), pp. 187-92. Ottawa.

Paquet, Gilles, and Jean-Pierre Wallot

"Aperçu sur le commerce international et les prix domestiques dans le Bas-Canada, 1793-1812," *Revue d'histoire de l'Amérique française*, Vol. 21, No. 3 (Dec. 1967), pp. 447-73. Montréal.

———. "Crise agricole et tensions socio-ethniques dans le Bas-Canada, 1802-1812: éléments pour une ré-interprétation," *Revue d'histoire de l'Amérique française*, Vol. 26, No. 2 (Sept. 1972), pp. 185-237. Montréal.

———. "Les inventaires après-décès à Montréal au tournant du XIXe siècle: préliminaires à une analyse," *Revue d'histoire de l'Amérique française*, Vol. 30, No. 2 (Sept. 1976), pp. 163-221. Montréal.

Teisseyre-Sallmann, Line

"Urbanisme et société; l'exemple de Nîmes aux XVIIe et XVIIIe siècles," *Annales E.S.C.*, Vol. 35. No. 4 (July-August 1980), pp. 965-86. Paris.

Turgeon, Laurier

"Consommation de morue et sensibilité alimentaire en France au XVIIIe siècle," *Historical Papers/Communications historiques* (1984), pp. 21-41. Ottawa.